Penguin Education

Penguin Critical Anthologies

General Editor: Christopher Ricks

Andrew Marvell

Edited by John Carey

Andrew Marvell

A critical anthology

edited by John Carey

Penguin Books

Penguin Books Ltd, Harmondsworth,
Middlesex, England
Penguin Books Inc., 7110 Ambassador Road,
Baltimore, Md 21207, U.S.A.
Penguin Books Australia Ltd, Ringwood,
Victoria, Australia

First published 1969
This selection copyright © John Carey, 1969
Introduction and notes copyright © John Carey, 1969

Made and printed in Great Britain by
Hazell Watson & Viney Ltd,
Aylesbury, Bucks
Set in Monotype Bembo

Contents

6   Contents

Part Two **Modern Views**

Introduction   61

The Setting

General Estimates

7 Contents

9 Contents

The Satires

Abbreviations

The following abbreviations have been used for journals.

E. in C.	Essays in Criticism
E.L.H.	English Literary History
E.S.	English Studies
H.L.Q.	Huntingdon Library Quarterly
J.E.L.H.	Journal of English Literary History
J.H.I.	Journal of the History of Ideas
M.P.	Modern Philology
N. & Q.	Notes and Queries
P.M.L.A.	Publications of the Modern Language Association
P.Q.	Philological Quarterly
R.E.S.	Review of English Studies
S.E.L.	Studies in English Literature 1500–1900
S.P.	Studies in Philology
T.L.S.	Times Literary Supplement

Preface

An editor who wants to reprint pieces of modern criticism is dependent on the goodwill of the authors and copyright-holders concerned. In this case the publishers were able to get permission to include nearly all the passages I originally selected. A list of acknowledgements is given on pp. 327–8.

The exception to this general cooperativeness was Dr F. R. Leavis. This fact is not recorded resentfully. It is rather that I wish to avoid the impression that Dr Leavis has been deliberately left out. I had meant to include two excerpts from Dr Leavis. The first, from *Revaluation*, 1936, pp. 24–8, criticized T. S. Eliot for suggesting that the wit of Marvell's *Horatian Ode* was similar to that in the songs in Milton's *Comus*. Dr Leavis, in reply, quoted not from the *Horatian Ode* or *Comus* but from the *Dialogue between the Resolved Soul and Created Pleasure*, and declared that Marvell presented his moral theme 'in relation to a wide range of varied and maturely valued interests' while Milton presented his with 'single-minded seriousness'. The second passage criticized Mr Bateson. It was from *Scrutiny*, vol. 19, 1953, pp. 162–83, and I have indicated its drift on p. 64. The controversy with Mr Bateson is reprinted, with the omission of Mr Bateson's original case, in *A Selection from Scrutiny*, compiled by F. R. Leavis, Cambridge University Press, 1968, vol. 2, pp. 280–315.

Throughout this volume excerpts from Marvell and from other seventeenth-century writers are given in modern spelling. Apart from this, the text of Marvell's poems followed is that in H. M. Margoliouth's edition of the *Poems and Letters*, Oxford University Press, second edition, 1952. Quotations from Marvell in the anthologized passages have been corrected where necessary to conform with Margoliouth. This has been done silently unless the divergence was thought interesting enough to warrant a footnote. T. S. Eliot, for example, failing to get a passage from *Appleton House* right, and yet presuming to call it 'immediately and unintentionally ridiculous' (p. 51), plainly comes into this category, and so does Edgar Allan Poe being misled by S. C. Hall's text of the *Nymph* into commending the 'exceeding vigor and beauty' of a line Marvell did not write (p. 39).

I have received expert and friendly help from Martin Lightfoot and Christopher Ricks, and should like to record my thanks to them both.

St John's College, Oxford   J.C.

Table of Dates

1621   Andrew Marvell born at Winestead, near Hull, son of the local clergyman.

1624   Family (Marvell, parents, and three older sisters) moves to Hull on appointment of father as Lecturer at Holy Trinity Church.

1633   From Hull Grammar School to Trinity College, Cambridge.

1637   Contributes Greek and Latin verses to Cambridge volume congratulating Charles I on birth of daughter.

1638   Mother dies (April); father remarries (November).

c.1639 Temporarily converted to Catholicism; runs away to London; recaptured by father.

1641   Father drowned crossing Humber. Marvell abandons Cambridge M.A. course.

1642–8 Travels for four years in Holland, France, Italy, Spain; learns languages and fencing. Writes, now or earlier, *A Dialogue between Thyrsis and Dorinda* (set to music by William Lawes before 1645). Visits Richard Flecknoe in Rome between 1645 and 1647; then or later writes *Flecknoe, an English Priest at Rome*.

1646   Perhaps writes *To his Coy Mistress* (thinks E. E. Duncan-Jones, *T.L.S.*, 5 December 1958, p. 705; but R. Sharrock, *T.L.S.*, 31 October 1958, p. 625 and 16 January 1959, p. 33 suggests *c.*1653).

1648   Writes (probably before February) *To his Noble Friend Mr Richard Lovelace*, printed in *Lucasta*, 1649. Writes (if it is Marvell's) anti-Parliamentarian *Elegy upon the Death of my Lord Francis Villiers*, printed and published without date, probably 1648.

1649   Writes *Upon the Death of the Lord Hastings*, printed in *Lachrymae Musarum*, 1649.

1650   Appointed (June or later) language tutor to Mary Fairfax; goes to live with Fairfaxes in Yorkshire. Writes (June or July) *An Horatian Ode upon Cromwell's Return from Ireland* and (November or later) anti-Parliamentarian *Tom May's Death*.

1650–52 Usually assumed, without evidence, to be writing major lyric poetry, *The Garden*, Mower poems, *Upon Appleton House*, etc.

1651   Writes (February or March) Latin verses flattering
        Parliament's ambassador to the United Provinces, *In
        Legationem Domini Oliveri St John*.

1653   (February) Writes *The Character of Holland*; Milton tries
        to get Marvell (who has recently left Fairfaxes) job as
        assistant secretary to Council of State: unsuccessful.
        Appointed (July or earlier) tutor to Cromwell's protégé
        William Dutton; moves to John Oxenbridge's house at
        Eton. (*Bermudas* is usually dated hereabouts because
        Oxenbridge had lived in Bermuda.)

1653–4 Writes (Winter) Cromwellian diplomatic poems: *A Letter to
        Dr Ingelo, then with my Lord Whitelocke, Ambassador from
        the Protector to the Queen of Sweden*, and two sets of Latin
        verses about Cromwell's portrait sent to Queen Christina
        in April 1654.

1654   Writes (December) Cromwellian court poem, *The First
        Anniversary*.

1655   *The First Anniversary ... Printed by Thomas Newcomb ...
        1655* published.

1656   In France (January to August) at Saumur, with Dutton.

1657   Writes (June or July) Cromwellian court poem, *On the
        Victory obtained by Blake over the Spaniards*. Appointed
        (September) Latin secretary to Council of State (£200 a
        year). Writes (November) *Two Songs at the Marriage of the
        Lord Fauconberg and the Lady Mary Cromwell* (Cromwell's
        third daughter).

1658   Writes (September) *A Poem upon the Death of Oliver
        Cromwell*.

1659   Elected (January) M.P. for Hull (remains one of the Hull
        members from now until his death). *A Dialogue between
        Thyrsis and Dorinda* printed with music in John Gamble's
        Airs and Dialogues.

1662–3 Spends eleven months in Holland (spying or diplomacy).

1663   Leaves (July) on embassy to Russia, Sweden and Denmark
        as secretary to Earl of Carlisle.

1665   Returns (January) to England. *The Character of Holland.
        Printed by T. Mabb for Robert Horn ... 1665* published
        (June); comprises lines 1–100 of Marvell's poem and eight-
        line conclusion, probably not his, suitable to circumstances
        of Dutch War of 1665–7: anonymous.

1667   Dutch fleet sails up Medway (June). Writes satires against
Clarendon: *Clarendon's House Warming* (July), *Upon his
House*, *Upon his Grand Children* (all three printed anony-
mously in *Directions To A Painter . . . Being The Last
Works of Sir John Denham Whereunto is annexed, Clarendon's
House Warming. By an Unknown Author . . . 1667*), and
(between August and November) *The Last Instructions to a
Painter* (perhaps printed now, but no printed copy survives
with a date earlier than 1689). Speaks (October to
November) four times against Clarendon in House of
Commons.

1668   Criticizes (February) in House of Commons the inefficiency
of English espionage abroad.

1669–70 Writes *The Loyal Scot*.

1670   Writes (if it is Marvell's) *The King's Vows* (May).

1671   Writes (if they are Marvell's) *Further Advice to a Painter*
and *Nostradamus's Prophecy* (both January). Writes (May)
Latin epigram on Colonel Thomas Blood's attempt to steal
Crown Jewels.

1672   (Autumn) *The Rehearsal Transprosed . . . Printed by A.B.
. . . 1672* published. Two further issues, also without
Marvell's or printer's name appear before the end of 1672.

1672–3   Writes (if it is Marvell's) anti-Prelatical addition to *The
Loyal Scot* (lines 87–235).

1673–4   Marvell (code name 'Mr Thomas') operating with fifth
column promoting Dutch interests in England, in touch
with Dutch secret agents. (Winter) *The Rehearsal
Transprosed: The Second Part . . . by Andrew Marvell.
London, Printed for Nathaniel Ponder . . . 1673* published.

1674   Writes (if they are Marvell's) *Britannia and Raleigh* (Spring)
and (December) *Upon his Majesty's being made free of the
City. On the Victory obtained by Blake over the Spaniards*
printed (February) in *A New Collection of Poems and Songs*
(republished 1678 as *Melpomene: Or, the Muses' Delight*).
On Mr Milton's Paradise Lost printed in the second edition of
Paradise Lost. Second edition of *The Rehearsal Transprosed:
The Second Part* published.

1675   Writes (if they are Marvell's) *Nostradamus's Prophecy* (second
part) (April or later), *The Statue in Stocks Market*, *The
Statue at Charing Cross* (both July), *A Ballad called the
Chequer Inn* and *A Dialogue between the Two Horses*

(between November 1675 and January 1676). Writes (April)
parody, *His Majesty's most Gracious Speech to both Houses
of Parliament.*

1676   *Mr Smirk: Or, The Divine in Mode . . . Together with a
Short Historical Essay, concerning General Councils . . .
By Andreas Rivetus, Junior* [i.e. Marvell] published (June).
Two further editions appear before the end of 1676.

1677   Writes Latin poem admiring courage of James Mitchell,
would-be assassin of Archbishop Sharp. *An Account Of
the Growth of Popery, and Arbitrary Government In England*
published without Marvell's or printer's name.

1678   *London Gazette* (March) offers reward for information about
author or printer of *An Account.* (May) *Remarks Upon a Late
Disingenuous Discourse . . . By a Protestant.* [i.e. Marvell]
London, Printed . . . by Christopher Hussey published.
Marvell dies (16 August) of medical treatment prescribed
for tertian ague. Second edition of *An Account* published
with Marvell's name.

1681   *Miscellaneous Poems. By Andrew Marvell, Esq; Late Member
of the Honourable House of Commons. London, Printed for
Robert Boulter . . . 1681* published: *An Horatian Ode,
The First Anniversary* and *A Poem upon the Death of Oliver
Cromwell* were printed but removed before publication.
One extant copy (British Museum C 59.i.8) retains these
(the last incomplete), and another has the first two.
Otherwise the volume contains all Marvell's surviving
poetry except the post-Restoration satires, the Latin and
Greek verses printed in 1637, *To His Noble Friend Mr
Richard Lovelace* and the elegies on Hastings and Villiers.

1689   Several of the satires printed in *A Collection of Poems on
Affairs of State . . . By A*[ndrew] *M*[arvel]*l, Esq; and other
Eminent Wits.*

1697   Most of the satires printed in *Poems on Affairs of State:
From The Time of Oliver Cromwell, to the Abdication of
K. James the Second.*

1699   Satires reprinted in *Poems on Affairs of State . . . The Third
Edition* (there is a fourth edition in 1702, a fifth in 1703,
a sixth in 1710 and another, still called the sixth, in 1716).

1705   Satires reprinted in *A New Collection of Poems Relating to
State Affairs.*

Part One Contemporaneous Criticism, Neglect and Revival

Introduction

The one notable thing about contemporaneous criticism of Marvell's poetry is the lack of it. When the collected poems came out in 1681 they were 'cried up as excellent' by 'many persons of his persuasion', as Anthony à Wood disdainfully recalls. No further details of their reception survive. Certainly it does not seem to have struck readers that they had just come into a deathless bit of their literary heritage. Nor was the 1681 collection a response to any popular demand. Mary Palmer, Marvell's housekeeper, published it, signing the preface 'Mary Marvell', so as to make good her claim that she was his widow. Her idea was to get her hands on £500 which he had been keeping for two bankrupt friends. She put together whatever seemed suitable among the 'few books and papers of small value' she had come across in Marvell's lodging, added a portrait, and presented the whole in a handsome format. No doubt she hoped that this commemorative volume would attract enough of Marvell's political admirers to pay its way, and no doubt it did. The portrait, missing from most surviving copies, seems to have been especially sought after. There was no second edition.

There are plenty of contemporary manuscripts of Marvell's satires, but there are no manuscript copies of the non-political poems. In a century when manuscript circulation was so usual this state of affairs presumably reflects a deliberate decision on Marvell's part to keep his poetry to himself. The only exception is *A Dialogue between Thyrsis and Dorinda*, which William Lawes somehow got hold of in an early version, and set to music. It became a popular song. Even *An Horatian Ode* cannot be proved to have had a wider audience than Marvell himself. Cleanth Brooks's discovery that the ode's unusual stanza form was imitated in Sir Richard Fanshawe's translations of Horace will carry no weight. The translations may have been written twenty years before the ode, as William Simeone suggests (*N. & Q.*, vol. 197, 1952, pp. 316–18). Arguments based on echoes of the

ode in a poem of Robert Wild's (1651) or in Buckingham's
epitaph on Fairfax (1671–2) are subject to the inherent
doubtfulness of arguments based on echoes.

True, the author of *A Letter from Amsterdam* (1678), whoever
he was, sounds for a moment as if he has heard something about
Marvell's lyrics: ''Tis well he is now transprosed into politics,
they say he had much ado to live upon poetry.' But 'poetry'
probably means satires, as opposed to 'transprosing'.
Everyone knew Marvell wrote those. John Aubrey's notes are
more definite:

He was a great master of the Latin tongue; an excellent poet
in Latin or English: for Latin verses there was no man could
come into competition with him. . . . He kept bottles of wine
at his lodging, and many times he would drink liberally by
himself to refresh his spirits, and exalt his muse.

Aubrey had known Marvell, of course, but he was writing after
the 1681 volume had made the lyrics public property.

Even then, Aubrey's stress falls unmistakably on the Latin
verse. *The Garden* and *On a Drop of Dew* both started as Latin
poems (apparently Carl Bain is alone in thinking the English came
first, *P.Q.*, vol. 38, 1959, pp. 436–9). Perhaps the other English
lyrics were Latin lyrics first, too, and have survived in English
alone because Mary Palmer did not bother with the Latin versions.
Marvell's estimate of himself as a Latin poet was seemingly as
high as Aubrey's. In 1671 Louis XIV offered a thousand pistoles
for the best Latin couplet to go on the front of the Louvre. 'All
the wits' of France and Italy were 'very busy' for the prize,
according to the English diplomat William Perwich, and so was
Marvell. No one won, Professor Legouis says (*T.L.S.*, 26 April
1957, p. 593). Louis lost interest, and became engrossed with
Versailles instead. On the other hand Archbishop Sancroft quotes
the winning couplet in his commonplace book, now in the

Bodleian, and says the poet was given six hundred crowns a year. Unfortunately he omits his name. Anyway it was not Marvell. But about Latin versifying the Council of State was also of Aubrey's mind. In 1653 Marvell, not Milton, was chosen to write the Latin poem which accompanied Cromwell's portrait to the Swedish court.

As a satirist, of course, Marvell was universally known. His name appeared first on the title page, and 'other Eminent Wits' second, when his satires appeared in collections. They were reprinted frequently until 1716. Earlier, when they had to be circulated surreptitiously, no one was in two minds about the author. He was so plainly the leading satirist that other people's work was constantly being ascribed to him. Even in 1667, when he had hardly begun as a satirist, the 'Directions-to-a-Painter' satires, published as Sir John Denham's, were 'thought by many', Anthony à Wood says, to be Marvell's. They still are by some (the pros and cons are mulled over afresh in D. V. Erdman and E. G. Fogel, *Evidence for Authorship*, 1966).

But to his contemporaries Marvell was pre-eminently a great prose writer, not a poet. Gilbert Burnet, writing in 1687, called the two parts of the *Rehearsal Transprosed* 'the wittiest books that have appeared in this age.' Charles II, 'not a great reader of books', read them 'over and over again'. Rochester, who never notices the poetry, praised these in *Tunbridge Wells*. They were subjected at once to the minutest verbal criticism, as the poems are today. Their phrasing, their logic, their addiction to metaphor, their author's impotence, homosexuality and 'frenchified' manners were all topics of inquiry in the hostile pamphlets of 1672-3. Their stylistic affiliations were noted. It was the unknown Elizabethan master-satirist, 'Martin Marprelate', who had provided Marvell with the idea of using comic banter in controversy. The *Rehearsal Transprosed* justifies the practice word-for-word out of Martin. Samuel Parker, Marvell's

antagonist, spotted the allusion immediately, and insists wearisomely
on the parallel between the two writers in his *Reproof* (1673).
Dryden can still think of nothing better ten years later when the
preface to *Religio Laici* calls Martin Marprelate 'the Marvel of
those times . . . the first Presbyterian scribbler who sanctified libels
and scurrility to the use of the Good Old Cause.'

Marvell is not even mentioned as a poet in the epitaph his
nephew William Popple wrote for him. The brilliant success of
his prose in the last few years of his life may be the explanation.
Similarly the unknown elegist of *On his Excellent Friend Mr
Anth.* [sic] *Marvell*, printed in 1697, ignores the poetry. Marvell is
acclaimed as 'this island's watchful sentinel', its defence against
Rome and 'arbitrary power'. It was on the strength of the prose,
too, that Swift, Marvell's pupil in style, called him a 'great genius'.
'We still read Marvell's answer to Parker with pleasure, though the
book it answers be sunk long ago.' There is no question, it
seems, of anyone still reading *To his Coy Mistress* or *The Garden*.

Marvell's secretiveness about his poetry includes not talking
about it in his letters or elsewhere. Critics have picked hopefully
at the prose for oblique comments on the poems. In *Remarks
Upon a Late Disingenuous Discourse* Marvell mentions the
inappropriateness of an 'architect' sawing timber or cleaving
logs. This would be 'to debase and neglect his vocation'.
E. E. Duncan-Jones (*N. & Q.*, n.s. vol. 3, 1956, pp. 383–4) reads
this as a criticism of his own line, 'So architects do square and
hew', in *A Dialogue between the Soul and Body*. Maybe, but the
'foreign architect' who hews whole forests in the first stanza of
Upon Appleton House makes it more (though more dully)
probable that 'hew' just means 'cause to be hewn' in both places.
Ingenious misreading is all such speculations usually lead to.
Isabel G. MacCaffrey, for instance (in *M.P.*, vol. 61, 1964,
pp. 261–9), takes the image of a 'great iron nail' driven through
'the axletree of Nature' in the *Rehearsal Transprosed* as a 'more

explicit' version of the 'iron wedges' in *The Definition of Love*.
But nails are not more explicit wedges, they are quite different.
Nails join, wedges split; 'wedge' never meant 'nail'. The lovers in
The Definition are at the poles of the world's axle; the wedges are
not. Mrs MacCaffrey's research can only help readers get the
poem wrong.

We are thrown back on the few comments on his own art
Marvell did make. The longest is *On Mr Milton's Paradise Lost*.
This admires Milton for omitting everything 'improper', and
derides Dryden's operatic version (*The State of Innocence*). More
adventurously, it recalls Marvell's fears that when Milton got to
work on the 'sacred truths' they would disappear under classical
debris, and it fairly plainly condemns the 'spite' of the hero in
Samson Agonistes. Aubrey records another snatch of literary
criticism: 'I remember I heard him say that the Earl of
Rochester was the only man in England that had the true vein of
satire.' Another is in a letter of 1667 to Lord Wharton. Marvell
finds that some verses by Simon Ford 'strain for wit and conceit
more than becomes the gravity of the author or the sadness of the
subject.' It is a pity we do not know what verses he is talking
about. In *Tom May's Death* the poet's function is defined:

When the sword glitters o'er the judges' head,
And fear has coward churchmen silenced,
Then is the poet's time, 'tis then he draws,
And single fights forsaken virtue's cause.
He, when the wheel of empire whirleth back,
And though the world's disjointed axle crack,
Sings still of ancient rights and better times,
Seeks wretched good, arraigns successful crimes.

(63–70)

It is wonderfully public. Yet there is no trace of publication until
thirty years after it was written, nor the least evidence that it was

made public in manuscript. Marvell, so far as we know, was haranguing an empty room.

It looks, then, as if Marvell's best poetry was unknown to his contemporaries until after his death. If, when it was eventually published, debate had begun to develop around it, there would be some point in breaking off our account here so as to separate contemporary estimates from the gradual formation of a critical tradition. But what has to be recorded is two centuries of neglect. Accounting for this is a matter of guesswork. The reasons usually advanced merely rephrase the problem. There is talk of the waning popularity of metaphysical poetry, of the rise of satire at the expense of lyric. In this vein a recent inquirer, George de F. Lord, tells us that between the writing of Marvell's lyrics and their publication 'a revolution in taste had intervened'. Patently, but why? The Restoration had intervened, too; so had the beginning of the Royal Society, the Two Party System, Greenwich Observatory, and other items that can be made to look significant. But these, like the change in taste, must be symptoms, not causes. All that had actually changed, as usual, was the state of man's knowledge. Mathematics, particularly, was advancing. But it would take a determined theorist to dredge this up as an explanation of the failure to appreciate Marvell's poetry. If it was the 'age of science' that it failed to appeal to, why does it appeal to ours?

Besides, it is not just a question, as with Donne, of extremely popular poetry becoming less so. With Marvell we have masterpieces which no one noticed at all. The nearest parallel seems to be in another art and another country – Vermeer. His dates are about the same as Marvell's. The output of both was small, which naturally made them easier to overlook. Only two of Vermeer's contemporaries seem to have mentioned the fact that he was a painter, and as late as 1882 the *Head of a Girl with Pearl Ear Drops*, one of his most famous works, fetched 4s 6d at an auction in the Hague. Practising artists (Eliot with Marvell; Pissarro and

Van Gogh with Vermeer) played a part in both revivals. All
mere coincidence, of course. Still, there are a few other
similarities. Both artists can (and did) look commonplace: Marvell
just another Silver Poet of the Seventeenth Century; Vermeer
just another genre painter. Marvell was classed with, and a bit
below, Lovelace; Vermeer with Mieris and Metsu. 'It is just as
easy to find all Vermeer's accessories in works of his painter
contemporaries, as it is to discover that in his pictures everything
is different' (Ludwig Goldscheider). *Mutatis mutandis* it ideally
fits Marvell. And what makes him and Vermeer 'different' is
curiously, and similarly, hard to define. Art critics talk about the
uncanny significance Vermeer gives to the ordinary – a jug, a
folded cloth – simply by the way he paints it. Yet the way he
paints it – the enamel finish, the camera-like vision – hardly looks
mysterious in itself. The effect is of casual moments caught with
unsettling deliberation. Marvell, writing, say, on a girl and her
dead pet, has a comparable suggestiveness. Further, the discovery
of symbolic meanings in both artists is easy enough now and then.
Vermeer's *Lady Weighing Pearls*, for instance, has a picture of the
Last Judgement hanging on the wall behind her. But with neither
Vermeer nor Marvell can the individual power be attributed to
these traditional moral properties. It has to be accounted for in
painterly and literary terms: attention to the palette and the placing
of objects in Vermeer's case; to the vocabulary and the placing of
words in Marvell's. The results obtainable can be seen in, say,
Cleanth Brooks's piece on the *Horatian Ode* or Robert Ellrodt's on
time and space in Marvell. But by the time these were written the
poems had been waiting three hundred years.

   At all events when the eighteenth century thought of Marvell
it was not as a poet but as an incorruptible patriot, the Tyrant's
Foe. Legends gathered around him. A particular favourite told
how he had refused a £1,000 bribe and dined, the same evening,
off mutton stew. The earliest version, without the mutton stew,

occurred in Thomas Cooke's edition of the *Works* in 1726. Like
Captain Thompson's edition of 1776, Cooke's was a political
gesture rather than an edition. Dedicated to the Duke of
Devonshire, it was meant to connect the rule of the Whigs with
England's Aristides – Cooke's new name for Marvell. To the
poems, Cooke was not much attracted. He complained that they
were careless. The best, in his view, were the lines on *Paradise
Lost*, *Bludius et Corona* and *A Dialogue between the Two Horses*.
This was the Cooke who found a place in the *Dunciad*. Captain
Thompson's three handsome folios were a reply to a new political
situation: George III's determination to bridle the Whigs and
increase the royal powers. Wilkes, a friend of Thompson's, and
Burke were among the subscribers, and the Whig peers headed the
list. David Garrick appeared lower down. Thompson's
responsiveness to the poetry was small enough for him to include
as Marvell's some hymns of Addison's.

Like the two editions, most references to Marvell during the
century were political. In 1701 Defoe drew on *A Dialogue between
the Two Horses* for his *True Born Englishman*, countering
chauvinist prejudice against a foreign king. In 1735 the *Craftsman*,
the main Opposition paper, borrowed pugnacious quotations from
Marvell's prose. He figures as the hero of William Mason's ode
To Independency, 1756, and as an example of intrepid patriotism
in Charles Churchill's satire *The Author*, 1763. Churchill was
another of Wilkes's friends. Across the Atlantic, too, Marvell was
invoked to embarrass the authorities. In a dispute over the
construction of the new Philadelphia market in 1773 'Andrew
Marvell' is among the dissidents. It is surprising to find Voltaire
alluding to Marvell in 1748 as *fameux poète anglais*. No one in his
own country would have called him that.

There is little enough evidence that the poems were read at all.
Addison must have read *To his Coy Mistress* because he paraphrases
lines from it in a *Spectator* article in June 1711, apparently with no

suspicion they would be recognized. In 1716 Tonson's *Miscellany Poems* prints a few of the lyrics, cutting out stanzas here and there. Presumably as a result, Marvell gets a mention in Giles Jacob's *Historical Account of the Lives and Writings of Our Most Considerable English Poets*, 1720. Besides the satires, Jacob lists as Marvell's poems only *On Mr Milton's Paradise Lost* ('an excellent piece'), *Damon the Mower*, *Young Love* and *Music's Empire* ('one of the best of Mr Marvell's'). *The Garden* and *The Nymph Complaining for the Death of her Fawn* are overlooked, though they, too, were in Tonson's bunch. About 1721 Pope was reading and making ink marks in the 1705 *State Affairs* collection, which reprinted Marvell's satires. But he never alludes to Marvell. Johnson's *Lives of the Poets* (1779–81) recognizes Marvell only as Milton's friend. There is no word of the poems, though one or two quotations in Johnson's *Dictionary* show he had read them.

The Romantic poets are also disappointing witnesses. Coleridge, prophet of the metaphysical revival, jotted down quotations from the *Rehearsal Transprosed* in 1800, but gives no inkling that he has read the poems. Southey copied the lines on Charles's execution from the *Horatian Ode* into a commonplace book, without comment. One of Wordsworth's early notebooks contains the ode, and he had read the satires. Offering Scott a helping hand with his edition of Dryden in 1805, he advises him to have a look in Marvell's poems, 'which I have not seen these many years', for an allusion to the slitting of Sir John Coventry's nose (it is in *Further Advice to a Painter*). 'Many years' may be nine. Wordsworth had planned to feature Marvell as a middle-class patriot in a satire he was writing in 1796, but it came to nothing. The famous sonnet of 1802 lists Marvell merely as one of Milton's republican friends.

After Tonson's, Marvell did not appear again in an anthology until the second edition of George Ellis's *Specimens of the Early English Poets* in 1801. Ellis prints *Young Love* and *Daphnis and*

Chloe, so cut as to deprive it of point, with the information that
Marvell is 'principally distinguished by his inflexible patriotism'.
The improvement in Marvell's fortunes at the beginning of the
nineteenth century was not Ellis's doing but Charles Lamb's. A
letter of Lamb's to William Godwin in 1800 carries the news that
he is 'just going to possess' Marvell's poems. In two of the
Essays of Elia, first printed in the *London Magazine* in 1821 and
1824, Lamb quotes from *The Garden* and *Upon Appleton House*.
He speaks affectionately of 'that garden loving poet' and says –
the phrase became famous – that all Marvell's serious poetry is full
of a 'witty delicacy'. Lamb must take the credit, such as it is, for
introducing Hazlitt and Leigh Hunt to Marvell. Hunt recalls how
he and Lamb failed, not surprisingly, to persuade Hazlitt that
The Character of Holland was funny by 'laughing immeasurably'.
Hazlitt uses the poem to illustrate the 'forced and far-fetched
method' of Marvell's 'satires and witty pieces' in his *Lectures on
the English Comic Writers*. In his 1818 (and 1821) lectures, though,
Hazlitt applauded Marvell, and frowned upon readers for neglecting
him. He rather spoiled the effect by adding that he had not looked
at the *Horatian Ode*, though he had heard it praised. His own
favourites among the lyrics are indicated with some vagueness: 'his
boat song, his descriptions of a fawn, and his lines to Lady Vere'.
It sounds remarkably like Leigh Hunt's selection: 'his song about
the Bermudas boat, his lines on a wounded fawn, the verses in
which he mentions "Fairfax and the starry Vere".' Both,
probably, were recalling conversations with Lamb, rather than the
poems themselves. Hazlitt was wrong, anyway, in thinking there
were some 'lines to Lady Vere': the line Hunt quotes is from
Upon Appleton House. Later, bits from *The Character of Holland*
and *Flecknoe* appeared in Hunt's anthology of *Wit and Humour
from the English Poets*, 1846, but Marvell did not qualify for the
companion volume of *Imagination and Fancy*. Marvell 'wrote a
great deal better in prose than verse', said Hunt.

This view was perfectly commonplace in the first half of the century. Attention was still fixed, when fixed at all, on Marvell as statesman and controversialist. Isaac Disraeli, narrating the defeat of Parker in *Quarrels of Authors*, 1814, seems unaware that Marvell wrote poetry at all. John Dove's *Life of Andrew Marvell, the Celebrated Patriot*, 1832, has few notions about the poetry, and those it does have are copied from two unsigned articles that had appeared in the *Retrospective Review* in 1824–5. These, while regretting Marvell's 'vulgarism and commonplace similes' had quoted extensively from his lyrics and predicted that they would one day be part of our 'standard literature'. Hartley Coleridge's *Life* of Marvell in 1833 borrows liberally from Dove. Coleridge says he met with Marvell's poems 'only by accident', and thinks it 'disgraceful to English booksellers' they are so little known. He disposes of them, though, in a fraction of the space given to the politics. So does Henry Rogers in his essay on Marvell in the *Edinburgh Review*, January 1844. The 'best' poems in Thompson's edition, Rogers explains, have been proved not Marvell's anyway (i.e. Addison's hymns). Between 1824 and 1862 Marvell participated in five of Landor's *Imaginary Conversations*. This Marvell is essentially a staunch republican, though he enjoys some hearty literary chat with Milton – 'Alighieri wanted flexibility of muscle' – and agrees with Henry Marten that the metaphysical poets were too obscure.

Meanwhile there were some signs of awakening interest in Marvell's lyrics. Thomas Campbell included four in his *Specimens*, 1819, and S. C. Hall four in his *Book of Gems*, 1836. *Bermudas* and *The Nymph* are both specimens and gems, the first rapidly becoming Marvell's best-known poem. But Hall still thinks of Marvell as 'the leading prose wit of England', and confesses that as a poet 'he was not of the highest order, not perhaps in even a high order'. In 1825 John Clare, having read Ellis's *Specimens*, and heard that Marvell was 'a great advocate for liberty', wrote a poem called *Death*, 'sprinkling a few old words here and there', and sent it to William Hone's *Every-Day Book* as Marvell's. Hone, his knowledge of Marvell evidently as extensive as Clare's, printed it. George Craik's *Sketches of the History of Literature*, 1845, improves distinctly (it is not, perhaps, saying much) on anything that had gone before. Craik tends to quote rather than analyse, but he is alive to the 'vigorous humour' and 'extemporaneous style' of the satires and penetrating about the 'union of grace and force', the swift transitions from 'sparkling levity' to 'solemn pathos' in *To his Coy Mistress*. It is no surprise to learn that Grierson read Craik before writing his preface to *Metaphysical Lyrics* in 1921. At the time, though, Craik's insights had little effect. Mary Russell Mitford proceeded to recollect, improbably, the 'earnestness and heartiness' of Marvell's lyrics in *Recollections of a Literary Life*, 1852. The next year E. P. Hood's *Andrew Marvell: The Wit, Statesman and Poet* still claimed Addison's hymns as Marvell's. Hood settled for an autobiographical reading of the other poems, *The Definition of Love* reflecting suppressed longings for Mary Fairfax. He paints an enthusiastic picture of Marvell's later temptations: 'How many of those voluptuous houris who surrounded the court of the king might have been his slaves?'

The American reaction, in the meantime, was more intelligent. Emerson, at twenty-five, speaks of his admiration for 'Herbert, Shakespeare, Marvell, Herrick, Milton, Ben Jonson', beside whom 'Homer and Virgil and Dante and Tasso and Byron and Wordsworth' have a 'pale ineffectual fire'. Eight years later, in 1836, Poe's review of Hall's *Book of Gems* gets more out of *The Nymph Complaining for the Death of her Fawn* than Hall would have dreamed possible. John Greenleaf Whittier praises *The Nymph* and *The Garden* and *Upon Appleton House* and the 'splendid ode to Cromwell' in the *National Era* for May 1848. Whittier, to be sure, is attracted first to Marvell the patriot and prose writer. He reckons the parody speech from the throne the

finest piece of satire 'in the entire compass of our language'. In
Boston, in 1857, appeared the first edition of Marvell's *Poetical
Works* to be prompted by an interest in his poetical works. The
introduction, pointing out that his 'wit' was 'interfused with
feeling', foreshadows Grierson and Eliot. Marvell's popularity
continued. In 1870 James Russell Lowell declared *Upon the Death
of Oliver Cromwell* and *An Horatian Ode* 'worth more than all
Carlyle's biography'.

Back in England Marvell figured in George Gilfillan's *Specimens
of the Less Known British Poets*, 1860. It was Tennyson that changed
all that. He conveyed to Palgrave his 'special admiration' for
Marvell, and would recite the *Coy Mistress* to him, 'dwelling
more than once on the magnificent hyperbole, the powerful
union of pathos and humour', though instructing him that in
'Thorough the iron gates of life', '*grates* would have intensified
Marvell's image'. He insisted that *An Horatian Ode* should go into
the *Golden Treasury*. Matthew Arnold, dispatching a copy of the
newly-published *Treasury* to Sainte-Beuve, seized on the ode as
buried treasure: '*Tout le monde l'ignorait*.' Sainte-Beuve was to
pass this information on to his readers two years later, offering
samples of the ode in French prose. The poem's famous poise
seems to escape the French critic. He is struck by its '*feu
d'enthousiasme*'. Palgrave chose *Bermudas* and *The Garden* as well
for his collection, warning his audience that the second
constituted, like *Lycidas*, 'a test of any reader's insight into the most
poetical aspects of poetry.' He did not risk the *Coy Mistress* with the
Victorians. Nor did Richard Chenevix-Trench, Archbishop of
Dublin, in his *Household Book of English Poetry*, 1868, purged of
anything that might not be 'confidently placed in the hands of
every member of the household.' *Eyes and Tears*, *On a Drop of
Dew* and *An Horatian Ode* survive the Archbishop's scrutiny. The
last is recommended for giving members of the household
'unacquainted with Horace' an idea, albeit imperfect, of the real

thing. Marvell's stock was now rising. George Macdonald lets it be known in *England's Antiphon*, 1868, that 'some half dozen' of his poems are 'worth all the verse that Cowley ever made'. Next year John Ormsby writes an appreciation for the *Cornhill Magazine*, with illustrations from 'less known' poems like *To his Coy Mistress*. A year later Murrays put the Boston edition of the *Poetical Works* on the English market. In 1872 Grosart's edition begins to appear, prepared with the usual grandiose incompetence, and W. D. Christie alerts readers of the *Saturday Review* to the 'unmitigated filth' they will find in the satires Grosart includes. 'A most rich and nervous poet' is Gerard Manley Hopkins's verdict, delivered in a letter to R. W. Dixon in 1879. He admits that he has read only extracts.

The closing years of the century see Marvell taken up by the literati. Edmund Gosse explains to his American audience that Marvell is the last of the 'school of Donne', and that those who have come under the 'spell' of these poets cannot bear to hear them 'analyzed or even touched by unsympathetic people.' Gosse's hypersensitivity does not quite incapacitate him, and he is able to identify Donne's comparison of lovers to compasses as 'tawdry false jewellery', and Marvell's vigilant patrol of stars as 'infantile'. 'Waller and Denham had taught English people to outgrow these childish toys of fancy.' Aitken's edition of the poems, 1892, excludes the satires. The editor apologizes, too, for Marvell's 'conceits', 'so often found in Donne and his contemporaries.' Reviewing Aitken in the *Academy*, E. K. Chambers thinks that some 'conceits' are all right, but admits that *On a Drop of Dew* 'affords a terrible example'. The satires are 'not a subject to dwell upon with pleasure.' A. C. Benson in *Macmillan's Magazine* blames Milton. His 'poisonous advice' (about getting a job as secretary) has meant the 'loss of a great English poet'. We have the 'vile realism' of the satires instead of more lyrics inspired by 'that exquisite relation that may exist between a grown man, pure in heart, and a young girl [i.e. Mary Fairfax], when disparity of fortune and circumstance forbids all thought of marriage.' Benson's classical scholarship allows him, however, to correct readers' notions about the lyrics Marvell did manage to write. They are, he points out, 'vague and prolix'. 'A lover of proportion such as Gray' would have cut them down to size. Even the lines which Benson quotes as 'The grave's a fine and private place,|But none, methinks, do there embrace' are 'a mere pagan commonplace, however daintily expressed.' Thanks, perhaps, to this type of recommendation, *To his Coy Mistress* is still not among the poems 'with which everyone is familiar' in 1896, when J. Churton Collins includes it, for that reason, in his *Treasury of Minor British Poetry*. F. G. Walters, writing in the *Gentleman's Magazine* in 1900, can still call Marvell 'a forgotten poet and satirist'.

Nevertheless H. C. Beeching, opening twentieth-century Marvell criticism with an article in the *National Review*, July 1901, compliments his own generation on its 'superior poetical taste' in resurrecting Marvell's lyrics. *The Unfortunate Lover*, Beeching acknowledges, is 'probably the worst love poem ever written by a man of genius', and *The Definition of Love*, 'merely a study after Donne's *Valediction*.' Still, Marvell was partially saved from Donne's 'careless writing' by 'the study of Milton'. W. J. Courthope in his *History of English Poetry*, 1903, is scarcely more helpful than Beeching. Marvell, Courthope feels, was a sort of mixture of Donne, Vaughan and Herrick. With Augustine Birrell's biography in 1905 Marvell achieves the dignity of the 'English Men of Letters' series. Not that Birrell says much about the poems. 'The judicious reader will be able to supply his own reflections ... Poetry is a personal matter'. Personally Birrell reflects on Marvell's lack of finish. 'He could not write verses like his friend Lovelace.' Francis Thompson protested mildly in his *Academy* review, but offered, as an alternative, only the Courthope

Mixture Theory, with the qualification that Marvell 'does not actually rival' Herrick. The *Saturday Review* objected that Birrell was wasting its time. Marvell's work has 'neither quantity nor significance to warrant a regular biography.'

Not until after the Great War does the approach to Marvell's poetry become suddenly more searching. Obviously something had gone dreadfully wrong with European culture. Perhaps it was that we had lost the aptitude for thinking and feeling simultaneously. H. J. Massingham discovers this blend of 'intellect and sensitiveness' in Marvell. Introducing his *Treasury of Seventeenth Century English Verse*, 1919, he demonstrates that *To his Coy Mistress* is a 'beautiful composite' of experiences which we have come to think of as opposed. Grierson elaborated the theory in his *Metaphysical Lyrics*, 1921, naming *To his Coy Mistress* as 'the very roof and crown' of the metaphysical achievement. T. S. Eliot gave it its final form in his review of Grierson – the 'Metaphysical Poets' essay.

Meanwhile the tercentenary of Marvell's birth arrived. The literary papers published their tributes. In Hull Marvell tramcars appeared on the streets bearing 'an appropriate and dignified scheme of decoration' devised by the Principal of the Municipal School of Art. There was a sermon and a lunch. The Chairman of the Hull Luncheon Club congratulated Birrell, the guest of honour, on his 'great study', to which the 'increasing estimation' of Marvell was due. Birrell modestly attributed this to Marvell's 'sweet garden poetry' itself. The Oxford University Press brought out a commemoration volume edited by W. H. Bagguley. It reprinted tributes from various newspapers by Cyril Falls, H. J. Massingham, J. C. Squire and Edmund Gosse – all negligible – along with T. S. Eliot's 'Andrew Marvell' from the *T.L.S.* and an essay by Edward Wright from the *Bookman*. This contained a new idea. Marvell 'expressed into poetry a philosophy as large as that which Coleridge could not reduce into prose. He was a singing

Cambridge Platonist.' A good deal of modern Marvell criticism starts here.

Eliot's and Wright's discernment did not change the climate of opinion at once. Besides, Eliot had frowned upon the salmon fishers in *Upon Appleton House*, and this corroborated nineteenth-century smugness about Marvell's 'conceits'. Accordingly we find F. L. Lucas carrying on about Marvell's 'puerility' and 'enormities', the 'intellectual abortions' of *Upon Appleton House*, in the *New Statesman*, August 1923. Victoria Sackville-West lays about her with a similar confidence in *Andrew Marvell*, 1929. Marvell is a minor poet who 'had read too much Donne'. He writes 'preposterous rubbish'. His 'conceits' are a 'disfigurement'. In spite of his 'nature-mysticism' he is spiritually shallow. There are no 'moral reflections' such as Miss Sackville-West requires in 'all poetry of the noblest order'. His poems do not even show any 'underlying doubts'. He had 'a tame, somewhat smug, material outlook.' By this time the change of climate had come about, all the same. The need for more respect was conceded. Pierre Legouis's gruelling *André Marvell: poète, puritain, patriote*, 1928, announced the change as distinctly, in its way, as Eliot's essay or Margoliouth's edition. Eliot himself, reviewing the 1923 facsimile of Marvell's *Miscellaneous Poems*, observes that 'seventeenth century poetry is to be in fashion', and rapidly separates himself from the crowd. Marvell, he announces, is neither great nor individual enough to be given the kind of individual treatment the tercentenary essayists gave him. He is not even as great as Henry King. He and his contemporaries were all 'fantastical'. There is not one of them who is 'a safe model for study' like Chaucer or Pope. No one took any notice. The review (in the *Nation and Athenaeum*, 19 September 1923) was not reprinted. Eliot's 'Andrew Marvell' remained as the permanent influence.

John Milton

from a letter to John Bradshaw February 1653

There will be with you tomorrow upon some occasion of business a gentleman whose name is Mr Marvell; a man whom both by report, and the converse I have had with him, of singular desert for the state to make use of; who also offers himself, if there be any employment for him. His father was the Minister of Hull and he hath spent four years abroad in Holland, France, Italy and Spain, to very good purpose, as I believe, and the gaining of those four languages; besides he is a scholar and well read in the Latin and Greek authors, and no doubt of an approved conversation, for he comes now lately out of the house of the Lord Fairfax who was General, where he was entrusted to give some instructions in the languages to the Lady his daughter.

Samuel Parker

from *History of His Own Time* 1728

Among these saucy detractors, the most notorious was that vile fellow Marvell: whose life, from his youth upwards, was one scene of wickedness. He was naturally so pert and impudent, that he took upon him to write satires for the faction, in which there was more defamation than wit. His talent was in railing; in everything else he had a grovelling genius. Being out of favour with his father, and expelled the University, he had less regard to his conscience, than he had before to his reputation. He was a strolling, ragged, half starved poetaster; beaten at every tavern, and caned and kicked every day for his sauciness. At last, by Milton's interest (to whom he was agreeable, because he had such another ill-natured talent), he was made one of the under secretaries to Cromwell's secretary. Pleased with his advancement, he published a congratulatory poem in praise of the tyrant; but when, for a long time, he sat hatching a panegyric, he brought forth a satire against all monarchs, legally established. ...

But at the Restoration, this miserable wretch relapsing into his former poverty, procured himself, for the sake of a livelihood, to be chosen a Member for a small burough, in which his father had been a Presbyterian preacher in the rebellion, and was very serviceable to the party. . . . But these fellows could never carry one point in the House, for they were always treated with the utmost scorn and contempt; if they could do no good, they could do no hurt, for as soon as any one of them began to open his mouth, he was hissed; and as often as our poet spoke, he was cudgelled for it. For which reason, having often undergone that sort of discipline, he learned at last to hold his tongue: but when he was out of the House, he vented his spleen with great bitterness, when he could do it with impunity, and daily belched out his scurrilous libels against the King himself.

(214–16)

William Lisle Bowles

from his Introduction to *The Works of Alexander Pope, Esq.* 1806

Marvell abounds with conceits and false thoughts, but some of the descriptive touches are picturesque and beautiful. His description of a gently rising eminence is more picturesque, although not so elegantly and justly expressed, as the same subject is in Denham. I transcribe the following, as the poem is but little read. [Quotes *Upon the Hill and Grove at Billborow*, 17–20, 25–34.] Sometimes Marvell observes little circumstances of rural nature with the eye and feeling of a true poet:

Then as I careless on the bed
Of *gelid strawberries* do tread,
And through the hazels thick, espy,
The hatching throstle's shining eye.

(*Upon Appleton House*, 529–32)

The last circumstance is new, highly poetical, and could only have been described by one who was a real lover of nature, and a witness of her beauties in her most solitary retirement. It is the observation of such *circumstances* which can alone form an accurate descriptive rural poet. In this province of his art Pope therefore must evidently fail, as he could not describe what his physical infirmities prevented his observing. For the same reason Johnson, as a critic, was not a proper judge of this sort of poetry.

(I 123–4)

Mark Pattison

from *Essays*, edited by H. Nettleship 1889

Familiarity with the 'hatching throstle's shining eye' only proves that Bowles and Marvell had both been schoolboys and addicted to birds-nesting. But keen sympathy with Nature constitutes a positive disqualification for being a commentator on Pope, as it only quickens the sense of one of the deficiencies of Pope's school.

(II 374)

Hartley Coleridge

from *Biographia Borealis or Lives of Distinguished Northerns* 1833

We are sorry that Marvell had, by a satirical piece [*The Character of Holland*] (published probably during the Protectorate), contributed to influence the national prejudices of the vulgar against the Dutch, and what is still worse, he makes the natural disadvantages which it was the glory of that industrious race to have surmounted, a topic of ridicule and insult. . . .

The poems of Marvell are, for the most part, productions of his early youth. They have much of that over-activity of fancy, that remoteness of allusion, which distinguishes the school of Cowley; but they have also a heartfelt tenderness, a childish simplicity of feeling, among all their complication of thought, which would atone for all their conceits, if conceit were indeed as great an offence against poetic nature as Addison and other critics of the French school pretend. But though there are cold conceits, a conceit is not necessarily cold. The mind, in certain states of passion, finds comfort in playing with occult or casual resemblances, and dallies with the echo of a sound.

We confine our praise to the poems which he wrote for himself. As for those he made to order, for Fairfax or Cromwell, they are as dull as every true son of the muse would wish these things to be. Captain Edward Thom[p]son, who collected and published Marvell's works in 1776, has, with mischievous industry, scraped together, out of the state poems, and other common sewers, a quantity of obscene and scurrilous trash, which we are convinced Marvell did not write, and which, by whomsoever written, ought to be delivered over to condign oblivion.

(23, 63)

Edgar Allan Poe

from *Works*, edited by E. C. Stedman and G. E. Woodberry 1895 (from a review of S. C. Hall's *Book of Gems*, originally printed in the *Southern Literary Messenger,* August 1836)

How truthful an air of deep lamentation hangs here [in *The Nymph Complaining for the Death of her Fawn*] upon every gentle syllable! It pervades all. It comes over the sweet melody of the words, over the gentleness and grace which we fancy in the little maiden herself, – even over the half-playful, half-petulant air with which she lingers on the beauties and good qualities of her favorite, like the cool shadow of a summer cloud over a bed of lilies and violets, and 'all sweet flowers'. The whole thing is redolent with poetry of the very loftiest order. It is positively crowded with nature and with pathos. Every line is an idea, conveying either the beauty and playfulness of the fawn, or the artlessness of the maiden, or the love of the maiden, or her admiration, or her grief, or the fragrance, and sweet warmth, and perfect *appropriateness* of the little nest-like bed of lilies and roses, which the fawn devoured as it lay upon them, and could scarcely be distinguished from them by the once happy little damsel who went to seek her pet with an arch and rosy smile upon her face. Consider the great variety of *truth* and delicate thought in the few lines we have quoted – the *wonder* of the maiden at the fleetness of her favorite –

the 'little silver feet' – the fawn challenging his mistress to the race, 'with a pretty skipping grace', running on before, and then, with head turned back, awaiting her approach only to fly from it again – can we not distinctly perceive all these things? The exceeding vigor, too, and beauty of the line,

And trod as if on the four winds,[1]

(70)

which are vividly apparent when we regard the artless nature of the speaker, and the *four feet* of the favorite – *one for each wind*. Then the garden of '*my own*,' so overgrown – entangled – with lilies and roses as to be 'a little wilderness' – the fawn loving to be there and there '*only*' – the maiden seeking it 'where it *should* lie', and not being able to distinguish it from the flowers until 'itself would rise' – the lying among the lilies 'like a bank of lilies' – the loving to '*fill*' itself with roses,

And its pure virgin limbs to fold
In whitest sheets of lilies cold,

(89–90)

and these things being its '*chief*' delights – and then the pre-eminent beauty and naturalness of the concluding lines – whose very outrageous hyperbole and absurdity only render them the more true to nature and to propriety, when we consider the innocence, the artlessness, the enthusiasm, the passionate grief, and more passionate admiration of the bereaved child.

Had it lived long it would have been
Lilies without – roses within.

(91–2)
(II 287–8)

1 S. C. Hall had printed 'as if on' for Marvell's 'as on'. [Ed.]

Edward FitzGerald

from a letter to W. A. Wright 20 January 1872

By way of flourishing my eyes, I have been looking into Andrew
Marvell, an old favourite of mine, who led the way for Dryden in
verse, and Swift in prose, and was a much better fellow than the last,
at any rate. . . . Tennyson once said to me, some thirty years ago, or
more, in talking of Marvell's *Coy Mistress*, where it breaks in:

But at my back I always hear
Time's winged chariot hurrying near, etc.

'*That* strikes me as sublime, I can hardly tell why.' Of course, this
partly depends on its place in the poem.

Goldwin Smith

from 'Andrew Marvell' in *The English Poets. Selections with . . .
a General Introduction by Matthew Arnold*, edited by T. H. Ward
1880

As a poet Marvell is very unequal. He has depth of feeling, descriptive
power, melody; his study of the classics could not fail to teach him
form; sometimes we find in him an airy and tender grace which
remind us of the lighter manner of Milton: but art with him was only
an occasional recreation, not a regular pursuit; he is often slovenly,
sometimes intolerably diffuse, especially when he is seduced by the
facility of the octosyllabic couplet. He was also eminently afflicted with
the gift of 'wit' or ingenuity, much prized in his day. His conceits
vie with those of Donne or Cowley. He is capable of saying of the
Halcyon:

The viscous air wheres'e'er she fly,
Follows and sucks her azure dye;
The jellying stream compacts below,
If it might fix her shadow so.

(*Upon Appleton House*, 673–6)

And of Maria:

Maria such, and so doth hush
The world, and through the evening rush.
No new-born comet such a train
Draws through the sky, nor star new-slain.
For straight those giddy rockets fail,
Which from the putrid earth exhale,
But by her flames, in heaven tried,
Nature is wholly vitrified.

(*Upon Appleton House*, 681–8)

The Garden is an English version of a poem written in Latin by
Marvell himself. It may have gained by being cast originally in a
classical mould, which would repel prolixity and extravagant
conceits. In it Marvell has been said to approach Shelley: assuredly
he shows a depth of poetic feeling wonderful in a political gladiator.
The thoughts that dwell in 'a green shade' have never been more
charmingly expressed.

A Drop of Dew, like *The Garden*, was composed first in Latin. It is a
conceit, but a pretty conceit, gracefully as well as ingeniously worked
out, and forms a good example of the contrast between the philosophic poetry of those days, a play of intellectual fancy, and its more
spiritual and emotional counterpart in our own time. The concluding
lines, with their stroke of 'wit' about the manna are a sad fall.

The Bermudas was no doubt suggested by the history of the Oxen-
bridges. It is the 'holy and cheerful note' of a little band of exiles for
conscience sake wafted by Providence in their 'small boat' to a
home in a land of beauty.

Young Love is well known, and its merits speak for themselves. It is
marred by the intrusion in the third and fourth stanzas of the fiercer
and coarser passion.

The *Horatian Ode on Cromwell's Return from Ireland* cannot be positively proved to be the work of Marvell. Yet we can hardly doubt
that he was its author. The point of view and the sentiment, combining admiration of Cromwell with respect and pity for Charles,
are exactly his: the classical form would be natural to him; and so
would the philosophical conceit which disfigures the eleventh stanza.
The epithet *indefatigable* applied to Cromwell recurs in a poem which

is undoubtedly his; and so does the emphatic expression of belief that the hero could have been happier in private life, and that he sacrificed himself to the State in taking the supreme command. The compression and severity of style are not characteristic of Marvell; but they would be imposed on him in this case by his model. If the ode is really his, to take it from him would be to do him great wrong. It is one of the noblest in the English language, and worthily presents the figures and events of the great tragedy as they would impress themselves on the mind of an ideal spectator, at once feeling and dispassionate. The spirit of Revolution is described with a touch in the lines:

Though Justice against Fate complain,
And plead the ancient rights in vain:
   But those do hold or break
   As men are strong or weak.

(37–40)

Better than anything else in our language this poem gives an idea of a grand Horatian measure, as well as of the diction and spirit of an Horatian ode.

Of the lines *On Milton's Paradise Lost* some are vigorous; but they are chiefly interesting from having been written by one who had anxiously watched Milton's genius at work.

Marvell's amatory poems are cold; probably he was passionless. His pastorals are in the false classical style, and of little value. *Clorinda and Damon* is about the best of them, and about the best of that is

Near this, a fountain's liquid bell
Tinkles within the concave shell.

The Satires in their day were much admired and feared: they are now for the most part unreadable. The subjects of satire as a rule are ephemeral; but a great satirist like Juvenal or Dryden preserves his flies in the amber of his general sentiment. In Marvell's satires there is no amber: they are mere heaps of dead flies. Honest indignation against iniquity and lewdness in high places no doubt is there; but so are the meanness of Restoration politics and the dirtiness of Restoration thought. The curious may look at *The Character of Holland*, the jokes in which are as good or as bad as ever, though the cannon of Monk and De Ruyter have ceased to roar; and in *Britannia and*

Raleigh, the passage of which giving ironical advice to Charles II is a specimen of the banter which was deemed Marvell's peculiar gift, and in which Swift and Junius were his pupils.

Like Milton, Marvell wrote a number of Latin poems. One of them had the honour of being ascribed to Milton.

(II 382–4)

Alfred, Lord Tennyson

in conversation, from Hallam Tennyson's *Alfred Lord Tennyson. A Memoir* 1897

He would now [1887–8] quote long pieces from Andrew Marvell to us, *The Bermudas*, *The Garden*, and he told us that he had made Carlyle laugh for half an hour at the following line from *The Character of Holland*:

They, with mad labour, fish'd the land to shore

(10)

'And' he continued, 'about poetry or art Carlyle knew nothing. I would never have taken his word about either.'

(II 335)

Alice Meynell

from 'Andrew Marvell', *Pall Mall Gazette* 14 July 1897

'He earned the glorious name,' says a biographer of Andrew Marvell (editing an issue of that poet's works, which certainly has its faults), 'of the British Aristides.' The portly dullness of the mind that could make such a phrase, and, having made, award it, is not, in fairness, to affect a reader's thought of Marvell himself nor even of his time. Under correction, I should think that the award was not made in his own age; he did but live on the eve of the day that cumbered its mouth with phrases of such foolish burden and made literature stiff with them. He, doubtless, has moments of mediocre pomp, but even then it is Milton that he touches, and not anything more common; and he surely never even heard a threat of the pass that the English tongue should come to but a little later on.

Andrew Marvell's political rectitude, it is true, seems to have been of a robustious kind; but his poetry, at its rare best, has a 'wild civility', which might puzzle the triumph of him, whoever he was, who made a success of this phrase of the 'British Aristides'. Nay, it is difficult not to think that Marvell too, who was 'of middling stature, roundish-faced, cherry-cheeked', a healthy and active rather than a spiritual Aristides, might himself have been somewhat taken by surprise at the encounters of so subtle a muse. He, as a garden-poet, expected the accustomed Muse to lurk about the fountain-heads, within the caves, and by the walks and the statues of the gods, keeping the tryst of a seventeenth-century convention in which there were certainly no surprises. And for fear of the commonplaces of those visits Marvell sometimes outdoes the whole company of garden-poets in the difficult labours of the fancy. The reader treads with him a 'maze' most resolutely intricate, and is more than once obliged to turn back having been too much puzzled on the way to a small, visible, plain, and obvious goal of thought.

And yet this poet two or three times did meet a Muse he had hardly looked for among the trodden paths; a spiritual creature had been waiting behind a laurel or an apple tree. You find him coming away from such a divine ambush a wilder and a simpler man. All his garden had been made ready for poetry, and poetry was indeed there, but in unexpected hiding and in a strange form, looking rather like a fugitive, shy of the poet who was conscious of having her rules by heart, yet sweetly willing to be seen, for all her haste.

For it is only in those well-known poems, *The Garden*, translated from his own Latin, and *The Nymph Complaining for the Death of Her Fawn*, in that less familiar piece *The Mower Against Gardens*, in *The Picture of T.C. in a Prospect of Flowers*, with a few very brief passages in the course of duller verses, that Marvell comes into veritable possession of his own more interior powers – at least in the series of his garden lyrics. The political poems, needless to say, have an excellence of a different character and a higher degree. They have so much authentic dignity that 'the glorious name of the British Aristides' really seems duller when it is conferred as the earnings of the

Horatian Ode upon Cromwell's Return from Ireland than when it inappropriately clings to Andrew Marvell, cherry-cheeked, caught in the tendrils of his vines and melons. He shall be, therefore, the British Aristides in those moments of midsummer solitude; at least, the heavy phrase shall then have the smile it never sought.

Marvell can be tedious in these gardens – tedious with every ingenuity, refinement, and assiduity of invention. When he intends to flatter the owner of the *Hill and Grove at Billborow*, he is most deliberately silly, not as the eighteenth century was silly, but with a peculiar innocence. Unconsciousness there was not, assuredly; but the artificial phrases of Marvell had never been used by a Philistine; the artifices are freshly absurd, the cowardice before the plain face of commonplace is not vulgar, there is an evident simple pleasure in the successful evasion of simplicity, and all the anxiety of the poet comes to a happy issue before our eyes. He commends the Billborow hill because 'the stiffest compass could not strike' a more symmetrical and equal semi-circle than its form presents, and he rebukes the absent mountains because they deform the earth and affright the heavens. This hill, he says, with a little better fancy, only 'strives to raise the plain'. Lord Fairfax, to whose glory these virtues of the soil are dedicated, and whose own merit they illustrate, is then said to be admirable for the modesty whereby, having a hill, he has also a clump of trees on the top, wherein to sequester the honours of eminence. It is not too much to say that the whole of this poem is untouched by poetry.

So is almost that equally ingenious piece, *Appleton House*, addressed to the same friend. It chanced that Appleton House was small, and out of this plain little fact the British Aristides contrives to turn a sedulous series of compliments with fair success and with a most guileless face. What natural humility in the householder who builds in proportion to his body, and is contented like the tortoise and the bird! Further on, however, it appears that the admired house had been a convent, and that to the dispossessed nuns was due the praise of proportion; they do not get it, in any form, from Marvell. A pretty passage follows, on the wasting of gardens, and a lament over the passing away of some earlier England. . . . But nothing here is of the really fine quality of *The Picture of T.C.*, or *The Garden*, or *The Nymph Complaining for the Death of Her Fawn*.

In these three the presence of a furtive irony of the gentlest kind is the sure sign that they came of the visitings of the unlooked-for muse aforesaid. Marvell rallies his own 'Nymph', rallies his own soul for her clapping of silver wings in the solitude of summer trees; and more sweetly does he pretend to offer to the little girl 'T.C.' the prophetic homage of the habitual poets. . . .

The noble phrase of the *Horatian Ode* is not recovered again high or low throughout Marvell's book, if we except one single splendid and surpassing passage from *The Definition of Love*. The hopeless lover speaks:

Magnanimous despair alone
Could show me so divine a thing.

To his Coy Mistress is the only piece, not already named, altogether fine enough for an anthology. The Satires are, of course, out of reach for their inordinate length. The celebrated Satire on Holland certainly makes the utmost of the fun to be easily found in the physical facts of the country whose people 'with mad labour fished the land to shore'. The Satire on *Flecknoe* makes the utmost of another joke we know of – that of famine. Flecknoe, it will be remembered, was a poet, and poor; but the joke of his bad verses was hardly needed, so fine does Marvell find that of his hunger. Perhaps there is no age of English satire that does not give forth the sound of that laughter unknown to savages – that craven laughter.

(3)

T. S. Eliot

'Andrew Marvell', *Selected Essays* 1932 (first printed in the *Times Literary Supplement* 31 March 1921, pp. 201–2)

The tercentenary of the former member for Hull deserves not only the celebration proposed by that favoured borough, but a little serious reflection upon his writing. That is an act of piety, which is very different from the resurrection of a deceased reputation. Marvell has stood high for some years; his best poems are not very many, and not only must be well known, from the *Golden Treasury* and the *Oxford Book of English Verse*, but must also have been enjoyed by numerous readers. His grave needs neither rose nor rue nor laurel; there is no imaginary justice to be done; we may think about him, if there be need for thinking, for our own benefit, not his. To bring the poet back to life – the great, the perennial, task of criticism – is in this case to squeeze the drops of the essence of two or three poems; even confining ourselves to these, we may find some precious liquor unknown to the present age. Not to determine rank, but to isolate this quality, is the critical labour. The fact that of all Marvell's verse, which is itself not a great quantity, the really valuable part consists of a very few poems indicates that the unknown quality of which we speak is probably a literary rather than a personal quality; or, more truly, that it is a quality of a civilization, of a traditional habit of life. A poet like Donne, or like Baudelaire or Laforgue, may almost be considered the inventor of an attitude, a system of feeling or of morals. Donne is difficult to analyse: what appears at one time a curious personal point of view may at another time appear rather the precise concentration of a kind of feeling diffused in the air about him. Donne and his shroud, the shroud and his motive for wearing it, are inseparable, but they are not the same thing. The seventeenth century sometimes seems for more than a moment to gather up and to digest into its art all the experience of the human mind which (from the same point of view) the later centuries seem to have been partly engaged in repudiating. But Donne would have been an individual at any time and place; Marvell's best verse is the product of European, that is to say Latin, culture.

Out of that high style developed from Marlowe through Jonson (for Shakespeare does not lend himself to these genealogies) the seventeenth century separated two qualities: wit and magniloquence. Neither is as simple or as apprehensible as its name seems to imply, and the two are not in practice antithetical; both are conscious and cultivated, and the mind which cultivates one may cultivate the other. The actual poetry, of Marvell, of Cowley, of Milton, and of others, is a blend in varying proportions. And we must be on guard not to employ the terms with too wide a comprehension; for like the other fluid terms with which literary criticism deals, the meaning alters with the age, and for precision we must rely to some degree upon the literacy and good taste of the reader. The wit of the Caroline poets is not the wit of Shakespeare, and it is not the wit of Dryden, the great master of contempt, or of Pope, the great master of hatred, or of Swift, the great master of disgust. What is meant is some quality which is common to the songs in *Comus* and Cowley's *Anacreontics* and Marvell's *Horatian Ode*. It is more than a technical accomplishment, or the vocabulary and syntax of an epoch; it is, what we have designated tentatively as wit, a tough reasonableness beneath the slight lyric grace. You cannot find it in Shelley or Keats or Wordsworth; you cannot find more than an echo of it in Landor; still less in Tennyson or Browning; and among contemporaries Mr Yeats is an Irishman and Mr Hardy is a modern Englishman – that is to say, Mr Hardy is without it and Mr Yeats is outside of the tradition altogether. On the other hand, as it certainly exists in Lafontaine, there is a large part of it in Gautier. And of the magniloquence, the deliberate exploitation of the possibilities of magnificence in language which Milton used and abused, there is also use and even abuse in the poetry of Baudelaire.

Wit is not a quality that we are accustomed to associate with 'Puritan' literature, with Milton or with Marvell. But if so, we are at fault partly in our conception of wit and partly in our generalizations about the Puritans. And if the wit of Dryden or of Pope is not the only kind of wit in the language, the rest is not merely a little merriment or a little levity or a little impropriety or a little epigram. And, on the other hand, the sense in which a man like Marvell is a 'Puritan' is restricted. The persons who opposed Charles I and the persons who supported the Commonwealth were not all of the flock of Zeal-of-the-land Busy or the United Grand Junction Ebenezer Temperance Association. Many of them were gentlemen of the time who merely believed, with considerable show of reason, that government by a Parliament of gentlemen was better than government by a Stuart; though they were, to that extent, Liberal Practitioners, they could hardly foresee the tea-meeting and the Dissidence of Dissent. Being men of education and culture, even of travel, some of them were exposed to that spirit of the age which was coming to be the French spirit of the age. This spirit, curiously enough, was quite opposed to the tendencies latent or the forces active in Puritanism; the contest does great damage to the poetry of Milton; Marvell, an active servant of the public, but a lukewarm partisan, and a poet on a smaller scale, is far less injured by it. His line on the statue of Charles II, 'It is such

a King as no chisel can mend', may be set off against his criticism of
the Great Rebellion: 'Men . . . ought and might have trusted the
King.' Marvell, therefore, more a man of the century than a Puritan,
speaks more clearly and unequivocally with the voice of his literary
age than does Milton.

This voice speaks out uncommonly strong in the *Coy Mistress*. The
theme is one of the great traditional commonplaces of European
literature. It is the theme of 'O mistress mine', of 'Gather ye rosebuds'
of 'Go, lovely rose'; it is in the savage austerity of Lucretius and the
intense levity of Catullus. Where the wit of Marvell renews the
theme is in the variety and order of the images. In the first of the
three paragraphs Marvell plays with a fancy which begins by pleasing
and leads to astonishment.

Had we but world enough, and time,
This coyness, lady, were no crime,
                . . . I would
Love you ten years before the Flood:
And you should, if you please, refuse
Till the conversion of the Jews;
My vegetable love should grow
Vaster than empires and more slow. . . .

We notice the high speed, the succession of concentrated images, each
magnifying the original fancy. When this process has been carried to
the end and summed up, the poem turns suddenly with that surprise
which has been one of the most important means of poetic effect
since Homer:

But at my back I always hear
Time's wingèd chariot hurrying near:
And yonder all before us lie
Deserts of vast eternity.

A whole civilization resides in these lines:

Pallida Mors aequo pulsat pede pauperum tabernas,
Regumque turris. . . .[1]

1 Pale death with impartial foot knocks at poor huts and royal palaces. [Ed.]

And not only Horace but Catullus himself:

Nobis, cum semel occidit brevis lux,
Nox est perpetua una dormienda.[1]

The verse of Marvell has not the grand reverberation of Catullus's
Latin; but the image of Marvell is certainly more comprehensive and
penetrates greater depths than Horace's.

A modern poet, had he reached the height, would very likely have
closed on this moral reflection. But the three strophes of Marvell's
poem have something like a syllogistic relation to each other. After a
close approach to the mood of Donne,

       then worms shall try
That long-preserved virginity ...
The grave's a fine and private place,
But none, I think, do there embrace,

the conclusion,

Let us roll all our strength, and all
Our sweetness, up into one ball,
And tear our pleasures with rough strife,
Thorough the iron gates of life.

It will hardly be denied that this poem contains wit; but it may not
be evident that this wit forms the crescendo and diminuendo of a
scale of great imaginative power. The wit is not only combined with,
but fused into, the imagination. We can easily recognize a witty
fancy in the successive images ('my *vegetable* love', 'till the conversion
of the Jews'), but this fancy is not indulged, as it sometimes is by
Cowley or Cleveland, for its own sake. It is structural decoration of a
serious idea. In this it is superior to the fancy of *L'Allegro*, *Il Penseroso*,
or the lighter and less successful poems of Keats. In fact, this alliance
of levity and seriousness (by which the seriousness is intensified) is a
characteristic of the sort of wit we are trying to identify. It is found in

Le squelette était invisible
Au temps heureux de l'art païen!

1 For us, when the brief light has once faded, there is no unbroken night of
sleep. [Ed.]

of Gautier, and in the *dandysme* of Baudelaire and Laforgue. It is in the poem of Catullus which has been quoted, and in the variation by Ben Jonson:

Cannot we deceive the eyes
Of a few poor household spies?
'Tis no sin love's fruits to steal,
But that sweet sin to reveal,
To be taken, to be seen,
These have sins accounted been.

It is in Propertius and Ovid. It is a quality of a sophisticated literature; a quality which expands in English literature just at the moment before the English mind altered; it is not a quality which we should expect Puritanism to encourage. When we come to Gray and Collins, the sophistication remains only in the language, and has disappeared from the feeling. Gray and Collins were masters, but they had lost that hold on human values, that firm grasp of human experience, which is a formidable achievement of the Elizabethan and Jacobean poets. This wisdom, cynical perhaps but untired (in Shakespeare, a terrifying clairvoyance), leads towards, and is only completed by, the religious comprehension; it leads to the point of the *Ainsi tout leur a craqué dans la main* of Bouvard and Pécuchet.

The difference between imagination and fancy, in view of this poetry of wit, is a very narrow one. Obviously, an image which is immediately and unintentionally ridiculous is merely a fancy. In the poem *Upon Appleton House*, Marvell falls in with one of these undesirable images, describing the attitude of the house toward its master:

Yet thus the leaden[1] house does sweat,
And scarce endures the master great:
But where he comes the swelling hall
Stirs, and the square grows spherical;

(49–52)

which, whatever its intention, is more absurd than it was intended to be. Marvell also falls into the even commoner error of images which are over-developed or distracting; which support nothing but their own misshapen bodies:

1 'laden' in Marvell. [Ed.]

And[1] now the salmon-fishers moist
Their leathern boats begin to hoist;
And, like Antipodes in shoes,
Have shod their heads in their canoes.

(769–92)

Of this sort of image a choice collection may be found in Johnson's
Life of Cowley. But the images in the *Coy Mistress* are not only witty,
but satisfy the elucidation of Imagination given by Coleridge:

> This power ... reveals itself in the balance or reconcilement of
> opposite or discordant qualities: of sameness, with difference; of
> the general, with the concrete; the idea with the image; the
> individual with the representative; the sense of novelty and
> freshness with old and familiar objects; a more than usual state of
> emotion with more than usual order; judgement ever awake and
> steady self-possession with enthusiasm and feeling profound or
> vehement. ...

Coleridge's statement applies also to the following verses, which are
selected because of their similarity, and because they illustrate the
marked caesura which Marvell often introduces in a short line:

The tawny mowers enter next;
Who seem like Israelites to be,
Walking on foot through a green sea. ...

(*Upon Appleton House*, 388–90)

And now the meadows fresher dyed;
Whose grass, with moister colour dashed,
Seems as green silks but newly washed. ...

(*Upon Appleton House*, 626–8)

He hangs in shades the orange bright,
Like golden lamps in a green night. ...

(*Bermudas*, 18–19)

Annihilating all that's made
To a green thought in a green shade. ...

(*The Garden*, 47–8)

1 'But' in Marvell. [Ed.]

Had it lived long, it would have been
Lilies without, roses within.

(The Nymph Complaining, 91-2)

The whole poem, from which the last of these quotations is drawn
(*The Nymph and the Fawn*), is built upon a very slight foundation, and
we can imagine what some of our modern practitioners of slight
themes would have made of it. But we need not descend to an invi-
dious contemporaneity to point the difference. Here are six lines from
The Nymph and the Fawn:

I have a garden of my own,
But so with roses overgrown,
And lilies, that you would it guess
To be a little wilderness.
And all the spring-time of the year
It only lovèd to be there.

(71-6)

And here are five lines from *The Nymph's Song to Hylas* in the *Life
and Death of Jason*, by William Morris:

I know a little garden close
Set thick with lily and red rose,
Where I would wander if I might
From dewy dawn to dewy night,
And have one with me wandering.

So far the resemblance is more striking than the difference, although
we might just notice the vagueness of allusion in the last line to some
indefinite person, form, or phantom, compared with the more
explicit reference of emotion to object which we should expect from
Marvell. But in the latter part of the poem Morris divaricates widely:

Yet tottering as I am, and weak,
Still have I left a little breath
To seek within the jaws of death
An entrance to that happy place;
To seek the unforgotten face
Once seen, once kissed, once reft from me
Anigh the murmuring of the sea.

Here the resemblance, if there is any, is to the latter part of the *Coy Mistress*. As for the difference, it could not be more pronounced. The effect of Morris's charming poem depends upon the mistiness of the feeling and the vagueness of its object; the effect of Marvell's upon its bright, hard precision. And this precision is not due to the fact that Marvell is concerned with cruder or simpler or more carnal emotions. The emotion of Morris is not more refined or more spiritual; it is merely more vague: if anyone doubts whether the more refined or spiritual emotion can be precise, he should study the treatment of the varieties of discarnate emotion in the *Paradiso*. A curious result of the comparison of Morris's poem with Marvell's is that the former, though it appears to be more serious, is found to be the slighter; and Marvell's *Nymph and the Fawn*, appearing more slight, is the more serious.

So weeps the wounded balsam: so
The holy frankincense doth flow.
The brotherless Heliades
Melt in such amber tears as these.

(97–100)

These verses have the suggestiveness of true poetry; and the verses of Morris, which are nothing if not an attempt to suggest, really suggest nothing; and we are inclined to infer that the suggestiveness is the aura around a bright clear centre, that you cannot have the aura alone. The day-dreamy feeling of Morris is essentially a slight thing; Marvell takes a slight affair, the feeling of a girl for her pet, and gives it a connexion with that inexhaustible and terrible nebula of emotion which surrounds all our exact and practical passions and mingles with them. Again, Marvell does this in a poem which, because of its formal pastoral machinery, may appear a trifling object:

CLORINDA Near this, a fountain's liquid bell
Tinkles within the concave shell.
DAMON Might a soul bathe there and be clean,
Or slake its drought?

where we find that a metaphor has suddenly rapt us to the image of spiritual purgation. There is here the element of *surprise*, as when Villon says:

Necessité faict gens mesprendre
Et faim saillir le loup des boys,

the surprise which Poe considered of the highest importance, and also
the restraint and quietness of tone which make the surprise possible.
And in the verses of Marvell which have been quoted there is the
making the familiar strange, and the strange familiar, which Coleridge attributed to good poetry.

The effort to construct a dream world, which alters English poetry
so greatly in the nineteenth century, a dream world utterly different
from the visionary realities of the *Vita Nuova* or of the poetry of
Dante's contemporaries, is a problem of which various explanations
may no doubt be found; in any case, the result makes a poet of the
nineteenth century, of the same size as Marvell, a more trivial and less
serious figure. Marvell is no greater personality than William Morris,
but he had something much more solid behind him: he had the vast
and penetrating influence of Ben Jonson. Jonson never wrote anything purer than Marvell's *Horatian Ode*; this ode has that same quality
of wit which was diffused over the whole Elizabethan product and
concentrated in the work of Jonson. And, as was said before, this wit
which pervades the poetry of Marvell is more Latin, more refined,
than anything that succeeded it The great danger, as well as the great
interest and excitement, of English prose and verse, compared with
French, is that it permits and justifies an exaggeration of particular
qualities to the exclusion of others. Dryden was great in wit, as Milton
in magniloquence; but the former, by isolating this quality and making it by itself into great poetry, and the latter, by coming to dispense
with it altogether, may perhaps have injured the language. In Dryden
wit becomes almost fun, and thereby loses some contact with reality;
becomes pure fun, which French wit almost never is.

The midwife placed her hand on his thick skull,
With this prophetic blessing: Be thou dull. . . .
A numerous host of dreaming saints succeed,
Of the true old enthusiastic breed.

This is audacious and splendid; it belongs to satire beside which
Marvell's Satires are random babbling, but it is perhaps as exaggerated
as:

Oft he seems to hide his face,
But unexpectedly returns,
And to his faithful champion hath in place
Bore witness gloriously; whence Gaza mourns,
And all that band them to resist
His uncontrollable intent.

How oddly the sharp Dantesque phrase 'whence Gaza mourns'
springs out from the brilliant contortions[1] of Milton's sentence!

Who, from his private gardens, where
He lived reservèd and austere,
   As if his highest plot
   To plant the bergamot,
Could by industrious valour climb
To ruin the great work of Time,
   And cast the kingdom old
   Into another mould.

(29–36)

The Pict no shelter now shall find
Within his parti-coloured mind;
   But from this valour sad
   Shrink underneath the plaid:

(105–8)

There is here an equipoise, a balance and proportion of tones, which,
while it cannot raise Marvell to the level of Dryden or Milton,
extorts an approval which these poets do not receive from us, and
bestows a pleasure at least different in kind from any they can often
give. It is what makes Marvell a classic; or classic in a sense in which
Gray and Collins are not; for the latter, with all their accredited
purity, are comparatively poor in shades of feeling to contrast and
unite.

We are baffled in the attempt to translate the quality indicated by
the dim and antiquated term wit into the equally unsatisfactory
nomenclature of our own time. Even Cowley is only able to define it
by negatives:

1 Eliot's original version reads 'the brilliant but ridiculous contortions'. [Ed.]

Comely in thousand shapes appears;
  Yonder we saw it plain; and here 'tis now,
  Like spirits in a place, we know not how.

It has passed out of our critical coinage altogether, and no new term
has been struck to replace it; the quality seldom exists, and is never
recognized.

In a true piece of wit all things must be
  Yet all things there agree;
As in the ark, join'd without force or strife,
All creatures dwelt, all creatures that had life.
  Or as the primitive forms of all
  (If we compare great things with small)
Which, without discord or confusion, lie
In that strange mirror of the Deity.

So far Cowley has spoken well. But if we are to attempt even no
more than Cowley, we, placed in a retrospective attitude, must risk
much more than anxious generalizations. With our eye still on
Marvell, we can say that wit is not erudition; it is sometimes stifled
by erudition, as in much of Milton. It is not cynicism, though it has
a kind of toughness which may be confused with cynicism by the
tender-minded. It is confused with erudition because it belongs to an
educated mind, rich in generations of experience; and it is confused
with cynicism because it implies a constant inspection and criticism of
experience. It involves, probably, a recognition, implicit in the expression of every experience, of other kinds of experience which are
possible, which we find as clearly in the greatest as in poets like
Marvell. Such a general statement may seem to take us a long way
from *The Nymph and the Fawn* or even from the *Horatian Ode*; but
it is perhaps justified by the desire to account for that precise taste of
Marvell's which finds for him the proper degree of seriousness for
every subject which he treats. His errors of taste, when he trespasses,
are not sins against this virtue; they are conceits, distended metaphors
and similes, but they never consist in taking a subject too seriously or
too lightly. This virtue of wit is not a peculiar quality of minor poets,
or of the minor poets of one age or of one school; it is an intellectual
quality which perhaps only becomes noticeable by itself, in the work

of lesser poets. Furthermore, it is absent from the work of Wordsworth, Shelley, and Keats, on whose poetry nineteenth-century
criticism has unconsciously been based. To the best of their poetry
wit is irrelevant:

Art thou pale for weariness
Of climbing heaven and gazing on the earth,
Wandering companionless
Among the stars that have a different birth,
And ever changing, like a joyless eye,
That finds no object worth its constancy?

We should find it difficult to draw any useful comparison between
these lines of Shelley and anything by Marvell. But later poets, who
would have been the better for Marvell's quality, were without it;
even Browning seems oddly immature, in some way, beside Marvell.
And nowadays we find occasionally good irony, or satire, which lack
wit's internal equilibrium, because their voices are essentially protests
against some outside sentimentality or stupidity; or we find serious
poets who seem afraid of acquiring wit, lest they lose intensity. The
quality which Marvell had, this modest and certainly impersonal
virtue – whether we call it wit or reason, or even urbanity – we have
patently failed to define. By whatever name we call it, and however
we define that name, it is something precious and needed and
apparently extinct; it is what should preserve the reputation of
Marvell. *C'était une belle âme, comme on ne fait plus à Londres.*

(278–90)

T. S. Eliot

from 'Andrew Marvell', a review of the Nonesuch Edition of
Marvell, *The Nation and the Athenaeum* 29 September 1923

A year or two ago, after the City of Hull, with more gratitude
than most cities, had commemorated the tercentenary of a Parliamentarian who had served his constituency well, there appeared a
memorial volume which did more credit to the City which sub-
ventioned it than to the writers whose critical essays on Andrew

Marvell were there assembled. From such a collection some genuine agreement, or definite difference, concerning the place and significance in English literature of the author celebrated, ought to transpire: but it never does. Critics almost invariably treat a writer, on such solemn occasions, as if it were impiety to recognize that any other authors have existed, or have had any relation to the subject of the eulogy. Exactly the points which it is their business to ponder, and on which their consensus or discord would have some interest and value, are avoided; the critics neither agree nor disagree: they expatiate upon their own whimsies and fancies. Now, a poet must be very great, very individual indeed, for us to be more or less safe in isolating him in this way; and even then we have only the part of a true appreciation. And Marvell and his contemporaries are not in this class. There is no one of them who is a safe model for study, in the sense that Chaucer, that Pope, is a safe model. For they are all more or less fantastical. This is no censure; there is no reason why a poet should not be as fantastical as possible, if that is the only way for him. But fantasticality must be that proper to its age, and the fantastic which may be a proper expression for our own will not be the fantastic of any other. Our conceits cannot be those of Marvell; they will spring, equally genuine, from a different impulse, from a different level of feeling.

Marvell is, without doubt, a very conceited poet. In a conceit two things very different are brought together, and the spark of ecstasy generated in us is a perception of power in bringing them together. It is, in my opinion, a conceit of the very finest order when Marvell says, of a spring of clear water:

Might a soul bathe there and be clean,
Or slake its drought?

Our pleasure is in the suddenness of the transference from material to spiritual water. But when Shakespeare says:

She looks like sleep
As she would catch another Antony
In her strong toil of grace,

it is not a conceit. For instead of contrast we have fusion: a restoration of language to contact with things. Such words have the inevitability which make them appropriate to be spoken by any character. And when a greater than Marvell – Bishop King – says:

But hark! my pulse, like a soft drum,
Beats my approach, tells thee I come,

that also is a conceit. If the drum were left out it would cease to be a conceit – but it would lose the valuable associations which the drum gives it. But when Dante says:

Qual si fe Glauco, al gustar della erba,

or:
                    l'impresa
Che fe Nettuno ammirar l'ombra d'Argo,

or the best known:

si ver noi aguzzevan le ciglia,
come vecchio sartor fa nella cruna,

these are not conceits. They have a rational necessity as well as suggestiveness; they are, like the words of Shakespeare above, an *explication* of the meaning.

A conceit is not to be something practised by the poet and despised by the critic; it has its place; for a purpose, for a poet, for a whole age, it may be the proper thing. And we must understand that the conceits which seem to us to fail are formed by exactly the same method as the conceits which seem to us to succeed. For that understanding we must read the whole of Marvell. But we must not only read the whole of Marvell; we must read Cleveland as well. And for this reason, and for others, and for the simple pleasure in a well-made book, we hope that the Nonesuch Press will continue their editions of seventeenth-century poets.

(809)

Part Two Modern Views

Introduction

The amount of Marvell criticism is growing rapidly, and there is
more bad than good. Few will be surprised to hear that. It might
seem wisest to ignore the bad. Instead I shall be mostly – not
exclusively – concerned with it in this introduction. In selecting
the essays that follow, on the other hand, I have tried, by and
large, to avoid it. The idea is that the reader, taking introduction
and essays together, will be in possession of the whole field,
without having to trudge through acres of nonsense. This way, too,
he will be less at the mercy of editorial censorship. Besides, he
will be able to assess each reprinted essay against the wider background of critical opinion. Also he may learn, from the mistakes
of others, something about Marvell's poetry – its tendency, for
instance, to start philosophical hares, and its resistance to paraphrase.

Badness is not the same as wrongness. A critic may be wrong,
but enlightening. It is a question of whether he responds to the
poem. The essays selected include a number of collisions –
J.V. Cunningham against T.S. Eliot, for example, or Karina
Williamson against Edward Le Comte. In the nature of things,
one party (at least) must be wrong each time. But the result is still
gainful. Badness, on the other hand, happens when the response is
not to the poem but to something else – the need to be in fashion,
to show learning, to compete with science, to keep one's job.
Derivative, irrelevant, obscure or factitious criticism ensues.

In several modern treatments of Marvell dependence on Eliot
is large and shameless. George Williamson's *The Donne
Tradition*, 1930, hardly ventures to modify the Master's phrasing.
Marvell's poems 'seem distilled from the very air about him'
(in Eliot 'a kind of feeling diffused in the air about him'). They
show 'a certain susceptibility to the French spirit of the age'
(in Eliot 'that spirit of the age which was coming to be the
French spirit of the age'). And they possess, of course,
'sensuous apprehension of thought', 'tough reasonableness' and
'inextricably mingled levity and seriousness'. R.G. Cox and

F.W. Bradbrook in the *Pelican Guide to English Literature* (vol. 3, 1956) are equally loyal. Mr Cox can think of no poet in whom 'levity and seriousness' are 'more inextricably mingled'. He obediently pooh-poohs the *Appleton House* salmon fishers – 'fantastic extravagance'. 'Ludicrous', agrees John Press in his *Writers and Their Works* pamphlet, 1958.

Though these authors preserve the gospel they sometimes encounter trouble applying it. Mr Cox, believes that levity and seriousness are 'inextricably' mingled, but talks happily about the 'transitions' from one to the other. Mr Bradbrook quotes the text which says that 'the seriousness is intensified' by this mingling, but reads the poetry as 'comedy' and 'burlesque'.

Fewer critics have applied Eliot's remarks intelligently to the poems. One is S. Gorley Putt (in *English*, vol. 2, 1938–9, pp. 366–75), who tries to show how Marvell's 'previous impressions' were 'always present to modify or augment the new increment of material' (a paraphrase of Eliot's 'recognition, implicit in the expression of every experience, of other kinds of experience which are possible'). Another is Barbara Everett (in the *Critical Quarterly*, vol. 4, 1962, 219–24), who finds levity and seriousness so inextricable in *The Mower's Song* that we do not know eventually how to regard the singer.

There has been dissent from Eliot too, of course, conscious or otherwise. A. H. King (*E.S.*, vol. 20, 1938, pp. 118–21) has denied *The Garden* any serious purpose at all, and M. F. E. Rainbow (*Durham University Journal*, vol. 37, 1945, pp. 22–7) accuses Marvell of being emotionless, which presumably contradicts the claim that he fused thought and feeling. Frank Kermode is amused by Eliot's notion that there was a 'dissociation of sensibility' in the seventeenth century, and says so in the *Kenyon Review*, vol. 19, 1957, pp. 169–94 (reworked in *Romantic Image*, 1957, pp. 138–61). His amusement is mostly over the fact that others had thought of it before Eliot and located it at other points in history. As a purely stylistic description, he concedes, it would be possible, 'though very nasty', to retain 'dissociated in sensibility' even after reading his article.

A particular difficulty of Eliot's creed is that it pronounces Marvell's poetry both precise and nebulous. Indeed, nebulous *because* precise. It has a 'hard, bright precision' which somehow connects it with 'that inexhaustible and terrible nebula of emotion which surrounds all our exact and practical passions.' Apostles have found this a hard saying. Mr Williamson repeated it willingly enough. In the *Nymph* the 'emotion is unusually moving' because the images are so hard and precise. Put like that, the idea seemed questionable, though, and in a later study of the *Nymph* (in *The Proper Wit of Poetry*, 1961) Mr Williamson silently dropped it. Geoffrey Walton in *Metaphysical to Augustan*, 1955, dutifully discovers the 'bright precision' of the *Nymph* too. But he thinks it has a 'limiting effect'. This seems the exact opposite of Eliot's contention, though Mr Walton has not the air of one striking out on a new line.

Agreement about the 'precision' of Marvell's images is found alongside disagreement about what, precisely, they mean. The 'one ball' into which the lovers are to roll their strength and sweetness in *To his Coy Mistress* has been explained, for example, as a symbol of eternity, a pomander, a cannonball, a sweetmeat ball, a rubber ball, the lovers' own personal sun, Plato's original hermaphrodite, and the egg of myrrh which Herodotus says forms out of the ashes of the Phoenix. If this is precision we need a new word to describe clear, distinct visual images.

Whether Marvell writes in clear, distinct visual images at all was the subject of an exchange between F. W. Bateson and F. R. Leavis in 1953. Mr Bateson in his manifesto 'The Function of Criticism at the Present Time' denied the affinity suggested by Dr Leavis in *Revaluation* between Marvell's couplet in *A Dialogue between the Soul and Body*:

Tortured, besides each other part,
In a vain head, and double heart

and Pope's in the *Dunciad*:

Bounded by nature, narrow'd still by art
A trifling head, and a contracted heart.

(IV 503–4)

Marvell, Mr Bateson assured subscribers to *Essays in Criticism*, writes
in 'picture language'. He does this because his 'social context' was
one that retained confidence in physical appearances – 'banquets,
pageants and masques' – and emblem-books. Pope, on the other
hand, writes in 'grey abstractions' because his society distrusted
appearances, having 'learnt the lesson of the Civil War'. Dr
Leavis's tart rejoinder (*Scrutiny*, vol. 19, 1953, pp. 162–83) found
'picture language' a 'disconcertingly inappropriate' phrase.
Marvell's poem 'transcends visualization'. It is a profound inquiry
into the difficulty of distinction between soul and body. The
situation was almost too good to be true: two major critics
drawn up sharply on opposed sides of a given quotation. At last
we were to be shown that how to read a line of poetry was not a
subjective affair but susceptible of reasoned dispute and conclusion.
We were not, as it happened. Nothing further ensued beyond a
splutter of reassertion from each side (*Scrutiny*, vol. 19, 1953,
pp. 317–28). 'Dr Leavis did not meet my points either about
Marvell or about Pope' is Mr Bateson's last word on the
controversy – to date (F. R. Leavis, *A Selection from Scrutiny*,
1968, vol. 2, p. 316).

William Empson had helped to swing the emphasis away from
Marvell's 'precision' in the thirties. Plucking different meanings
out of 'Annihilating all that's made . . .' (*The Garden*, 47–8) he
could plead that even a decent plain scholar like H. M.

Margoliouth had found the lines ambiguous. *Seven Types of Ambiguity* uses Marvell to show how a seventeenth-century poet can turn out 'vague conceits', much like Shelley. Marvell's similes are muddled on top of each other, transient, unworked-out. He falls 'below the standard of precision that the metaphysicals set themselves.'

It was generally felt that Empson had been infuriatingly clever in *Seven Types*. The reaction took some twenty years to collect itself, however. Eventually two American ladies came forward to object that poems could not go on spawning meanings in this unprincipled way. These were Miss Rosemond Tuve in *Elizabethan and Metaphysial Imagery*, 1947, and Miss Ruth Wallerstein in *Studies in Seventeenth-Century Poetic*, 1950. Though neither had the gift of lucid exposition, their proposals were essentially straightforward. Miss Tuve's idea was that we should limit ourselves in talking of images to the categories the Elizabethan rhetoricians had devised. In this way we should cut out three centuries of thought about language, and so wonderfully simplify our discussions. Miss Wallerstein's idea was that instead of reading Marvell we should read St Bonaventura. If we persevered we should find, on returning to Marvell's poems, that we thought about St Bonaventura when reading them. Thus we should have succeeded in 'barring out too multiple associations from the images.' If we should still encounter any difficulty it would be 'reasonable', Miss Wallerstein decides, 'to use the more explicit views expressed in his prose of fifteen or twenty years later to know what the words of the poems mean.' To encourage us to attach no special importance to the words of the poems, Miss Wallerstein quotes the well-known lines from *To his Coy Mistress* as:

All around about us lie
Deserts of vast eternity.

Other critics have felt that Empson is right about the ambiguities, and that it is Marvell's fault for not being more careful. Pierre Legouis (*M.L.Q.*, vol. 21, 1960, pp. 30–32) is sorrowful about all the discussion over the meaning of the *Nymph*. There would be no excuse for it if Marvell had not been misled by the 'fatal facility' of the octosyllabic into writing the poem in the first place. Dennis Davison (in *The Poetry of Andrew Marvell*, 1964) is forced to agree with Empson that 'from pleasure less' (*The Garden*, 41) is ambiguous, but pronounces it 'unfortunate'.

A short step from Empson takes us to the New Critics scanning Marvell's poems for ambiguities which reveal 'tension' and 'irony'. Cleanth Brooks's reading of the *Horatian Ode* stirred up Douglas Bush and James F. Carens. Mr Carens is irked by his opponent's agility. Whatever excuses Brooks with his 'sleight of hand' may devise, the poem's extravagant praise of Cromwell is simply, he maintains, one of its 'aesthetic defects' (*Bucknell Review*, vol. 7, 1957, pp. 41–70). John E. Hardy's attempt to read *The Coronet* New Critically (in *The Curious Frame*, 1962) proves more of a strain than Brooks's piece on the *Ode*. Hardy finds himself having to paraphrase, for example, 'the fragrant towers| That once adorned my shepherdess's head' as 'ornaments borrowed from the finery of this recherché bawd.' A reader who could swallow that would be hardly worth convincing.

Meanwhile Miss Wallerstein's idea was becoming popular. St Bonaventura was not to everyone's taste, but there were plenty of other Neoplatonists to choose from. Selecting Plotinus, Milton Klonsky offers himself as 'A Guide through *The Garden*' in the *Sewanee Review*, vol. 58, 1950, pp. 16–35. The vital clue he has hit on is that Marvell's garden is not a garden at all but '*the neo-Platonic Realm of First Forms*' (Mr Klonsky's italics). This revelation came to him when he was reading a passage in Plotinus where the 'ideas streaming from Zeus' are called the 'garden of Zeus'. Admittedly, Plotinus's metaphor is nowhere stated in

Marvell's poem. Still, Mr Klonsky is convinced that we must
supply it. The rhapsodic muddle which follows does little to conceal
the shortcomings of our Guide. Even on his reading, Marvell's
body experiences 'sensuality' among the fruits and flowers of the
garden, which could hardly happen if they were Ideal Forms.

Undeterred by Mr Klonsky's guidance, Lawrence W. Hyman
also employs Plotinus in his explanation of The Garden (E.L.H.,
vol. 25, 1958, pp. 13–22). As he sees it, the poem's 'chief difficulty'
is that the man in it is not attracted by women but seems to be
getting sexually involved with plants (in stanza 5). Marvell later
says this 'garden state' was what it was like in Eden before the
creation of Eve. So we must, Mr Hyman concludes, read into the
poem the idea popular with the Neoplatonists that before the
creation of Eve Adam was 'androgynous' (i.e. a hermaphrodite;
containing both sexes). Miss Wallerstein had toyed with this as
well. What neither seems to appreciate is that being a
hermaphrodite means having sex with yourself not with a plant.
It has nothing to do with romping among the herbage. No one in
Marvell's poem has male and female organs as happens when
hermaphrodites really do turn up in Renaissance literature. (An
instance is the unexpurgated 1590 ending to the Faerie Queene
where Scudamour and Amoret copulating are mistaken for a
hermaphrodite.) Hopefully, we can forget about 'androgynous
Adam' when reading The Garden.

Instead Patrick G. Hogan uses Plotinus to illuminate To his Coy
Mistress (S.P., vol. 60, 1963, pp. 1–11). Where we have all been
going wrong, Mr Hogan explains, is in imagining that the Mistress
is a mistress. In fact it is Marvell's soul. In the poem Marvell talks
to it and directs its attention away from Nature ('vegetable love')
towards the Intellectual Principle. Though we might not have
guessed it, he is positively eager to enter the 'Deserts of vast
eternity'. They are 'the "There" of Plotinus'. As to why Marvell
chose to disguise this 'testament of faith' as a love poem, there

even Mr Hogan cannot help us. It is 'perhaps impossible to determine'.

The Definition of Love is a piece of disguised Plotinus, too, if Ann Evans Berthoff's insight is anything to go by – or, for that matter, the insight of the editor of the Review of English Studies and his counsellors, since they accepted her article (vol. 17, 1966, pp. 16–29). At all events, Mrs Berthoff maintains that The Definition of Love is not about love but about the desire the poet's 'temporal soul' feels for what Plotinus called its 'higher part'. This 'higher part' remains in heaven, only joining up again with the 'temporal soul' at death. Naturally so novel an interpretation cannot be reached without some firm handling of Marvell's often inconsiderate phrasing. Mrs Berthoff grapples stoutly. It is true that she overlooks the line where Marvell says that their loves 'Though infinite can never meet'. But since the higher and lower souls are going to meet at death, this line bids fair to wreck the whole theory, and is clearly best ignored.

Scholars dissatisfied with Plotinus have brought in Ficino and Hermes Trismegistus to help clear things up. Ruth Nevo (S.E.L., vol. 5, 1965, pp. 1–22) is convinced that Ficino is the key to The Nymph Complaining for the Death of her Fawn. The fawn is 'God's countenance in his handiwork', and the nymph's soul is contemplating it as Ficino says the soul does in old age. The nymph, to be sure, is not old, but she is disillusioned about Sylvio, which is the same thing. Miss Nevo records her debt to the 'overwhelming scholarship' of Miss Wallerstein, and her contempt for the 'tribe-of-Eliot critics'. Hermes's champion is Maren-Sofie Røstvig. Without Hermes, Miss Røstvig reasonably insists, we might never suspect that The Garden was an account of the Creation of Man, or Upon Appleton House a sermon on baptism (E.S., vol. 40, 1959, pp. 65–76, and The Happy Man, 1962, pp. 172–90). Unlike Mr Hogan, Miss Røstvig, can explain why Marvell wrote so deviously. Fairfax, she finds, was interested in

Hermes. Obviously Marvell, anxious to placate the General, devised verses he would enjoy unriddling.

H. E. Toliver, though, discovers in *Marvell's Ironic Vision*, 1965, that Marvell was nearer to Henry More than to any other Neoplatonist. Despite the efforts of Miss Tuve and Miss Wallerstein, this book is the first to adopt a style which does full justice to the impenetrability of its subject. Marvell is clarified in terms of 'strategical inversion' and 'oppositional calculus'. On the dustjacket Professor D.C. Allen applauds the passing of the 'amateur' approach to Renaissance poetry. Now no one can pretend that Professors of English are unnecessary.

The Neoplatonists cannot take all the credit for the effort to find a philosophical system which will allow us to dispense with Marvell's poems. The Pauline doctrine of salvation is what *The Garden* and the Mower poems expound, according to Geoffrey Hartman (*E.L.H.*, vol. 31, 1964, pp. 175–94). Daniel Stempel (*J.H.I.*, vol. 28, 1967, pp. 99–114) proposes Cartesian dualism. *An Horatian Ode*, J. A. Mazzeo finds out, is versified Machiavelli (*J.H.I.*, vol. 21, 1960, pp. 1–17). (Hans Baron politely corrects this view in *J.H.I.*, vol. 21, 1960, pp. 450–1.) Nor does this effort account for all the new ways of reading Marvell with which the last twenty years have provided us. At times a flash of private insight on the critic's part is all we have to thank. Thus T. A. Birrell is able to expose the depths to which Marvell has sunk in *A Dialogue between the Soul and Body*.

So architects do square and hew
Green trees that in the forest grew

is, Mr Birrell reveals, not part of the dialogue but Marvell's own 'callous and vicious' equation of theology with 'philosophical wrangling' (*Downside Review*, vol. 73, 1952, pp. 174–83). Similar breakthroughs, unaided by anything in the poems concerned, are Charles Mitchell's realization that the glow-worms in *The Mower to the Glow-worms* are women (*Explicator*, vol. 18, 1960, item 50), and John Wheatcroft's 'rather certain' feeling that the Coy Mistress is not a woman but Marvell's Muse (*Bucknell Review*, vol. 6, 1956, pp. 22–53).

Less inspired are the critics who relate Marvell to his 'literary background'. Professor Allen (in *Image and Meaning*, 1960) is tireless at guessing what might or might not cross the mind of a reader of Marvell if he were also a reader of classical literature, the Church Fathers and medieval hagiography. Professor Kermode (*N. & Q.*, vol. 197, 1952, pp. 136–7, and *E. in C.*, vol. 2, 1952, pp. 225–41) believes that Marvell wrote 'most of his lyric poetry' in order to 'refute' immoral poetic themes. Not that this 'refutation' was itself moral. Marvell was not advancing 'ethical propositions', just turning fashionable 'genres' round for a change. *The Definition of Love* calls into question whether Marvell's sense of genre was as exact as Professor Kermode's. He admits that it does not obey the rules of the Definition Genre, but suggests the title got attached to it by mistake (*R.E.S.*, n.s. vol. 7, 1956, pp. 183–5).

Finally, we have the source-hunters and echo-hearers. Credulity is their strong point. Katherine Garvin, for example, fancies a resemblance to *The Garden* in the *Ancren Riwle* (*T.L.S.*, 11 August 1950, p. 508). Unable to suggest how Marvell could have come across this, she luckily recalls that Nun Appleton was once a convent: 'It is not uncommon for a poet to think conventual thoughts while walking in a former convent garden.' Echoes of Drayton, Quarles, Habington, Lovelace and Crashaw are accounted for less desperately. There is an argument about whether *The Definition of Love* echoes more clearly Sidney's *Arcadia* or Massinger's *Maid of Honour* (*R.E.S.*, vol. 23, 1947, pp. 63–5; n.s. vol. 2, 1951, pp. 374–5; n.s. vol. 3, 1952, p. 375). Each is pretty close, but if we are to eliminate one as mere coincidence there seems no reason why we should not eliminate both. Echo-hearers rarely ask themselves what bearing their conjectures have on the value or meaning of any poem. An exception is R. H. Syfret (*R.E.S.*, vol. 12, 1961, pp. 160–72). She reviews the phrases from May's translation of Lucan embedded in *An Horatian Ode* and assumes that they are meant to direct the reader's sympathies in the same way as they did in their original setting. Dennis Davison also uses echoes to emend Marvell's meaning. Readers who want the 'iron gates of life' to be the entrance to the Coy Mistress's womb will be grateful to him for finding that Lovelace's Lucasta had 'rosy gates' in the same place (*N. & Q.*, n.s., vol. 5, 1958, p. 521). Miss Røstvig claims less for her parallels between Marvell and the once-famous Latin poems of a Polish Jesuit, Casimir Sarbiewski (*H.L.Q.*, vol. 18, 1954, pp. 13–35). These fit Marvell into the European neo-Latin milieu, though, and so are at least more interesting than that he had read some English poetry.

Obscurity and misplaced erudition are pervasive faults in modern Marvell criticism. Some critics are misled by a desire to appear scholarly. Others, by a suspicion that their subject does not seem difficult enough. Some write obscurely because they have not fully thought out what they wish to say, and hope the reader will discover profundity where there is only muddle. Crudity is another fault. Criticism is taken to consist in showing that a poem 'really means' something entirely different from what had been assumed. Often it is apparent that the critic is criticizing a prose paraphrase of the poem. Readers exasperated by these faults may indulge in vengeful speculations: they may question the way we distribute the money available for education; they may decide that in English studies the 'scholarly periodical' has outlived its usefulness. They are probably right to do both, but the situation has its brighter side. More has been written about Marvell's poems in the last twenty years than in the whole of the eighteenth and nineteenth centuries. That must be better than their being ignored.

The Setting

Christopher Hill

'Society and Andrew Marvell', *Puritanism and Revolution* 1958
(first printed in *Modern Quarterly*, no. 4, 1946, pp. 6–31)

I

At first sight the poetry of Andrew Marvell seems to bear little
relation to the age in which he lived. Marvell wrote a good deal of
political satire, which is of considerable interest to the historian, but
of less poetic value; his greatest poems (except the *Horatian Ode upon
Cromwell's Return from Ireland*) have no direct reference to the political
and social revolution of the seventeenth century. Yet this revolution
transformed the lives of Englishmen; it faced them with intellectual
and moral decisions which it was difficult to evade. I believe that if
we study Marvell with a knowledge of the political background of his
life we can discover in the great lyrics new complexities which will
increase our appreciation of those very sensitive and civilized poems.

Marvell was born near Hull in 1621, his father being a clergyman
whom Andrew described as 'a conformist to the established rites of
the Church of England, though none of the most over-running or
eager in them.'[1] Marvell went to Cambridge, then much the more
Puritan of the two universities, and remained there until 1640. He
then travelled on the Continent for four or five years, during which
period the Civil War between Charles I and his Parliament broke out.
Most of Marvell's friends at this time seem to have been aristocratic
young cavaliers of the type he was likely to meet in continental
salons; and when he returned to England his own sympathies were
apparently Royalist. But we have no real evidence for his activities,
and little for his views, until 1650, the year after the execution of
Charles I. Then he wrote the *Horatian Ode upon Cromwell's Return
from Ireland*, from which it is clear that he was prepared to accept the
triumphant revolution. In the following year he became tutor to
Mary Fairfax, daughter of the famous general who had led the
Parliamentary armies to victory.[2] This suggests that he was already

[1] *The Works of Andrew Marvell*, ed. Grosart, vol. 3, p. 322.
[2] Alas! the girl whom Marvell used as a symbol of ideal virtue in *Upon
Appleton House* (see below) came to no good end. She was married to the second

accepted as a sound Parliamentarian. The period in Yorkshire with the Fairfaxes and the years immediately following seem to have been those in which his greatest poetry was written.

In his early thirties Marvell emerged as a more active supporter of the new government. In 1653 he was personally recommended by no less a person than Milton as his assistant in the secretaryship for foreign tongues. Marvell failed to get this post then, becoming tutor to a ward of Oliver Cromwell instead. But in 1657 Marvell became Milton's colleague in the Foreign or Latin secretaryship. Like Pepys, he was one of the new type of civilian middle-class official who came into their own after the Civil War, during the soberer years of the Protectorate. In 1658 Marvell was elected M.P. for Hull, for which he continued to serve in successive parliaments until his death in 1678. His correspondence shows him to have been an indefatigable defender of the interests of his constituency. But his main activity was as a pamphleteer for the Parliamentary opposition to Charles II's governments and as a defender of religious liberty and freedom of thought, the struggle for which had originally attracted Milton and no doubt Marvell to the Parliamentary side.

Despite his early Royalist phase, then, Marvell became decidedly a partisan of the cause of Parliament: he was intimate with its noblest figures. He was not only the protégé of Milton, but also the friend of Harrington, shrewdest of the Parliamentarian political thinkers, and of Baxter, most resolute of Nonconformist divines. Marvell accepted the Revolution only in his late twenties; he was no juvenile or light-hearted enthusiast. But unlike Dryden, who took service under the Protectorate at the same time as Marvell, and who wrote eulogies of Oliver Cromwell which afterwards proved embarrassing, Marvell did not leave the ship when it began to sink. In the dark days after 1660 he retained his dangerous friendship with Milton, and his

Duke of Buckingham (Dryden's Zimri) in 1657. The marriage caused something of a sensation at the time. For Buckingham, son of Charles I's hated minister and himself a notorious Cavalier, used the Fairfax marriage as a means for recovering his confiscated estates, the General giving Parliament his personal security for his son-in-law's good behaviour. It was hoped that other Royalists would follow Buckingham's example in thus making terms with the Protectorate. But Oliver Cromwell died in 1658, and after the Restoration Buckingham in his turn was able to protect Fairfax.

partisanship became increasingly open. He invented the nickname Cabal, which has stuck to the government of Clifford, Arlington, Buckingham, Ashley, and Lauderdale. Marvell dealt roughly with the sycophantic Samuel Parker, and he ran great risks by the outspokenness of his attacks on the cynical extravagance of the court, the brutalities of the advocates of religious persecution and the treacherous activities of the pro-French party at court.

Marvell's oft-quoted remark about the Civil War, 'The Cause was too good to have been fought for', does not mean what those who cite it out of its context appear to think – that Marvell was disavowing 'the Good Old Cause'. He meant, on the contrary, that the war *should* not have been fought because it *need* not have been fought, because the victory of Parliament was inevitable, war or no war. Here Marvell was following the historical and political theory of his friend James Harrington,[1] in just the same way as Halifax did later in his *Letter to a Dissenter*:

You act very unskilfully against your visible interest, if you throw away the advantages, of which you can hardly fail in the next probable revolution. Things tend naturally to what you would have, if you would let them alone, and not by an unseasonable activity lose the influences of your good star, which promiseth you every thing that is prosperous.[2]

For Marvell, after saying the cause was too good to have been fought for, continued – with an exaggeration pardonable if we recollect that he was writing under Charles II's censorship –

The King himself, being of so accurate and piercing a judgement, would soon have felt where it stuck. For men may spare their pains when Nature is at work, and the world will not go the faster for our driving. Even as our present Majesty's happy restoration did itself come, all things else happen in their best and proper time, without any need of officiousness.[3]

1 Marvell was a member of Harrington's Rota Club in 1659–60.
2 The Marquess of Halifax, *Complete Works*, 1912, pp. 139–40.
3 *Works*, vol. 3, p. 212. Marvell's view of history is further analysed in sections VI and VII below.

II

'The war was begun in our streets before the King or Parliament had any armies,' wrote Baxter,[1] another of Marvell's friends, in whose defence some of his greatest pamphlets were later to be written. As the tension within society became more acute, so a new type of lyric arose, charged with the most intense feeling of the age. These lyrics, unlike the Elizabethan, were no longer intended to be sung: they had lost their social function, and existed only to resolve the conflict within the poet's mind. The poet has become an isolated individual in a divided society, and his own mind is divided too: we find this internal conflict in poets so dissimilar as Marvell's early friend Lovelace, Crashaw, and Vaughan.

A characteristic of the conceit, indeed, from Donne to Traherne (precisely the revolutionary period) is that it lays incompatibles side by side, that it unites the apparently unrelated and indeed the logically contradictory, that it obtains its effects by forcing things different in kind on to the same plane of reference. In this broad sense we may speak of the lyric of conflict, whose characteristics are an awareness in the poet's mind of the new and troubling (especially the new scientific discoveries) as well as the old and familiar, and an effort to fit them into a common scheme – first by the violent and forced juxtaposition of Donne, then by the unresolved conflict of the later metaphysicals; until finally, after the victory of the new political and intellectual forces, we get a new type of poetry drawing on new philosophical assumptions, and disturbed by none of the doubts which have tormented the sensitive since the days of Shakespeare.[2] The tortured conceit gives way to the neatly balanced rhymed couplet. This new equilibrium satisfied poets less and less in the second half of the eighteenth century but was not finally upset until the fresh social and political crisis of the French Revolution – and Wordsworth.

The existence of a conflict of some sort in Marvell is apparent from the most careless reading of his poems. At the risk of alienating readers by an excessively crude and oversimplified statement, I wish to say

1 *A Holy Commonwealth* (written by Richard Baxter at the invitation of James Harrington, Esq., 1659), p. 457.
2 Swift, of course, is an exception to this general acceptance of the new synthesis; but I think his personal and political abnormalities could be explained in terms which would confirm rather than weaken the generalization.

briefly and dogmatically what I think may have underlain this conflict, and then to try to prove and illustrate this thesis. The suggestion is that Marvell's poetry is shot through with consciousness of a conflict between subjective and objective, between the idea and the reality, which it is perhaps not too far-fetched to link up (very indirectly of course) with the social and political problems of his time. This conflict takes many forms, but we can trace a repeated pattern, a related series of symbols, which suggests that fundamentally all the conflicts are interrelated, and that this 'double heart' (Marvell's phrase) is as much the product of a sensitive mind in a divided society as is Day Lewis's 'divided heart'.[1] That of course is one reason why Marvell and the other 'metaphysical' poets have so attracted our generation.

One of Marvell's qualities which is most sympathetic to us is his humour, his refusal to take his agonies too seriously. This is in itself one of the aspects of the 'double heart', Marvell's ability to see both sides; but it also shows his attempt to come to terms with and to control the contradictions between his desires and the world he has to live in, his ideals and the brutal realities of the Civil War. Humour is for Marvell one way of bearing the unbearable: it is a sign of his enviable maturity, besides which Waller, Cowley, Dryden, and the other ex-Royalist and future Royalist panegyrists of Cromwell look so shabby. The opening lines of the *Horatian Ode* perfectly illustrate this aspect of Marvell's manner:

The forward youth that would appear
Must now forsake his Muses dear,
Nor in the shadows sing
His numbers languishing.

Less than three years after writing these lines Marvell offered his services to the Parliamentary cause, which he was never to desert in the remaining twenty-five years of his life. The light touch, the self-mockery, the hatred of the portentous which are obvious in these lines should not obscure for us the genuine doubts and struggles, conflicts and despairs, which had preceded Marvell's acceptance of the

1 Cf. Richard Sibbes: 'A kind of doubleness of heart, whereby we would bring two things together that cannot suit' (*The Soul's Conflict*, 1635, p. 469). The phrase no doubt derives from *James* i, 8.

position which he here states with an irony made possible only by deep conviction. Marvell has come through when he has gained this tone.

III

But I propose to defer consideration of the *Horatian Ode* until after we have looked at some of the lyrics, in which the political approach is less obvious. Let us begin with *The Definition of Love*, for here the points can be made merely by quotation:

My love is of a birth as rare
As 'tis for object strange and high:
It was begotten by Despair
Upon Impossibility.

Magnanimous Despair alone
Could show me so divine a thing,
Where feeble Hope could ne'er have flown
But vainly flapped its tinsel wing.

And yet I quickly might arrive
Where my extended soul is fixed,
But Fate does iron wedges drive,
And always crowds itself betwixt. . . .

And therefore her decrees of steel
Us as the distant poles have plac'd,
(Though Love's whole world on us doth wheel)
Not by themselves to be embrac'd. . . .

As lines so loves oblique may well
Themselves in every angle greet:
But ours so truly parallel,
Though infinite can never meet.

Therefore the love which us doth bind,
But Fate so enviously debars,
Is the conjunction of the mind,
And opposition of the stars.

This is a very sophisticated poem, playing about with newly fashionable geometrical theories. The main point, obviously, is the one that
I have already suggested as typical of Marvell – the conflict between
Love and Fate, desire and possibility. Fate 'defines' Love in both
senses of the word – it both limits it and expresses its full significance.
But the poem is far more than a clever conceit. The image in lines 11
and 12 is perfect for the age of Civil War. Fate is symbolized by the
products of one of the industries which were transforming rural
Britain, by the conventional symbol for warlike arms; and it 'crowds
itself betwixt' with irresistible force: here Fate is thought of as a
tumultuous multitude of human individuals, as well as abstract
military and industrial processes. Nor is Fate merely an external
force. As Miss Bradbrook and Miss Lloyd Thomas said,

Material Fate and spiritual Love, though apparently in complete
opposition, are in reality two aspects of the same situation:

Magnanimous Despair alone
Could show me so divine a thing.

If the 'stars' were not so completely opposed, the love could not
reach such heroic stature.[1]

The individual exposed to and triumphing over and through the
buffetings of Fate is the theme of the bombastic rhodomontade of
The Unfortunate Lover:

See how he nak'd and fierce does stand,
Cuffing the thunder with one hand;
While with the other he does lock,
And grapple, with the stubborn rock: ...

. . . .

This is the only banneret
That ever Love created yet:
Who though, by the malignant stars,
Forced to live in storms and wars:

1 M. C. Bradbrook and M. G. Lloyd Thomas, *Andrew Marvell*, p. 45. Their
whole analysis of the dialectics of this intricate poem is most interesting.

Yet dying leaves a perfume here,
And music within every ear:
And he in story only rules,
In a field sable a lover gules.

Marvell too had been forced 'by the malignant stars' 'to live in
storms and wars'; his finest music was wrung out of him in the
grapple with a stubborn world.

Let us examine some of the other poems with these symbols and
our main thesis in mind.

The titles of many speak for themselves: *A Dialogue Between the
Resolved Soul, and Created Pleasure, A Dialogue between the Soul and
Body*. In the first of these the conflict is between a militantly Puritan
soul, conscious of its mission, its calling, its arduous pilgrimage to
heaven, on the one hand, and the distracting and illusory pleasures of
the senses and of idleness on the other. In the second poem the conflict
is more subtle:

SOUL: O who shall, from this dungeon, raise
       A soul enslav'd so many ways?
       With bolts of bones, that fetter'd stands
       In feet; and manacled in hands.
       Here blinded with an eye; and there
       Deaf with the drumming of an ear.
       A soul hung up, as 'twere, in chains
       Of nerves, and arteries, and veins.[1]
       Tortur'd, besides each other part,
       In a vain head, and double heart. . . .

BODY: But physic yet could never reach
       The maladies thou me dost teach;
       Whom first the cramp of hope does tear:
       And then the palsy shakes of fear.
       The pestilence of love does heat:
       Or hatred's hidden ulcer eat.
       Joy's cheerful madness does perplex:
       Or sorrow's other madness vex.

1 In one of Quarles's *Emblems* (v 7) the soul is shown literally imprisoned
within a skeleton, crying out 'who shall deliver me from the body of this
death?' Cf. Rosemary Freeman, *English Emblem Books*, p. 119.

> Which knowledge forces me to know;
> And memory will not forgo.
> What but a soul could have the wit
> To build me up for sin so fit?
> So architects do square and hew,
> Green trees that in the forest grew.

Here the antithesis is not just between soul and body, for the soul may betray the body as well as the body the soul; it is a complex, four-handed conflict, which blends the familiar themes of puritan asceticism against sensual pleasure with action against rest. (The symbolism of the last two lines is a favourite of Marvell's: the loss of certain natural qualities that the civilizing process makes inevitable. There seems, as will be shown later, to be a direct connexion between this symbolism and the more obvious conflict of the Civil War.) Marvell's sympathies are here less decisively on one side than they were in the *Dialogue Between the Resolved Soul and Created Pleasure*, where the moral issue was clear: here opposite concepts are jostling in Marvell's mind. (He is indeed one of the few Parliamentarian writers – if we except Winstanley on the extreme left – who frankly enjoys and praises the pleasures of the body.)[1]

The same complexity occurs in *Upon Appleton House*:

> As first our Flesh corrupt within
> Tempts impotent and bashful Sin.
>
> (555–6)

This is not just good against evil, but evil that is also good against good that is also evil. In these complicated problems and relationships there are no easy solutions or evasions:

> To what cool cave shall I descend,
> Or to what gelid fountain bend?
> Alas! I look for ease in vain,
> When remedies themselves complain,

cried Damon the Mower. The Soul lamented to the Body that it was

1 Aubrey tells us of Marvell that 'he kept bottles of wine at his lodging, and many times he would drink liberally by himself to refresh his spirits and exalt his muse' (*Letters from the Bodleian*, vol. 2, p. 437).

Constrained not only to endure
Diseases, but, what's worse, the cure.

Again, in complex form, though with a different solution, conflict pervades *To his Coy Mistress*. It is no longer soul against body, but the sensual pleasures up against the hard facts of an uncongenial world in which effort is demanded. The moral is not 'Gather ye rosebuds while ye may.' It is

Let us roll all our strength, and all
Our sweetness, up into one ball:
And tear our pleasures with rough strife,
Thorough the iron gates of life.
Thus, though we cannot make our sun
Stand still, yet we will make him run.

That, as has been well said, is a Puritan rather than a libertine conclusion:[1] the sensual pleasures are put into a subordinate place:

Had we but world enough, and time,
This coyness, Lady, were no crime.

But as we have neither world nor time enough, coyness *is* a crime. The gates of life are iron, time's winged chariot is hurrying near:

And yonder all before us lie
Deserts of vast eternity.

We may compare Marvell's own lines on *The First Anniversary of the Government under O. C.*:

Tis he the force of scattered time contracts,
And in one year the work of ages acts:
While heavy monarchs make a wide return,
Longer, and more malignant than Saturn:
And though they all Platonic years should reign,
In the same posture would be found again.

1 Cf. Bishop Joseph Hall: 'A good man must not be like Ezechia's sun, that went backward, nor like Joshua's sun, that stood still, but David's sun, that (like a bridegroom) comes out of his chamber, and as a champion rejoiceth to run his race' (*Meditations and Vows*, 1901, p. 7). Cf. also the *Enchiridion* of Francis Quarles, first published in 1641: 'He only (if any) hath the art to lengthen out his taper, that puts it to the best advantage' (fourth century, no. 55).

It should not surprise us by now to find Marvell censuring 'heavy monarchs' in the same vein as a coy mistress, or praising Cromwell's political activity in the same terms as those in which he had invited the lady to 'sport us while we may'.

To his Coy Mistress strikes a note we shall find repeated. The individual and his desires come up against the outer world, life and time. The mock-serious moral of that flippant and very un-Puritan poem, *Daphnis and Chloe*, is the obverse of that of *To his Coy Mistress*; it is better to forgo a pleasure than to be casual or half-hearted about it.

> Gentler times for love are meant
> Who for parting pleasure strain
> Gather roses in the rain,
> Wet themselves and spoil their scent.
>
> (85–8)

In the *Coy Mistress* mere epicureanism is *rejected* for a more rigorous coming to terms with reality. The laxity and ease of the *rentier* ruling class are contrasted with the effort, asceticism, concentration typical of Puritanism and commercialism. And again iron symbolizes the harshness and impersonality of this world which we *must* accept.

IV

The Mower, whose iron scythe cuts down himself as well as the grass, the innocent as well as the guilty, is a favourite symbol with Marvell. He appears in *The Mower against Gardens, Damon the Mower, The Mower to the Glow-worms, The Mower's Song*, and *Upon Appleton House*. The theme of *The Mower against Gardens* is one which frequently recurs: it contrasts natural and artificial cultivation; the coarse toil and sweat of the mowers is set against the leisured sophistication, the luxury products of the garden. 'Luxurious man', the Mower says

> . . . first enclosed within the garden's square
>   A dead and standing pool of air:
> And a more luscious earth for them did knead,
>   Which stupified them while it fed.

The pink grew then as double as his mind. ...
'Tis all enforced; the fountain and the grot;
  While the sweet fields do lie forgot.

And over all this ostentatious opulence the Mower stands brooding like Fate, confident in his power:

The Gods themselves with us do dwell

But the nostalgia for a simpler pre-commercial age is qualified by an irony of humorous over-statement which shows that Marvell was arguing a case in which he did not wholly believe:

And fauns and fairies do the meadows till,
More by their presence than their skill.

There is the same semi-serious regret in *The Nymph Complaining for the Death of her Fawn.*

The formal garden, as something essential to any gentleman's mansion, was relatively new in seventeenth-century England. There was still something exotically luxurious about it. 'God Almighty first planted a garden,' but they began to become common in England as a result of the Tudor peace, of the internal order and security which allowed manor houses to replace baronial castles and created the conditions in which lesser gentry, yeomen, and merchants were able to prosper. In *The Faerie Queene* the garden is a symbol of the sheltered and opulent life of courtly society: Spenser follows in this the tradition of the medieval allegory of love.[1] Bacon wrote his essay to tell the very wealthy how a garden should be laid out. Stuart gardens, as the Mower has already told us, were still very formal: they were 'the greatest refreshment to the spirit of man,' as Bacon put it, *because* of their contrast with rude Nature in the unenclosed waste outside. It is thus easy to see how the garden became a symbol of security, property, ease, repose, and escape:[2] it was shut

1 C. S. Lewis, *The Allegory of Love,* p. 119.
2 'I ... write ... to those only, that are weatherbeaten in the sea of this world, such as having lost the sight of their gardens and groves study to sail on a right course among rocks and quicksands' (Sir Fulke Greville, *Life of Sir Philip Sidney,* 1907, p. 224). Cf. also Shakespeare's *Richard II,* III, iv. George Puttenham, *The Art of English Poesy* (1589) compared the poet to a gardener

off from the commons, the open fields, the sweaty vulgar outside, from the Mower. For other seventeenth-century poets as well as Marvell and Milton the garden is normally Eden rather than Gethsemane.[1]

If we take the garden as Marvell's equivalent of the ivory tower, the mere title of *The Mower against Gardens* is a political tract in itself. The Mower symbolizes Fate, the historic process which lowers over these artificial and walled-off paradises, as Milton's Satan broods over the Garden of Eden.

The Mower is always a portentous figure:

Sharp like his scythe his sorrow was,
And wither'd like his hopes the grass.

(*Damon the Mower*)

When he is lost he is guided by glow-worms:

... country comets, that portend
No war, nor prince's funeral,
Shining unto no higher end
Than to presage the grass's fall.

(*The Mower to the Glow-worms*)

---

who improved on nature. The garden as an image of order and harmony was a favourite of Bunyan's (J. Brown, *John Bunyan*, pp. 50–51; H. Talon, *John Bunyan*, pp. 302–3). Cf. also Gerrard Winstanley, *Fire in the Bush*, 1650, *passim*. John Evelyn's *Elysium Britannicum*, begun about 1653, compared England to the Garden of Eden.
1 Maren-Sofie Røstvig, in *The Happy Man*, Oslo, 1954, studies the evolution of the cult of rural retirement in seventeenth-century England. She dates its beginning from the political crisis of the late sixteen-twenties and -thirties, rising to its peak in the forties and fifties with Mildmay Fane, Edward Benlowes and Henry Vaughan. She quotes a wide range of poets who deal with garden themes in the second quarter of the century. I would add to her list only Nathaniel Whiting, *Upon Bellama's Walking in the Garden* (*Albino and Bellama*, 1638), George Wither, Hymn 30 (*Hallelujah*, 1641), Shirley *The Garden* (*Poems*, 1646), Nicholas Hookes, *To Amanda Walking in the Garden* (*Amanda*, 1653). I should not myself altogether agree with Miss Røstvig's absolute opposition of the Royalist 'Hortulan Saint' to 'the grim figure of the Puritan pilgrim' (*The Happy Man*, p. 441). The case of Marvell suggests that it was more complicated than that.

War and the death of kings are never very far away, even if they only point a contrast. In this poem and in *The Mower's Song* the Mower is overcome by the power of love: Juliana –

What I do to the grass, does to my thoughts and me.

(cf. the Fate and Love motive in *The Definition of Love* and *The Unfortunate Lover*). But in *Upon Appleton House*, as we shall shortly see, the Mower is directly related to the blind forces of the Civil War.[1]

The garden had its deep attractions for Marvell in the years before he plunged into public life. For he had his escapism, of which the opening of *The Garden* is typical:

How vainly men themselves amaze
To win the palm, the oak, or bays;
And their uncessant labours see
Crowned from some single herb or tree.
Whose short and narrow vergéd shade
Does prudently their toils upbraid;
While all flowers and all trees do close
To weave the garlands of repose.

But even here the poet is tripped up: 'Ensnared with flowers, I fall on grass.' The calm and peace are transient, an interlude: ' *Temporis O suaves lapsus!* '[2] says the Latin version. The garden is a place of temporary repose and refreshment, not a permanent haven. The mind seeks an intenser satisfaction than the merely physical pleasures of the garden: it

. . . creates, transcending these,
Far other worlds, and other seas.

The soul looks forward to further activity even while the body is at rest:

1 All Marvell's symbols, of course, are used partly unconsciously, and so their significance varies: the Mower is now the power of Love, now the scythe of Death or Fate; now the armies of the Civil War; at other times he stands for a pre-commercial simplicity which acquires an elemental force in contrast to the sophistication of the garden. So too the garden itself stands for different things in different poems: but I do not think this makes analysis impossible, provided we are careful to apply no rule-of-thumb symbol-equivalents. All Marvell's writing is packed with alternative meanings.
2 O sweet lapses of time. [Ed.]

Casting the body's vest aside,
My soul into the boughs does glide:
There like a bird it sits, and sings,
Then whets, and combs its silver wings;
And, till prepared for longer flight,
Waves in its plumes the various light.

Whilst the soul thus anticipates eternity, the garden itself recalls
Paradise before the Fall. But the ambiguous phrase 'Garden-state'
hints at England, and the terms of the comparison remind us that
Marvell's garden is in and of this world:

. . . 'Twas beyond a mortal's share
To wander solitary there.

'Society is all but rude'; yet its needs impinge remorselessly upon the
ideal world of escape, prevent it being final. Already in the second
verse Marvell had doubted whether quiet and innocence were to be
found at all on earth. The poem began by mocking at the vanity of
human effort; in the last verse 'th' industrious bee' is introduced, who
– lest we should have missed the significance of the adjective – 'com-
putes its time as well as we.' The garden clock, for all its fragrance,
reminds us of 'Time's winged chariot'. We cannot think ourselves
out of time any more than we can escape from fallen humanity.

The Nymph Complaining for the Death of her Fawn pictures a garden-
Eden shattered by violence from without: the violence of soldiers:

The wanton troopers riding by
Have shot my fawn and it will die.

(1–2)

Marvell plays with the idea later to be elaborated in the Horatian Ode,
of the innocent victim sacrificially redeeming the users of violence,
but here rejects it:

Though they should wash their guilty hands
In this warm life-blood, which doth part
From thine, and wound me to the heart,

Yet could they not be clean: their stain
Is dyed in such a purple grain.
There is not such another in
The world, to offer for their sin.

(18–24)

There is no easy redemption. But the tone of the complaint is curious:
'Ev'n beasts must be with justice slain.' The Fawn symbolizes an
escape, and is not uncritically regarded:

Thenceforth I set myself to play
My solitary time away,
With this: and very well content,
Could so mine idle life have spent. . . .
Had it lived long, I do not know
Whether it too might have done so
As Sylvio did: his gifts might be
Perhaps as false or more than he.

(37–40, 47–50)

As always in Marvell, the conflict is far from simple: he cannot
wholly praise 'a fugitive and cloistered virtue'.

In *The Coronet*, the poet seeks 'through every garden, every mead'
for flowers to crown his Saviour (flowers 'that once adorned my
shepherdess's head'). But –

Alas I find the serpent old
That, twining in his speckled breast,
About the flow'rs disguised does fold,
With wreaths of fame and interest.

And the conclusion is

. . . let these wither, so that he may die,
Though set with skill and chosen out with care.

The garden is not enough.

V

In *Upon Appleton House*, Marvell's longest poem, all this symbolism
becomes specific. The house had been a nunnery, which had come

to the Fairfax family at the Reformation. In the poem the retirement, the cultured and indeed opulent ease of the nunnery is frankly opposed to the claims of a Protestant and commercial civilization. The words which Marvell writes of the earlier Fairfax who acquired the Church lands clearly presage the dilemma of the Fairfaxes, father and son, when they had to take sides in the Civil War:

What should he do ? He would respect
Religion, but not right neglect.

> (225-6)

The elder Fairfax built his family mansion and his fortune on the site of the nunnery; the younger Fairfaxes took up arms in the name of liberty against the Lord's Anointed.

In the poem England before the Civil War is depicted as a garden, in which Fairfax

... did with his utmost skill,
Ambition weed, but conscience till.

> (353-4)

(That other great Parliamentary general, Oliver Cromwell left 'his private gardens, where He lived reserved and austere', at the call of duty in the Civil War.)

Fairfax's garden (or England) is clearly linked up with the Garden of Eden (stanzas 41-3), concluding:

What luckless apple did we taste,
To make us mortal, and thee waste?

> (327-8)

The symbolism of the Mower, who blindly massacres all that he meets in 'the abyss ... of that unfathomable grass', is repeated in stanzas 46-53, and the reference to the Civil War is again explicit:

The mower now commands the field; ...
A camp of battle newly fought:
Where, as the meads with hay, the plain
Lies quilted o'er with bodies slain:

The women that with forks it fling,
Do represent the pillaging.[1]

(418–24)

War is no respecter of persons, cuts down the innocent and uncon-
cerned together with the guilty:

Unhappy birds! what does it boot
To build below the grass's root;
Where lowness is unsafe as height,
And chance o'ertakes what scapeth spite? . . .

(409–12)

Or sooner hatch or higher build. . . .

(417)

The Levellers 'take pattern at' 'this naked equal flat', – 'A new and
empty face of things'.

The villagers in common chase
Their cattle, which it closer raze;
And what below the scythe increased
Is pinched yet nearer by the beast.

(451–4)

This direct reference to the Levellers, and hint at the destructive
communism of 'the many-headed monster', is symbolically followed
by a sudden inundation. Marvell 'takes sanctuary in the wood.' But
escapism brings no neutrality: the forces shaping our lives can neither
be controlled nor evaded. This reintroduces Marvell's other theme of
the need for equalizing desire and opportunity, the conflict brought
to a crisis by the brutal external force of the Mower. Thus Marvell's
key ideas are linked in one symbol, suggesting the possibility that all
his poems really deal with a single complex of problems.

1 At Edgehill, Royalist Welsh infantry, very badly equipped 'with scythes,
pitchforks and even sickles, . . . cheerfully took the field, and literally like
reapers descend[ed] to that harvest of death' (quoted in J. R. Phillips, *Memoirs
of the Civil War in Wales and the Marches*, vol. 1, p. 128). In 1649 scythes were a
part of the equipment sent over to the English army in Ireland, for the rather
different purpose of cutting down corn in order to starve the Irish into submission (J. P. Prendergast, *The Cromwellian Settlement of Ireland*. p. 14).

In *Upon Appleton House* there is humorously ironical escapism again (stanzas 71–81). The whole passage is of the greatest interest as evidence of Marvell's 'double heart'. On a careless reading the picture is one of ideal happiness, a Garden-of-Eden life, an escape, particularly, from war:

How safe, methinks, and strong, behind
These trees have I encamp'd my mind;
Where beauty, aiming at the heart,
Bends in some tree its useless dart;
And where the world no certain shot
Can make, or me it toucheth not.
But I on it securely play,
And gall its horsemen all the day.

(601–8)

But again Marvell makes continual digs at his own dream-world:

Strange prophecies my fancy weaves. . . .

(578)

I in this light mosaic read.
Thrice happy he who, not mistook,
Hath read in nature's mystic book.

(582–4)

(The heavy emphasis their position gives to 'methinks' and 'not mistook' can hardly be entirely without significance.)

Thus I, easy philosopher,
Among the birds and trees confer. . . .

(581–2)

The oak leaves me embroider all,
Between which caterpillars crawl:
And ivy, with familiar trails,
Me licks, and clasps, and curls, and hales.
Under this antic cope I move
Like some great prelate of the grove.

(587–92)

'Easy' prepares us for incomplete acceptance, and the political note would strike for contemporaries the requisite undertone of disapproval in the last lines quoted, even without the hint of 'caterpillars.'

A bishop and his vestments could not but call up reactions of hostility in a good Parliamentarian (cf. 'Safe from the storms, and prelate's rage' in *Bermudas*).

There is a snare hinted in the very placidity of this garden-world, in the attractions of its philosophy:

> And where I language want, my signs
> The bird upon the bough divines;
> And more attentive there doth sit
> Than if she were with lime-twigs knit.
>
> (571-4)

(Cf. *The Garden* and the passage about the falconer in the *Horatian Ode*.) For all its fair seeming, this Eden does not really satisfy the poet:

> ... languishing with ease, I toss
> On pallets swoll'n of velvet moss;
> While the wind, cooling through the boughs,
> Flatters with air my panting brows.
>
> (593-7)

('In this time', Hobbes wrote in 1651, 'that men call not only for peace, but also for truth',[1] flattery was not enough.) Chains are not less chains because men cling to them, nor are half-truths truths because sincerely held:

> Bind me ye woodbines in your twines,
> Curl me about ye gadding vines,
> And O so close your circles lace,
> That I may never leave this place:
> But, lest your fetters prove too weak,
> Ere I your silken bondage break,
> Do you, O brambles, chain me too,
> And courteous briars nail me through.
>
> (609-16)

The idyllic scene suddenly suggests the Crucifixion.[2] And the succeeding stanzas show that escapism is not in fact Marvell's ultimate ideal.

1 *Leviathan*, p. 390.
2 Cf. Lewis Bayley, 'A Divine Colloquy between the Soul and her Saviour': 'Soul – Lord wherefore wouldest thou begin thy passion in a garden? Christ – Because that in a garden thy sin took first beginning' (*The Practice of Piety*, 55th edn, 1723, p. 451).

It is not the highest wisdom to discover 'I was but an inverted tree.' For now Mary Fairfax enters. Whatever she symbolizes (and it is clear from stanza 91 that she is associated with Puritan 'Goodness' as well as Fairfaxian 'Discipline'), there can be no doubt of the condemnation of 'loose Nature' (cf. 'easy philosopher') in the lines describing her advent:

See how loose Nature, in respect
To her, itself doth recollect;
And everything so whisht and fine,
Starts forth with to its bonne mine. . . .
(657–60)

But by her flames, in Heaven tri'd,
Nature is wholly vitrifi'd.
'Tis she that to these gardens gave
That wondrous beauty which they have;
She straightness on the woods bestows; . . .
She yet more pure, sweet, straight, and fair,
Than gardens, woods, meads, rivers are. . . .
For she, to higher beauties rais'd,
Disdains to be for lesser prais'd.
She counts her beauty to converse
In all the languages as hers.
(705–8)

Her wisdom subsumes and includes the wisdom of the garden, just as her discipline and morals reduce its luxuriance to order.[1]

Go now fond sex that on your face
Do all your useless study place,
Nor once at vice your brows dare knit
Lest the smooth forehead wrinkled sit:
Yet your own face shall at you grin,
Thorough the black bag of your skin;

1 Similarly, 'little T. C.' had been adjured to 'reform the errors of the spring;' and the mind in *The Garden* created worlds and seas which transcended reality. Cf. Lancelot Andrewes: 'Christ rising was indeed a gardener. . . . He it is that . . . shall turn all our grass into garden-plots' (*XCVI Sermons*, 2nd edn, 1631, p. 538).

When knowledge only could have fill'd
And virtue all those furrows till'd.[1]

(789–36)

The new standards and discipline transmute the old cosmos by
putting it into its place, and a new reality emerges, so different that
we might be at the Antipodes:

'Tis not, what once it was, the world;
But a rude heap together hurl'd;
All negligently overthrown,
Gulfs, deserts, precipices, stone.
Your lesser world contains the same,
But in more decent order tame;
You Heaven's centre, nature's lap,
And Paradise's only map.

(761–8)

(cf. *Clorinda and Damon* –

DAMON: These once had been enticing things,
           Clorinda, pastures, caves, and springs.
CLORINDA: And what late change?
DAMON: The other day
           Pan met me. . . .)

In many of the poems Marvell is concerned to show the mutual
indispensability of apparent opposites. He says of Fairfax in *The Hill
and Grove at Billborow* –

Therefore to your obscurer seats
From his own brightness he retreats:
Nor he the hills without the groves,
Nor height but with retirement loves.

(77–80)

In *Bermudas* the garden-island (which is also an idealized England) is
not an escape from struggle, but its reward. It is 'far kinder' than the
prelates' England, but the emigrants have had to pass through storms

1 Black bag = mask. Death, the final external reality, equally reinforces the
moral whether the invitation – as here – is to virtue, or – as in the *Coy Mistress*
– to pleasure.

to reach it, and the song is sung by men at work. The picture of the perfect haven is set between two quatrains which remind us unobtrusively of the difficulty of getting there.[1]

VI

The conflict in the poet's own mind between the attractions of evading reality in communion with Nature, and the necessity of coming to terms with the world, is shown in its most interesting form in the *Horatian Ode upon Cromwell's Return from Ireland*. This poem was probably written before the great lyrics, before Marvell entered the Fairfax household, but it is convenient to consider it here since to some extent it sums up the argument by its direct political reference.

The forward youth that would appear
Must now forsake his Muses dear,
   Nor in the shadows sing
   His numbers languishing . . .
'Tis madness to resist or blame
The force of angry Heaven's flame:
   And, if we would speak true,
   Much to the man is due,
Who, from his private gardens, where
He liv'd reserved and austere,
   As if his highest plot
   To plant the bergamot,
Could by industrious valour climb
To ruin the great work of time,
   And cast the kingdom old
   Into another mould.
Though Justice against Fate complain,
And plead the ancient rights in vain:
   But those do hold or break
   As men are strong or weak.

                              (1–40)

1 I owe some of these points to Mr C. H. Hobday.

The poet is clearly arguing with himself rather than with Cromwell; note the garden symbol again. Then there comes the famous passage in which the Parliamentarian Marvell shows his sympathy for the old-world virtues of the executed Charles I,[1] consoling himself with the vision of new life through sacrificial death:

A bleeding head where they begun,
Did fright the architects to run;
   And yet in that the state
   Foresaw its happy fate.

(69-72)

Again Marvell takes up the struggle with himself, and hints back at the lost ideals of the Garden in a passage where the needs of the state are again shown as triumphing over the private interests of the individual:

So when the falcon high
   Falls heavy from the sky,
She, having kill'd, no more does search,
But on the next green bough to perch;
   Where, when he first does lure,
   The falconer has her sure.

(91-6)

1 Did Marvell see the execution? The lines –

Nor call'd the gods with vulgar spite
To vindicate his helpless right,
   But bow'd his comely head,
   Down as upon a bed

(61-4)

read like an eyewitness's recollection of a fact recorded by the Venetian Ambassador which Marvell's editors seem to have missed: 'As they doubted that His Majesty might resist the execution of the sentence, refusing to lay his neck upon the block, they fixed into the block at his feet two iron rings through which they passed a cord which, placed on His Majesty's neck, would necessarily make him bend by force, and offer his head to the axe, if he did not voluntarily resign himself to the humiliation of the fatal blow. But the King, warned of this, without coming to such extremes, said that they should use no violence; he would readily submit to the laws of necessity and the rigours of force' (E. Momigliano, *Cromwell*, English translation, p. 282; cf. also Sir P. Warwick, *Memoirs of the Reign of Charles I*, p. 385, and E. Warburton, *Memoirs of Prince Rupert and the Cavaliers*, vol. 3, p. 400).

(The falconer is England, the state; but he is also Fate, the reality
which has to be accepted, the historical process: he recalls the Mower.)
Marvell concludes reasonably on the side of action, the impossibility
of neutrality:

But thou the wars' and fortune's son
March indefatigably on;
   And for the last effect
   Still keep thy sword erect:
Besides the force it has to fright
The spirits of the shady night,
   The same arts that did gain
   A pow'r must it maintain.

(113–20)

('Shady,' it will be observed, continues the symbolism; cf. 'shadows'
in line 3.)

Critics have frequently commented on the rather left-handed
compliment to Cromwell in this poem: his use of force and fraud is
indeed a little openly praised. I suggest that this is part of Marvell's
own internal struggle, and is evidence of his desire to be honest with
himself. The artist in him dislikes the unpleasant actions which alone
can 'cast the kingdom old into another mould'; but like his master,
Milton, Marvell has come to realize that the immortal garland is to
be run for not without dust and heat. He has come down from the
ivory tower into the arena.

In so far as Marvell is thinking of Cromwell at all, he is not treating
him as an individual: the general is for the poet the personification of
the Revolution, of victory over the King.

Nature that hateth emptiness,
Allows of penetration less;
   And therefore must make room
   Where greater spirits come.

(41–4)

Cromwell draws his greatness from the events of which he has been
the instrument – a view of history with which the Protector would
have agreed and which Milton assumes in *Samson Agonistes*. For
Marvell the Revolution is 'the force of angry Heaven's flame,'
ruining 'the great work of Time,' something real which must

inevitably be accepted, which cannot be wished away nor even excluded from the garden. "Tis madness to resist or blame' an elemental power of this kind. 'The world will not go the faster for our driving,' but it will also not go the slower for our regrets. Wisdom is 'To make their destiny their choice'.[1] In the *Horatian Ode* Marvell is clearly aware of a fusion of opposites: the life of the community demands the death of the individual, rest is obtainable only through and by means of effort, eternal vigilance is the price of liberty, freedom is the knowledge of necessity.[2]

But this paradox, this dialectical thought, recurs throughout Marvell's poems. The soul, in *On a Drop of Dew*,

Does, in its pure and circling thoughts, express
The greater heaven in an heaven less. . . .
  Moving but on a point below,
  It all about does upwards bend. . . .
Congeal'd on earth: but does, dissolving, run
Into the glories of th' Almighty Sun.

We find it in *Ametas and Thestylis making Hay-Ropes*, ironically, as in the *Coy Mistress* seriously. The solution of the conflict may not be the victory of either side, but a fusion of aspects of both from which something new emerges. We find the synthesis again in *Eyes and Tears*:

How wisely Nature did decree,
With the same eyes to weep and see!
That, having view'd the object vain,
They might be ready to complain. . . .

I have through every garden been,
Amongst the red, the white, the green;
And yet, from all the flow'rs I saw,
No honey, but these tears could draw. . . .[3]

1 *Upon Appleton House*, line 744.
2 'The thesis is the impersonal power of Cromwell. . . . The antithesis is the personal dignity and comeliness of Charles, which may offset Cromwell's achievement: and the synthesis is the acceptance of Cromwell, both his "forc'd pow'r" and his personal unattractiveness. . . . The poem may well represent the steps of reasoning by which the friend of Lovelace threw in his lot with the Roundheads' (Bradbrook and Lloyd Thomas, op. cit., p. 73).
3 Here again the garden fails to meet the poet's needs.

Thus let your streams o'erflow your springs,
Till eyes and tears be the same things:
And each the other's difference bears;
These weeping eyes, those seeing tears.

VII

The suggestion then is that all Marvell's problems are interconnected.
They are the problems of an individual in an age of revolutionary
change. I do not think the following lines from *The Fair Singer* were
intended to be taken at more than their surface value (though one
never knows with Marvell); but they could be interpreted as a perfect
allegory of the influence of society on the individual:

I could have fled from one but singly fair:
My disentangled soul itself might save,
Breaking the curled trammels of her hair.
But how should I avoid to be her slave,
Whose subtle art invisibly can wreathe
My fetters of the very air I breathe ?[1]

Soul and body, Love and Fate, illusion and reality, escape or action –
all the poems in the last analysis deal with the adjustment of individual
conduct to external conditions and forces. Marvell's life and his
poetry form a single whole. I would also suggest that the resolution
of the personal conflict revealed in the lyrics is almost exactly parallel
to the resolution of the political conflict revealed in the political
poems: the individual soul never can disentangle itself from society,
never can save itself in isolation; 'the very air I breathe' even in the
remotest garden comes from outside. Since we cannot escape we must
submit.

The significance of this solution of his own crisis for Marvell is
shown by the number of times he recurs to it. The moral of *The
First Anniversary of the Government under O.C.* is exactly the same as
that of the *Horatian Ode*:

1 Marvell may have noticed 'curl'd trammels of thy hair' in Drayton's *Second
Nymphal.*

For all delight of life thou then didst lose,
When to command, thou didst thyself depose;
Resigning up thy privacy so dear,
To turn the headstrong people's charioteer;
For to be Cromwell was a greater thing,
Than aught below, or yet above a King:
Therefore thou rather didst thyself depress,
Yielding to rule, because it made thee less.[1]

(221–8)

The subordination of self to political purposes which he believed to be right: that is the lesson Marvell had taught himself once he found that he could not escape from the disagreeable realities of the world. It was not only Cromwell

... whom Nature all for peace had made,
But angry Heaven unto war had sway'd.

(*Poem upon the Death of O.C.*, 15–16)

Like so many other Parliamentarians, Marvell had been pushed reluctantly to approve of revolution and regicide since otherwise 'religion and liberty' could not be secured. Here again the wise and virtuous man 'makes his destiny his choice.'

Far different motives yet, engag'd them thus,
Necessity did them, but choice did us.

(*On Blake's Victory over the Spaniards*, 141–2)

Marvell was a true Cromwellian, truer perhaps than Milton, who could not accept the new tactics of the Restoration. For Marvell, as we have seen, the Restoration illustrated the point that 'things happen ... without any need of officiousness.' He had Cromwell's carelessness of forms of government, provided the root of the matter were secure. Yet Marvell had Milton's sense – a conception surely born of the agonies and triumphs and sufferings of the Revolution? – of good through evil, of the impossibility of good without evil, of the meaninglessness of rejecting good because of concomitant evil. It

1 Cf. *A Letter to Doctor Ingelo*, where Cromwell is described as *Ducere sive sequi nobile laetus iter*: on a noble course his joy was equal whether leading or following.

was from the rind of one apple tasted in a garden that the knowledge of good and evil came into the world. Tearing our pleasures 'with rough strife|Thorough the iron gates of life' makes them greater, not less.

> Thus, though we cannot make our sun
> Stand still, yet we will make him run.

That is the final triumph over circumstance. The highest praise of Cromwell was that he

> As the angel of our Commonweal,
> Troubling the waters, yearly mak'st them heal.
> (*The First Anniversary*, 401-2)

Or as Endymion, who wanted the moon, said to Cynthia:

> Though I so high may not pretend,
> It is the same so you descend.
> (*Marriage of Lord Fauconberg and*
> *Lady Mary Cromwell*, 41-2)

By the time of *The First Anniversary* and *On Blake's Victory over the Spaniards* all Marvell's problems are solved: and the great poetry ceases.[1] Marvell became a public servant, and his experience in writing compact business prose helped him, with Pepys and Dryden, to contribute a fresh element of conciseness and clarity to English prose style. Though the Restoration was to bring new complications, the inward assurance Marvell had so hardly won in the fifties was never lost. The poet became a pamphleteer as soon as he saw some of the returned Cavaliers trying to set the clock back to before 1640, trying to interfere with liberty of thought. With a purity of style reminiscent of Pascal, Marvell laughed down the enemies of religious

---

[1] We do not *know* this. Miss Bradbrook and Miss Lloyd Thomas point out that some of the religious and philosophical poems might be dated after Marvell's state service began (op. cit., p. 9). But I think the indirect internal evidence is strong enough to justify allotting all the great poems to the same period, roughly 1650-55.

I should like to think that the order of the lyrical poems in the 1681 edition (which Margoliouth uses) is chronological. Then we could trace the chronological as well as the logical sequence of Marvell's inner struggles. But the point is not material.

toleration. The irreligious fashionable world enjoyed his polished and sophisticated wit no less than Paris had enjoyed the *Lettres Provinciales* in which Pascal had exposed the Jesuits. It is no part of my purpose to discuss Marvell's admirable prose, but it is perhaps worth recording the judgement of Miss Bradbrook and Miss Lloyd Thomas that its wit and ridicule are based on 'a security of unquestioned and untroubled belief which gives him a standard by which he can relate the different levels of feeling, with their intensity,'[1] That is what we should have expected from our study of the poems.

This security, this stability in his political principles, this poised maturity and urbanity, are Marvell's peculiar strength: and they were won in the conflicts of the early fifties to which the great lyrics testify. In a lengthy simile in *The First Anniversary*, primitive man, terrified by the setting of the sun and the shadows, continues to look for light in the west, and is beginning to despair –

When straight the sun behind him he descri'd,
Smiling serenely from the further side.

(341–2)

That is the dialectic of life and change as Marvell came to know it.
(337–66)

F. W. Bateson

from *English Poetry: A Critical Introduction*   1950

What, however, is it in the social order that is projected in the poetry? It is time to come down to the brass tacks. Two recent comments on the poetry of Andrew Marvell will provide a convenient test-case. Obviously the American professor who thinks that *The Nymph Complaining for the Death of her Fawn* may represent 'an Anglican's grief for the stricken Church' is talking through his Yankee hat.[2] Obviously the Marxist who equates Marvell's 'Mower'

1 op. cit., p. 116. They contrast Swift – but that is another story. Swift, incidentally, was a great admirer of Marvell's prose.
2 Douglas Bush, *English Literature in the Earlier Seventeenth Century*, 1945, p. 161. It is only fair to add that this is an isolated lunacy. The book is a sensible, if somewhat superficial, guide-book to the period.

impartially with 'the power of Love', 'the scythe of Death or Fate', 'the revolutionary armies', 'the productive classes as against the drones', and 'a pre-commercial simplicity', is also seeing things that aren't really all of them there.[1] But it is easier to feel that this sort of thing is wrong than to be able to say specifically why it is wrong. The fundamental error, it seems to me, lies in identifying a social order with the concrete particulars, human or institutional, that make up its cogs and shafts, instead of with its prime mover, the basic human incentive that is ultimately responsible for setting in motion the particular manifestations, political, economic, religious and literary.[2] The social order that finds its expression in Marvell's lyrics cannot be defined in terms of social cogs like the Anglican Church and the New Model Army. To do so is to confuse effects with their causes. Even the political and economic systems of the English Renaissance are not the essential features of its social order. The fundamental question is a 'Why'. Why was the English ruling class the agent of such systems? The formula that we need must be one that defines the human motives that controlled the social behaviour of this dominant group.

What was the motivating force *par excellence* of the English Renaissance? I believe the one-word answer to this question is 'self-interest'. The self-interest, however, of the new ruling class of the 'King's Servants', who had displaced the feudal aristocracy of the Middle Ages, was neither narrow nor calculated. The sheep-farming that created deserted villages and the usury that financed piracy and the slave-trade were accompanied by more reputable titillations of the

1 Christopher Hill, 'Society and Andrew Marvell', *The Modern Quarterly*, no. 4, 1946, p. 18 [pp. 73–102 in this edition]. In spite of some rather wild identifications this is a most interesting article.
2 It is the failure to realize this that vitiates L. C. Knights's *Drama and Society in the Age of Jonson*, 1937, the most ambitious attempt since Buckle and Taine to relate English literature to the social background. Knights provides an admirable summary of English economic history, 1550–1650, and follows this with two excellent critical essays on Ben Jonson and some rather more perfunctory ones on Dekker, Heywood, Middleton and Massinger. The idea is that the economic analysis will illuminate the literary criticism. In fact, however, the two halves of the book do not coalesce, and the reader lays it down with a feeling that the claims made in the Introduction have not been justified. Knights handicapped himself unnecessarily by excluding the political and religious influences.

ego – among them military and athletic prowess, the art of dress, the patronage of culture, the ability to write a love-poem, the ambition of universal learning, and the delights of introspection. Unlike nineteenth-century individualism the individualism of the Renaissance was not specialized or one-sided. According to the theory of the handbooks of 'courtesy,' like Castiglione's *Il Libro del Cortegiano* and Peacham's *The Complete Gentleman*, success in the competition for the Prince's favour went to the accomplished individual, the man who had brought to perfection all the different sides of his personality. And during the reigns of the Tudors at any rate the theory had a certain basis in fact. The careers of Leicester, Sidney, Raleigh and Essex were, up to a point, an exemplification of it. Even more important, however, than the many-sidedness of Renaissance individualism is its mysticism. The *étalage du moi* was not a deliberate exploitation of the anti-social instincts, but a spontaneous response to a universe that had suddenly become increasingly unpredictable. The destruction of the feudal and ecclesiastical hierarchies of the Middle Ages had knocked the bottom out of the 'chain of being' explanation of the world and its associated doctrines.[1] On the political plane, instead of the hierarchical series of villein: manorial lord: feudal magnate: king, or family: tithing: hundred: county: kingdom,

There was naught but a naked people under a naked crown.

And Protestantism was also busy removing the theological inter-mediaries – Pope, saints and angels – between God and the individual worshipper. In the end, indeed, there were only four certainties left – God, the Prince, the head of the family and the ego. In every other province of human life *anything* might be true. Hence the omni-vorous curiosity and credulity of the Elizabethans. Hence too the new fear of witchcraft and the growth of interest in alchemy and astrology. The wildcat speculations and the financial extravagance, the travellers' tales and the sensational news-sheets, the eccentric

1 E. M. W. Tillyard, *The Elizabethan World Picture*, 1943, and Hardin Craig, *The Enchanted Glass*, 1936, stress the persistence of the theory. It survived in the sense in which the Christianity of *Hymns Ancient and Modern* survives today – as popular mythology, part of the fabric of thinking. Its fantastic correspon-dences (flames, blood, gold, mint, crocodiles and swans were some of the things that were 'solary', i.e. attracting to oneself the virtue of the sun) were a gift to the poets, but only the cranks took them seriously.

religious sects and the 'Heath Robinson' inventions were only different aspects of the same exuberant irrationality. It was a world in a
state of nature in which everything was possible, if only four things
were certain.

It was this world-picture that was displaced in the 1650s by the
man-made world of the scientists and of 'common sense', in which
probability was the guide of life and there were no certainties outside
mathematics. Here is the background against which Marvell's lyrics
must be read. They were written in the late 1640s and early 1650s by a
man whose heart and head were divided. Marvell's heart was with
the old world of mystical individualism which he associated with the
unconscious life of young growing things (flowers, fawns, children,
and grass, especially grass) and with their custodians, the mowers
and gardeners. His enemies were those who interfere with nature –
the lovers who cut their names on trees, the architects who 'square
and hew' the green trees of the forest, the troopers who shoot the
nymph's fawn. It is all summarized in *The Mower against Gardens*:

Luxurious man, to bring his vice in use,
Did after him the world seduce:
And from the fields the flowers and plants allure,
Where Nature was most plain and pure.

So much for the heart. Marvell's head was on the other side. Politically
he was a Parliamentarian, intellectually he was a rationalist, tempera-
mentally he was a satirist. And the head refused to allow the heart to
take itself too seriously. The mower's case against gardens is so overstated that it is clear it is largely only a pretext to describe their charm.
Marvell's irony enabled him to have it both ways. He retained the
mystical individualism of the Renaissance while recognizing its
inadequacy, and as a consequence a tension is generated in his poetry
comparable to that in the later poems of Yeats, who also had a foot
in two cultural camps.

There may well be details in the preceding analysis that can be
questioned, but it is at this level of abstraction at any rate that the
social significance of Marvell's poems, and indeed of all poems, must
be determined. The principle is inherent in the nature of poetry. The
subject-matter of poetry is not 'things,' but conflicting moods and
attitudes, *human nature in its social relations*. Even important 'things,'

like an economic or political system, cannot be the subject-matter of poetry except as the objects of human emotions and reflections. The inner meaning of a poem is the synthesis of conflicting attitudes and not the conflict of institutions. To interpret a poem as an allegory of incidents on the political scene, like the Puritan attack on the Anglican Church, or on the economic scene, like the struggle between capitalism and pre-commercial morality, is really to condemn it as poetry and reduce it to *roman à clef*. All that the poet can do *qua* poet is to dramatize the basic human attitudes that have been institutionalized as Anglicanism or Puritanism or whatever it is. This is what Marvell has done in *A Dialogue between the Resolved Soul and Created Pleasure*, a poem with far more strictly social significance than *The Nymph Complaining for the Death of her Fawn* or the 'Mower' poems. In this poem Marvell introduces a 'Soul' which rejects seriatim the temptations dangled before it by 'Pleasure'. The temptations begin with the pleasures of the senses (taste, touch, smell, sight and sound in that order) and conclude with the lusts for feminine beauty, gold, power and knowledge. The poem is clearly intended to symbolize Marvell's rejection of the Renaissance world (it was to satisfy precisely these lusts that Faustus had sold his soul to Lucifer), and it is reasonable to describe it as an exposition of an intellectual Puritanism. But this is a very different thing from the disguised history of the Civil War that the writers I have referred to wish to ascribe to him.

My conclusion, therefore, is that the social content of poetry must not be identified with the concrete particulars of everyday life. There is no reason why teapots, Proportional Representation and the Crystal Palace should not be introduced into a poem, but again there is no reason why they should be. The imprint of the social order must be looked for at a higher level of abstraction, and to the casual reader it may easily not be visible at all. It will normally be concerned with the basic incentives, the human prime mover, that a particular society offers its members. In English Renaissance poetry its centre of interest seems to lie in variations round the theme of a mystical individualism.

(96–101)

Patrick Cruttwell

from 'The Civil War and the Split in the Age', *The Shakespearean Moment* 1954

The Civil War then, forced writers to 'take sides'. It did this more extensively and harmfully than simply by enlisting them as propagandists. It has already been suggested that the imaginations of the Elizabethans anticipated the reality of civil war which their grandchildren suffered; what is more, the ideological shape which the war took, and in particular its two central human figures, Cromwell and the King, made realities, and gave to those realities enormous emotional force, out of two of the most vital imaginative and drama-tic *personae* of the age. Cromwell embodied the military hero, the self-made conquering usurper; Charles the legitimate anointed monarch, the King by the Grace of God. These two figures are of enormous importance to Elizabethan and Jacobean drama; the struggle between them makes the backbone of Marlowe's *Tamburlaine*, of Shakespeare's English histories, and of *Macbeth*. The former stood for and satisfied the age's craving for individualist self-expression, for the great man who could revolt against the controls of orthodoxy, and defeat them; the latter was the central symbol of the other part of the age's mind, its deep reverence for order and tradition.

How completely Cromwell fulfilled the role of self-made hero, already worked out for him in the drama, will be seen in a moment; as for Charles, it is clear that his death became for the Royalists an event which concentrated all those feelings for Church-and-State-as-one which we have found to be dominant in the Shakespearean moment and its society. The 'Martyr King' was not merely a figure of speech, as it is nowadays for all but a few determined eccentrics who confuse what they would like to feel with what they do feel; on the figure of Charles was focused all that desire to *have* 'martyrs' and 'saints', and to celebrate them according to the Catholic pattern, which existed, in spite of Protestant qualms, in Shakespeare and Donne. The intensive cult of 'relics' of the executed King is one proof of it; another is the drawing of parallels – sometimes hinted, sometimes explicit – between Charles's fate and that of Christ. Both friends and enemies made of him a religious symbol; against the

Puritans' Man of Blood, the royalists made him a Man of Sorrows.
This comparison, which to us may seem blasphemous, was quite
clearly in Charles's own mind; when Bishop Juxon, on the morning
of the execution, read the Lesson for the day, the 27th chapter of
St Matthew, 'which relateth the Passion of our blessed Saviour',
Charles inquired if he had picked out that chapter on purpose, as
'being so applicable to his present condition'. And in *Eikon Basilike*
the parallel is often suggested – in the prayer in the 26th chapter:

O let not my blood be upon them and their children, whom
the fraud and faction of some, not the malice of all, have
excited to *crucify* me

and in the verses printed at the end of the book:

With such a bloody method and behaviour,
Their ancestors did crucify our Saviour.[1]

Such an identification, between the deposed and martyred King-by-
divine-Grace and the divine victim himself, was not in the least a
new creation, invented for the special benefit of Charles; it was the
natural outcome of a whole tradition, exactly anticipated in the words
of Shakespeare's Richard II, speaking to the men who had deposed,
and were to murder, him:

Nay, all of you, that stand and look upon me,
Whilst that my wretchedness doth bait myself,
Though some of you, with Pilate, wash your hands,
Showing an outward pity: yet you Pilates
Have here deliver'd me to my sour cross,
And water cannot wash away your sin.
(IV I)

By such a particular point as this can be justified the assertion that the
dramatists anticipated in imagination what the later generation would
experience, and by this anticipation helped to set the pattern of
thought and emotion which determined how that generation would

1 *Eikon Basilike*, it seems conclusively established by now, was not Charles's
own work: but the argument is not affected. It hit to a hair's-breadth – as its
huge success demonstrated – what the royalists wanted to feel.

react to its experience. The same is true – exactly the same – if we look at the other great figure, both symbolic and real: Cromwell, the usurping hero.

For the type he came to fulfil, Marlowe's *Tamburlaine* is the starting-point in dramatic poetry: the perfect expression, in its clear outline and brilliant colouring, of the dream of the conqueror. But Tamburlaine the hero is a far more subtle, more intelligent creation than his Technicolor trappings may suggest; he is built on ideas, precise and intellectual. He is, above all, the self-made man, the climber from obscurity to greatness. 'But tell me, Madam,' he asks of the captured Zenocrate, 'is your grace betroth'd?' 'I am (my Lord),' she answers, 'for so you do import'; and he replies

I am a Lord, for so my deeds shall prove,
And yet a shepherd by my parentage.

This self-made man is above Fate and Fortune; the powers that control lesser men are controlled by him:

I hold the Fates bound fast in iron chains,
And with my hand turn Fortune's wheel about.[1]

Nature too joins in to help him:

Nature doth strive with Fortune and his stars
To make him famous in accomplished worth.

And in Menaphon's description of the hero – a description which seems to suggest a superhuman robot rather than a man – the meta-

[1] Cf. *Jew of Malta*, at the end of which the Governor of Malta (the legitimate ruler, who has defeated the self-made usurper of that play, Barabas) explicitly rejects the forces that Tamburlaine relies on, and appeals instead to God:

So march away, and let due praise be given
Neither to Fate nor Fortune, but to Heaven.

This view of the conqueror as especially 'fortunate' descends from the Romans. That Pompey was *felix* is one of the grounds advanced by Cicero (*Pro Lege Manilia*) in support of his appointment to high command. *Felix* meant 'favoured by fortune', but it implied also that such a condition was more than just a chance; it was a personal quality, and it was one of the qualifications for being a hero. So (in *Antony and Cleopatra*) Antony reluctantly endorses, as valid evidence against himself, so to speak, the soothsayer's observation that Octavius always defeats him at games of chance.

phor hints that the planets themselves, the whole divine order, are moving at his command and for his advancement:

... Wherein by curious sovereignty of art,
Are fixed his piercing instruments of sight:
Whose fiery circles bear encompassed
A heaven of heavenly bodies in their spheres:
That guides his steps and actions to the throne,
Where honour sits invested royally.

The conqueror has, for his special function, that of the usurper, the destroyer of legitimacy, of those who rule by divine right and by the traditional sanctions and loyalties. In the comic cowardice of Mycetes, the King of Persia –

Away, I am the King: go, touch me not.
Thou break'st the law of arms unless thou kneel,
And cry me mercy, noble King

– it is the untouchability of divine right (what Claudius in *Hamlet* appeals to) that is ridiculed, and also the feudal obligation of loyalty ('the law of arms'). So, too, when Cosroe, now king himself, learns that Tamburlaine has turned against him, he bases his defiance of the upstart on 'love of honour and defence of right', and when he too has met with defeat, he simply cannot understand, this feeble representative of the old order, the new spirit of individualist rebellion: 'the *strangest* men', he cries in puzzled despair –

The strangest men that ever nature made,
I know not how to take their tyrannies.

From enemy of legitimate ruler to enemy of orthodox religion was a short and inevitable step. And Tamburlaine is both. The Emperor Bajazeth, next victim on the hero's list, as he and his future conqueror are indulging in the flyting that precedes the battle, appeals to his State religion:

By Mahomet, my kinsman's sepulchre,
And by the holy Alcaron I swear ...

but Tamburlaine answers with an appeal to his own native strength:

By this my sword that conquer'd Persia . . .

When the battle has been fought, and Bajazeth is a prisoner, he is still appealing, and still in vain, to the priests of his orthodoxy, invoking their powers of magic:

Ye holy priests of heavenly Mahomet,
That sacrificing slice and cut your flesh,
Staining his altars with your purple blood:
Make heaven to frown and every fixed star
To suck up poison from the moorish fens,
And pour it in this glorious tyrant's throat.

And now Tamburlaine answers with a confident assertion (it is not a prayer, and it is not in vain) that a God who is higher than mere 'religions', a sort of Stoic or deist First Cause, is his protector and favourer:

The chiefest God, First Mover of that sphere,
Enchas'd with thousands ever shining lamps,
Will sooner burn the glorious frame of heaven,
Than it should so conspire my overthrow.

In the key of mockery, the same point is made through the jeers of Tamburlaine's followers:

– Dost thou think that Mahomet will suffer this?
– 'Tis like he will, when he cannot let it.

The religion, in fact, is discredited because its anointed representative is defeated and humbled. 'No king, no bishop': Marlowe is endorsing King James's dictum; but Marlowe is all for it.

Tamburlaine's 'morality' – for he has one, he is not just a conqueror for the sake of conquering – is like his God, more Roman than modern. 'Virtue' and 'worth' are words he is always invoking; and the sense of his use of the former is far closer to the Latin *virtus* (manly accomplishment) than it is to moral 'goodness'. He defeats the legitimate Emperor, becoming Emperor himself, but still (though Zenocrate hopefully talks of his '*sacred* person' and begs him to give up his soldiering) he regards himself as dedicated to arms, he is still

the champion of individualism and rejects the convention of primo-
geniture, saying to his youngest son

If thou exceed thy elder brothers' worth,
And shine in complete virtue more than they,
Thou shalt be king before them, and thy seed
Shall issue crowned from their mother's womb.

So, in the lines that end his most famous tirade –

... Shall give the world to note for all my birth,
That virtue solely is the sum of glory,
And fashions men with true nobility

– the context makes it painfully clear that 'virtue' does not mean
goodness; for the speech is sandwiched between the brutal killing of
the virgins sent to beg peace for Damascus ('what, have your horsemen shown the virgins Death?') and the mocking of Bajazeth in his
cage.

Tamburlaine, in fact, is something of a Whiggish hero, and the
Marlowe who created him[1] is almost a proto-Whig; sceptical of
organized religion, contemptuous of traditional loyalties, advocate of
la carrière ouverte aux talents. The line he began continues through the
century; and when it encountered the person of Cromwell, it found
at once that to praise the real hero the same terms were called for as
had served for the fictional. Marlowe is to Tamburlaine as Milton is
to Cromwell. Just as Tamburlaine had claimed to be in command of
Fortune –

And with my hand turn Fortune's wheel about

so Milton claims for Cromwell, that he

on the neck of crowned Fortune proud

has 'rear'd God's trophies'. Marvell has the same in the *Horatian Ode*:
'the wars' and Fortune's son'. Cowley echoes Marvell: 'this son of

1 But not the Marlowe of *Faustus* and *Edward II*, who is far more critical, more
traditional, and – possibly – more Christian.

Fortune'; Dryden and Bishop Sprat, that dexterous pair of turncoats,
complete the chorus. 'For he was great,' says Dryden, 'ere Fortune
made him so'; and the Bishop sings in tune:

Though Fortune did hang on thy sword,
   And did obey thy mighty word,
   Though Fortune, for thy side and thee,
   Forgot her lov'd inconstancy . . .[1]

They are, indeed, remarkably unanimous, the contemporary cele-
brators of the Lord Protector, whatever their judgements on his
doings. They unite in putting, at the head of their accounts of him,
his rise from obscurity to greatness ('who, from a Scythian shepherd,
by his rare and wonderful conquests, became a most puissant and
mighty monarch' is how the title-page of *Tamburlaine* – first edition
of Part I – expresses it). Marvell's English verse in the *Horatian Ode* –

Who from his private gardens, where
He liv'd reserved and austere

(29–30)

– and Clarendon's English prose in the *History* (Book 15) –

. . . who from a *private* and obscure birth, (though of a good
family), without interest of estate, alliance, or friendships, could
raise himself to such a height . . . yet as he grew into place and
authority, his parts seemed to be renewed, as if he had had
concealed faculties till he had occasion to use them

run parallel with Milton's Latin in the *Defensio Secunda* –

He grew up in concealment [*in occulto*] at home, and coming
to mature and settled years, lived still a private person
[*privatus*], chiefly known for observance of the purer religion,
and for integrity. Awaiting some great crisis, he cherished his

1 Milton: *Sonnet on the Lord Protector*; Cowley: *Discourse by way of Vision
Concerning the Government of Oliver Cromwell*; Dryden: *Heroic Stanzas on the
Death of the Lord Protector*; Sprat: *To the Happy Memory of the late Lord Pro-
tector*.

confidence in God, and his great spirit, in silence [*tacito
pectore*].[1] [Editor's translation.]

The standpoints and conclusions of these three witnesses are entirely
different. Clarendon, the royalist, condemns; Milton, the Puritan,
approves; Marvell, the quasi-Puritan humanist, is balanced. Their
agreement is all the more striking.

Tamburlaine, we have seen, was above all the destroyer of old-
established things. And so was Cromwell, in the eyes of his contemporaries. Marvell's brief and pregnant phrases –

Could by industrious valour climb
To ruin the great work of Time,
    And cast the Kingdoms[2] old
    Into another mould

(33–6)

– are echoed in Cowley's prose:

What can be more extraordinary than that a person of mean
birth, no fortune, no eminent qualities of body . . . should have the
courage to attempt, and the happiness to succeed in, so improbable
a design, as the destruction of one of the most ancient and most
solidly founded monarchies upon the earth?[3]

And just as Tamburlaine tells his Zenocrate that no success, no
assumption of 'sacred' legitimacy, will induce him to cease from his

1 To these could be added Waller (*Panegyric to my Lord Protector*):

Oft have we wonder'd, how you hid in peace
A mind proportion'd to such things as these

and Bishop Sprat (op. cit.):

So whilst but private walls did know
What we to such a mighty mind should owe,
    Then the same virtues did appear,
Though in a less and more contracted sphere,
As full, though not as large, as since they were.

2 Grosart's reading, Margoliouth prints 'Kingdom'. [Ed.]
3 This is spoken not by Cowley in *propria persona*, but by the 'devil' with
whom he debates in the *Discourse by way of Vision*. But since it is a comment on
the extraordinary nature of Cromwell's achievement, not a moral judgement
on it, we may conclude that on this point Cowley and his devil are at one.

conquering career, so Clarendon reaches, with explicit condemnation, the conclusion that Marvell arrives at with judgement reserved:

They who enter upon unwarrantable enterprises, must pursue many unwarrantable ways to preserve themselves from the penalty of the first guilt.[1]

The same arts that did gain
A power, must it maintain.

(119–20)

The Wallers, Drydens and Bishop Sprats need not greatly concern us; they were time-servers, from whom obsequious panegyric could always be expected for whatever, and whoever, occupied the seats of the mighty. It is only in Marlowe and Milton that uncompromising approval of the conquering usurper is completely sincere; for both of them were, if not fanatics, at least revolutionaries, men with very strongly-held and clear-cut opinions, which made it difficult for Marlowe, impossible for Milton, to do any sort of sympathetic justice to the other side. But there was also another way of looking at the usurping hero, a way different from both hired adulation and revolutionary fervour: the balanced, half-critical and half-admiring way, which is seen supremely in Shakespeare and in Marvell's *Horatian Ode*, the characteristically 'double-faced' way of the mature Shakespearean and metaphysical manner. It sees and judges the conqueror's destructiveness as well as his greatness; it feels the case for traditional loyalties as strongly as that for the upstart; it views the hero with irony as much as with admiration; it is willing to agree that he is fortunate, but will never claim (as Milton does for Cromwell) that his trophies are also God's. Contrast, for example, Marvell with Dryden, each describing the speed of Cromwell's victorious campaigns:

Then burning through the air he went
And palaces and temples rent.

(21–2)

Swift and resistless through the land he past,
    Like that bold Greek who did the East subdue;

1 *History*, Book 10. The comment is made *à propos* of Cromwell.

And made to battle such heroic haste,
  As if on wings of victory he flew.

Marvell's image (Cromwell has just been compared with the 'three-fork'd lightning') is full of the sense of a destructiveness terrible and indiscriminate – and almost devilish, for 'temples' are destroyed by it; Dryden has nothing of this. Dryden, again, uncritically asserts that Cromwell was guiltless of ambition – 'and yet dominion was not his design'; Marvell, always equivocal, implies the opposite:

So *restless* Cromwell *could not* cease
In the inglorious arts of peace.

(9–10)

Dryden swallows, without a hint of reservation, Cromwell's claim to be fighting a 'war to end war' – 'he fought to end our fighting' – Marvell, as noted above, obliquely warns his hero that they who won power by the sword must maintain it by the sword. Milton affirms the purity of Cromwell's religion; Marvell, on that, is most diplomatically silent.[1] If Milton is to Cromwell as Marlowe to Tamburlaine, then Marvell is to Cromwell as Shakespeare to Coriolanus. As Shakespeare, indeed, is to all his warlike heroes or self-made usurpers, to Bolingbroke and Hotspur, Coriolanus and Antony; the balance of admiration and criticism is always preserved. Bolingbroke is certainly meant to be admired; the weakness and foolishness of the king whom he deposes are relentlessly shown; yet the case for legitimacy, and the consequences of usurpation, are stated by the Bishop of Carlisle with a vigour as great as anything in the play ('The blood of English shall manure the ground, And future ages groan for his foul act'); and even the usurper's son, on the eve of his greatest triumph, is haunted by the guilt which his father incurred. Such balance, such freedom from engagement, is clearly the exact equivalent of Marvell's supremely generous tribute to Charles's conduct on the scaffold, and his plain assertion (in a poem ostensibly celebrating Charles's destroyer) that

1 Richard Baxter – like Marvell, a Commonwealth-man but no fanatic – had similar doubts: 'Hereupon Cromwell's general religious zeal, giveth away to the power of that ambition, which still increaseth as his successes do increase. . . . He meaneth well in all this at the beginning, and thinketh he doth all for the safety of the godly, and the public good, but not without an eye to himself.' (*Reliquiae Baxterianae*, lib. 1, part i).

'Justice' is with the loser;[1] just as Marlowe's caricaturing of Tamburlaine's enemies is the parallel of Milton's harsh contempt for the King. Or consider – this may seem irrelevant but in fact is the same – the subtle Shakespearean use of his keyword 'noble' in *Julius Caesar*. 'Noble' is, above all words, *the* word for the killers of Caesar, the idealist slayers for liberty's sake, and especially the word for the most idealist, for Brutus himself. It is, says Cassius, the quality that Rome, under Caesar, has lost – 'Rome, thou hast lost the breed of noble bloods.' It is the epithet that Antony, talking to Caesar, awards to Cassius – 'he is a noble Roman, and well given.' Cassius gives it to Brutus, prodding him up to the sticking-point – 'well *Brutus*, thou art noble: yet I see ...' – but here already it has a tinge of irony, the practical man regarding the lofty hesitant idealist. The irony thickens, to explicit mockery, when Antony repeats it to the Roman mob:

The noble Brutus,
Hath told you Caesar was ambitious ...

– the equivocation is driven home when that same mob, turned inside out by Antony's rhetoric, transfers the word to Antony himself – 'there's not a nobler man in Rome than Antony' – so that when we reach the final use of it –

This was the noblest Roman of them all

– can we be sure (remembering that this is a 'set speech' and that Antony's cynical cunning as a rhetorician has been well established) if true admiration or mocking irony is the dominant note?

This is the attitude, and therefore the kind of art, that the Civil War rendered impossible. By embodying in contemporary events both symbolic figures, conquering individualist usurper and divinely-sanctioned King, by forcing men to choose one or the other, the war brought to an end the conditions which made such a balance tenable. As long as these two figures were not in head-on and contemporary collision, it was possible for men to enjoy, in imagination, the tension between them and the tensions within their own minds of which the figures were embodiments, and to make from it all a tense but un-

1 Though Justice against Fate complain,
  And plead the ancient rights in vain.

(37–8)

distorted poetry; but as soon as they *were* in collision, there came, inevitably, the propagandist's lop-sided viewpoint. Imagine a *Macbeth* written after the execution of King Charles. It would then have been quite impossible to preserve, as Shakespeare does, both the mystical reverence for legitimate kingship, the sense that its destruction involves a violation of the divine and the natural orders, and the sympathetic dramatic presentation of the murderous usurper. One or the other would have had to go; what *is* a tragedy would be turned into a piece of propaganda. (This is not to argue that propaganda – that is, work intended to enforce a particular viewpoint – cannot be real art. It can be: but it can *not* be true tragedy.) Of the balanced view Marvell's *Horatian Ode* is perhaps the last achievement; an astonishing achievement, considering its date – two years after the King's execution. But even Marvell could not hold it for long or with comfort: many of his other poems – *Appleton House*, for example, and those like it, which develop his special world of garden, country-house fantasy – have a strong tinge of escape; they seem the poetry of a man deeply disturbed by the chaos and horrors around him, who has managed, for a time, to construct a world of the imagination to keep out the conflict. But its fragility is evident even in the symbols which are used to create it; the garden-wall is no real defence against 'ambition's heat' (Cromwell, after all, had begun in a garden, where he 'tended the bergamot'), and the 'sweet militia' of the flowers is perfectly realized to be only a wishful fantasy. 'O happy! *could* we but restore That sweet militia once more ...' – but he knows quite well that we can't.

It is in Marvell and Milton that we can best study the effects of the Civil War on poetic sensibility, for it happens that they are the only poets of the first quality whose careers span this watershed of the century; the others are either entirely before it, like Donne and Herbert, or almost entirely after it, like Dryden. On Marvell the effect seems to have been a total destruction: the end of what had been one of the most delicate and exquisite sensibilities in the language. No poet's career provides a more striking, or more depressing, contrast than his does between his real poetry and the Satires which were apparently his only work in verse written after the Restoration. What impresses one in those satires, if one comes to them from *Appleton House* and *The Garden* and the *Coy Mistress*, is the coarseness and crudity of the wit and emotion, it is not merely that Marvell has become a propagandist and nothing but a propagandist, but that in so doing he has lost all the qualities which had made him a great poet. Dryden – with less to lose – loses a good deal less when *he* turns to propaganda; and the cause is this, that Dryden, a man of a later generation, with none but the most superficial traces of the earlier kind of sensibility, was not wronging the best part of his nature when he 'to party gave up what was meant for mankind'. Marvell *was* doing that wrong, for he had been a true son of the Shakespearean moment. The sense of tragedy is lost, succeeded by a bitter one-eyed railing; the metaphysical wit, never divorced from feeling, is displaced by the kind of wit which aims at nothing more than creating contempt and dislike; above all, there is lost the ability to stand aside from contemporary events even while writing of them and judging them. That ability the *Horatian Ode* had shown supremely; its quality comes from the fact that – partly by the aid of the 'Horatian' form, partly by the parallels with Roman history – Marvell was able to place the conflict between Charles and Cromwell in the perspective of history. But now, after the Restoration, he is totally involved: up to the neck in it, a Party man.

(187–200)

J. B. Leishman

'Some Themes and Variations in the Poetry of Andrew Marvell', *Proceedings of the British Academy*, vol. 47   1961

If, then, which is by no means certain, *The Match* and *The Unfortunate Lover* are early poems, they are not like Donne, and Marvell did not begin as a disciple of Donne. It would be more possible to maintain that he began as a disciple of Crashaw and of those neo-Latin epigrammatists whom Crashaw often imitated. Consider for a moment the poem *Eyes and Tears*. It was almost certainly suggested by Crashaw's *The Weeper*, and the fourteen stanzas into which its fifty-six octosyllabic couplets are divided are as loosely connected and as transposable as those of Crashaw's poem, each of them developing more cerebrally and definingly and less pictorially

than Crashaw, some ingenious metaphor or simile to express the
superiority of tears to any other terrestrial sight and of sorrow to any
other human emotion: laughter turns to tears; the sun, after distilling
the world all day, is left with nothing but moisture, which he rains
back in pity; stars appear beautiful only as the tears of light, and so on.
The eighth stanza,

> So Magdalen, in tears more wise
> Dissolved those captivating eyes,
> Whose liquid chains could flowing meet
> To fetter her redeemer's feet,

might almost be regarded as a complimentary allusion to Crashaw's
weeping Magdalene, and at the end of his poem Marvell has added a
translation of this stanza into Latin elegiacs which would not have
been out of place in *Epigrammata Sacra*, the little collection of Latin
epigrams on sacred subjects which Crashaw published in 1634. The
poem *Mourning*, which, in nine octosyllabic quatrains, attempts to
say, by means of ingenious similes and metaphors, what Chlora's
tears are, recalls, more immediately than do any of Marvell's more
individual and characteristic poems, various things in the enormous
and enormously popular collections of Renaissance Latin epigrams.
Étienne Pasquier (1529–1615), for example, has a poem entitled *De
Amoena Vidua*, 'On Amoena,[1] having lost her husband', which
contains the lines:

> His tamen in lachrimis nihil est ornatius illa,
>   Perpetuusque subest eius in ore nitor.
> Siccine, defunctum quae deperit orba maritum,
>   Semper aget viduo foemina maesta thoro?
> Quae flet culta, suum non luget, Amoena, maritum;
>   Quid facit ergo? alium quaerit Amoena virum.

(Yet, amid these tears, nothing could be handsomer than she, and
there lurks a perpetual brightness in her face. Will she, who pines
in her bereavement for her dead husband, always be thus enacting
the mourner on a widowed bed? One, Amoena, who weeps with

1 Pasquier is using the adjective *amoena* ('lovely', 'charming') as a proper
noun.

elegance is not mourning her husband. What, then, is she doing?
Amoena, she's looking for another.)[1]

... Is Marvell ever really like Donne? His *Definition of Love*,[2]
although its last stanza, almost certainly the germ from which the
whole poem sprang, was suggested by the third stanza of a not very
good poem in Cowley's *The Mistress* entitled *Impossibilities* – his
Definition of Love is, as many readers must have felt, more like
Donne's *A Valediction: forbidding mourning* than perhaps any other
single seventeenth-century poem is like any one of Donne's *Songs
and Sonnets*: 'like', not as a deliberate and inferior imitation, as are so
many of the poems in Cowley's *Mistress*, but like with the likeness of
a peer. Certainly, without the example of Donne's *Valediction* I
doubt whether Marvell's poem could have been what it is. In what
might be called (though I do not much like the phrase) its concrete
intellectuality, the way in which it intellectualizes feeling or sensation
into conceptions, into more or less abstract ideas, which still retain
the vividness of perceptions, the style of Marvell's poem strikingly
resembles Donne's; and yet, below the surface, is there not a fundamental difference? Let us place three stanzas from each poem side by
side.

Dull sublunary lovers' love
  (Whose soul is sense) cannot admit
Absence, because it doth remove
  Those things which elemented it.

But we, by a love so much refined
  That our selves know not what it is,
Inter-assured of the mind,
  Care less, eyes, lips, and hands to miss.

Our two souls therefore, which are one,
  Though I must go, endure not yet
A breach, but an expansion,
  Like gold to airy thinness beat.

1 *Deliciae C[entum] Poetarum Gallorum*, ed. R. Gherus, 1609, ii 875.
2 In what I have to say about this poem I am greatly indebted to some remarks
by Professor R. Ellrodt, *Les Poètes métaphysiques anglais*, première partie, tome
2, 1960, pp. 123 and 148.

Donne, as in nearly all the more serious of the *Songs and Sonnets*, is here analysing his immediate experience of a particular situation, real or imagined, and developing the paradox that for true lovers absence is not incompatible with presence. Now listen to Marvell:

For Fate with jealous eyes does see
Two perfect loves; nor lets them close:
Their union would her ruin be,
And her tyrannic power depose.

And therefore her decrees of steel
Us as the distant poles have placed,
(Though Love's whole world on us doth wheel)
Not by themselves to be embraced,

Unless the giddy heaven fall,
And earth some new convulsion tear;
And, us to join, the world should all
Be cramped into a planisphere.[1]

Marvell is not starting from the immediate experience of a particular situation, is not really being analytic and psychological and paradoxical like Donne, but is simply performing, with characteristically seventeenth-century intellectuality, ingenuity, hyperbole, and antithesis, an elaborate series of variations on the ancient theme of star-crossed lovers. While Donne, not merely in the stanzas I quoted but throughout his poem, is developing an argument ('Even though physically parted, we can remain spiritually united'), Marvell is simply saying over and over again, in various ingenious ways, 'we can never meet'. He is not really, like Donne, being paradoxical: what at first sight looks like paradox appears, when we examine it more closely, to be merely antithesis:

Their union would her ruin be,
And her tyrannic power depose.

And that characteristically exhilarating piece of semi-burlesque hyperbole, that the poles-apart lovers could only be joined if the

1 A map or chart formed by the projection of a sphere, or part of one, on a plane. *O.E.D.* quotes from Thomas Blundeville's *Exercises*, 1594: 'Astrolabe . . . is called of some a planisphere, because it is both flat and round, representing the globe or sphere, having both his poles clapped flat together.'

world were 'cramped into a planisphere' – what is it but our old friend the catalogue of impossibilities, ἀδύνατα ('till oaks sweat honey', 'till fish scale the mountains', etc.), so familiar in Greek and Roman poetry, brought up to date? This is one of the great differences between Donne and Marvell: while Donne, one might almost say, devised entirely new ways of saying entirely new things, Marvell assimilated, recombined, and perfected from his contemporaries various new ways of saying old ones.

In what, after the Cromwell ode, is perhaps Marvell's finest single poem, *To his Coy Mistress*, it can be shown that throughout he is doing very old and traditional things in a new way, and that he is only being very superficially like Donne. The poem is indeed, like many of Donne's and unlike *The Definition of Love*, a continuous argument, and even a more rigidly syllogistic argument than I think we shall find in any of the more serious of the *Songs and Sonnets*, where Donne is usually concerned with analysis rather than with demonstration.

If we had infinite time, I should be happy to court you at leisure;
But our life lasts only for a moment:
Therefore, in order to live, we must seize the moment as it flies.

It is only, I think, in such fundamentally unserious poems as *The Will* that we shall find Donne being as neatly syllogistic as this. Where this poem most resembles Donne, and is perhaps more fundamentally indebted to his example than any other of Marvell's poems, is in its essentially dramatic tone (more dramatic than in any other of Marvell's poems), in the way in which it makes us feel that we are overhearing one of the speakers in a dialogue. But, before proceeding, let us make sure that we have the poem vividly in our minds: [quotes lines 1–33]. Marvell reaches the conclusion of his semi-syllogistic argument, and, after some lines which are poetically rather below the general level of his poem, magnificently concludes:

Let us roll all our strength, and all
Our sweetness, up into one ball:
And tear our pleasures with rough strife,
Thorough the iron gates of life.
Thus, though we cannot make our sun
Stand still, yet we will make him run.

The tempo, *allegro molto* at least, is much faster than that of any of the more serious of Donne's *Songs and Sonnets*, and, both in its speed, its mock-serious argument and its witty hyperbole, the poem might seem to have some affinity with Donne's tone and manner in some of his more exuberant elegies. The hyperbole, though – often, like that in *A Definition of Love*, approaching burlesque – is not, as I shall try to show later, really like Donne's, and the argument, although I have called it 'mock-serious', is really more serious, less paradoxical, than the sort of argument Donne conducts in the Elegies. It is also, I think, an argument which Donne would have regarded as too traditional and literary – the argument of Catullus'

Vivamus, mea Lesbia, atque amemus . . .
Soles occidere et redire possunt:
nobis cum semel occidit brevis lux,
nox est perpetua una dormienda,

which Ben Jonson so delightfully paraphrased as:

Come my Celia, let us prove,
While we may, the sports of love;
Time will not be ours for ever:
He, at length, our good will sever.
Spend not then his gifts in vain.
Suns, that set, may rise again:
But if once we lose this light,
'Tis, with us, perpetual night.

On this ancient theme Marvell has executed a series of brilliant seventeenth-century variations, which were partly suggested to him by the last stanza of a poem in Cowley's *The Mistress* entitled *My Diet*, a stanza from which Marvell has borrowed and made unforgettable the phrase 'vast eternity'[1]:

1 Cowley, too, evidently thought the phrase a good one, for he used it again in the penultimate line of his ode *Sitting and Drinking in the Chair made out of the Relics of Sir Francis Drake's Ship*, first printed in *Verses lately written upon several Occasions*, 1663:

The straits of time too narrow are for thee,
Launch forth into an indiscovered sea,
And steer the endless course of vast eternity,
Take for thy sail this verse, and for thy pilot me.

On 'a sigh of pity I a year can live,
   One tear will keep me twenty 'at least,
   Fifty a gentle look will give:
An hundred years on one kind word I'll feast:
   A thousand more will added be,
If you an inclination have for me;
And all beyond is vast eternity.

Cowley was by no means the first to introduce arithmetic into love-poetry, but he has here exploited its possibilities in a way that seems to be original. The earliest of these arithmetical amorists, so far as I know, was an anonymous Alexandrian imitator of Anacreon, who, anticipating Leporello's catalogue of his master's conquests in Mozart's *Don Giovanni*, wrote a poem which begins: 'If you can count the leaves of all trees and the waves of the whole ocean, then I will make you sole reckoner of my loves. First set down twenty from Athens and add to them fifteen. Then set down whole chains of loves from Corinth, for it is in Achaea, where women are beautiful.'[1] Catullus, at the conclusion of *Vivamus mea Lesbia*, seems to have been the first poet to write arithmetically of kisses:

Da mi basia mille, deinde centum,
dein mille altera, dein secunda centum –

... Like Johannes Secundus[2] before him, the French Renaissance Latin poet Étienne Pasquier, whom I have already quoted on the subject of a lovely widow, combined, in a poem *Ad Sabinam*, this osculatory arithmetic, or arithmetical osculation, with one of the most popular themes of classical and Renaissance love-poetry, the catalogue of a mistress's charms, declaring that he would print a thousand kisses on every part of Sabina's body:

Quid reniteris? obstinatiora
Carpo basia mille singulatim.
Labris millia, millia en ocellis,
Genis millia, millia en papillis,
Obsignabo, licet puella nolit.[3]

1 *Anacreontea* 14, Εἰ φύλλα πάντα δένδρων.
2 *Basia* 7.
3 *Deliciae C[entum] Poetarum Gallorum*, ed. R. Gherus, 1609, ii 1000.

(Why do you resist? I snatch my kisses all the more resolutely,
a thousand at a time. Thousands on lips, thousands on eyes,
thousands on cheeks, thousands on breasts I will implant –
unwilling though the girl may be.)

Throughout the first twenty lines of his poem Marvell is making a
brilliantly original use of the time-measuring arithmetic in that
stanza of Cowley's from which he borrowed the phrase 'vast eternity'.
In the passage beginning

An hundred years should go to praise
Thine eyes, and on thy forehead gaze,

he has applied it to that traditional and popular topic, the catalogue
of a mistress's charms – a novel combination, I think, although it may
have been suggested to him by Pasquier's combination of that traditional catalogue with the osculatory arithmetic of Catullus. In the
exuberant hyperbole and antithesis of his opening lines, declaring that,
had they but world enough and time, he would be willing to court
her and be refused by her from ten years before the Flood until the
conversion of the Jews, Marvell is not only being original, but
writing in a manner in which no poets except those of the English
seventeenth century ever wrote. When ancient poets handled the
topics of *carpe diem* and *carpe florem*, when they pointed to the contrast between the returning anise and parsley, the returning seasons,
the returning sun and moon and the unreturning lives of men, or
when they exhorted some unresponsive girl or boy to learn a lesson
from the withering and neglected rose, they nearly always wrote with
an undiluted pathos and seriousness and even solemnity; or, if any
trace of a smile was there, it was a sad one. And the Renaissance
Italian and French poets, when they handled these topics, nearly
always preserved a similar tone. It was only certain English poets of
the earlier seventeenth century who expanded and varied these and
other traditional topics with the witty, elaborate, and sometimes
positively hilarious ingenuity of Marvell in this poem.

This does not mean that Marvell's poem is, in comparison, slight
or unserious or superficial, for in its central section it sounds notes as
deep as those of any ancient poetry on the topics of *carpe diem* and
carpe florem. [Quotes lines 21–32]. 'Your quaint honour': that indeed

is a characteristically post-classical conception, with a faint echo of
the *Roman de la Rose* and a much stronger one of a famous chorus in
Tasso's pastoral drama *Aminta*, celebrating that *bel età del oro* when *il
gigante Onor* was unknown. But behind the rest of this passage lies, I
feel almost sure, either directly or indirectly (for it was imitated by
several Renaissance poets, both Latin and vernacular), something
much more ancient: an epigram by Asclepiades in the Greek Anthology (v 85):

Φείδῃ παρθενίης· καὶ τί πλέον; οὐ γὰρ ἐς Ἅδην
    ἐλθοῦσ' εὑρήσεις τὸν φιλέοντα, κόρη.
ἐν ζωοῖσι τὰ τερπνὰ τὰ Κύπριδος· ἐν δ' Ἀχέροντι
    ὀστέα καὶ σποδιή, παρθένε, κεισόμεθα.

Hoarding your maidenhood – and why? For not when to Hades
    You've gone down shall you find, maiden, the lover you lack.
Only among the alive are the joys of Cypris, and only,
    Maiden, as bones and dust shall we in Acheron lie.

Here, as so often, out of something old Marvell has made something
entirely new – or, what amounts to the same thing, something that
gives the impression of being entirely new.

ἐν δ' Ἀχέροντι
ὀστέα καὶ σποδιή, παρθένε, κεισόμεθα

The grave's a fine and private place,
But none I think do there embrace:

had he not known that epigram of Asclepiades, I doubt whether
Marvell would, or perhaps could, have written those lines; and yet
their irony, their concentration, their colloquial vigour are absolutely
Marvellian and absolutely seventeenth century: they could have
been written at no other period, and probably by no other poet. How
pale and thin and unmemorable in comparison (to mention two of the
most famous poets of the preceding century) is Johannes Secundus's
imitation of this epigram in one of his Elegies (1 v) and Ronsard's
imitation of Secundus's imitation in his *Ode à sa maîtresse*![1] While

1 In his *Poèmes* of 1569 Ronsard published an undistinguished translation of this
epigram of Asclepiades, beginning 'Dame au gros cœur, pourquoy t'es-
pargnes-tu?', and a not much more distinguished expansion of it into a sonnet,
beginning 'Douce beauté, meurdrière de ma vie.'

Marvell remains absolutely contemporary, Ronsard brings in Pluto and Charon's skiff:

Pour qui gardes-tu tes yeux,
Et ton sein délicieux,
Ta joue et ta bouche belle?
En veux-tu baiser Pluton,
Là-bas, après que Caron
T'aura mise en sa nacelle?

While Ronsard's lines are no more than an agreeable example of neo-classic imitation, such as any other member of the Pléiade could have produced, what Marvell has given us is not so much an imitation as a transmutation. And, indeed, his whole poem is a superb example of what I meant when I said that his poetry, although in the highest degree original, would have been impossible without the numerous literary sources from which he derived inspiration, stimulation, and suggestion. A stanza of Cowley's, a poem of Catullus, a Greek epigram, possibly a neo-Latin one – we can see how they all played an essential part in the genesis of Marvell's poem, and yet, at the same time, we can also see that he has transmuted them into something unmistakably his own. This is indeed originality, but it is a different kind of originality from that which Donne wanted to achieve.

(226–38)

Susan Shrapnel

from 'Seeing into a Brick Wall', a review of Pierre Legouis' *Andrew Marvell* and J. B. Leishman's *The Art of Marvell's Poetry*, *Cambridge Quarterly*, vol. 1   1966

If Marvell's excellence is only excellence at synthesizing material on given topics, through the force of poetic energy, then his preference for certain topics, and the attitudes that emerge on them, are only his unconsciously, and only relate to his age as symptoms of it. If on the other hand one is persuaded, as I am (though in so little space I can only say it and not demonstrate it), that the ordering power in Marvell's poetry is a greater understanding than that shown by his contemporaries of the importance of the traditional themes – if one sees him as reacting to the pressures of the time in a highly conscious way – then it is at this point that the wall between Mary Fairfax's tutor, who wrote lyrics, and the Parliamentarian and satirist, must come down, and we must extend our sense of the way in which Marvell, as a lyric poet, was 'of his age'. The danger of over-sophistication and cynical sensuality, feeling that we had advanced so much beyond our animal nature that we could afford to use it impersonally; the danger of partisanship and blindness to truth; the danger of chaos – we see Marvell resisting these, using his extra-ordinary mobility between sense and abstraction, using the con-templative retreat of Appleton and the disciplined nature of his gardens. And we value his poetry partly because of his just perception of what was worth preserving.

(407–8)

General Estimates

William Empson

from *Seven Types of Ambiguity* 1961 (first published 1930, revised edition 1947)

It is tactful, when making an obscure reference, to arrange that the verse shall be intelligible even when the reference is not understood. Thus many conceits are prepared to be treated as subdued conceits, though in themselves they have been fully worked out. Consider as the simplest kind of example

The brotherless Heliades
Melt in such amber tears as these.
(*The Nymph Complaining*, 99–100)

If you have forgotten, as I had myself, who their brother was, and look it up, the poetry will scarcely seem more beautiful; such of the myth as is wanted is implied. It is for reasons of this sort that poetry has so much equilibrium, and is so much less dependent on notes than one would suppose. But something has happened after you have looked up the Heliades; the couplet has been justified. Marvell has claimed to make a classical reference and it has turned out to be all right; this is of importance, because it was only because you had faith in Marvell's classical references that you felt as you did, that this mode of admiring nature seemed witty, sensitive, and cultured. If you had expected, or if you had discovered, that Marvell had made the myth up, the couplet might still be admired but the situation would be different; for instance, you would want the *brother* to be more relevant to the matter in hand. Lyly continually invents fabulous beasts for his own stylistic convenience, and this gives him a childish, didactic, and exquisite air, merely because one gives his statements an unusual degree of disbelief. This is, of course, legitimate, and in an odd way courtly, because it treats the reader as a patron of learning without threatening to assume things that he ought already to know. More definitely it is a colloquial or prose device, intended to convey its point at a single reading; all that is relevant about the beast must be said at once, because from the nature of the case it is impossible to find out any more about him. But from a writer whose references are to be relied upon one expects a use of them which will repay study; one expects a simile with reserves of meaning and at any rate the first type of ambiguity.

I have suggested here a few ways in which conceits might become vaguer than they need be; I shall now consider a couple of vague conceits by Marvell, which fall below the standard of precision that the metaphysicals set themselves, and try to explain how in effect they are so powerful. One difficulty about this is that I must assume they are peculiar, whereas the history of English literature has been such that to a modern reader they will seem more normal than the style from which they diverge. I must try, then, to show also that lines which approach towards the nineteenth-century 'simplicity' are, in fact, more complicated than the normal metaphysical conceit, though their machinery and its strangeness are less insistent, and though they move as though something simple was being conveyed. Marvell is a convenient person for this plan; as a metaphysical poet who had not forgotten the Elizabethans he is sensitive to a variety of influences, and one can watch the conceit at the beginning of its decay. From the elegy *Upon the Death of the Lord Hastings*:

The gods themselves cannot their joy conceal
But draw their veils, and their pure beams reveal:
Only they drooping Hymeneus note,
Who for sad purple, tears his saffron coat,
And trails his torches through the starry hall
Reversed, at his darling's funeral.

An extreme, a direct, an unambiguous beauty wells up in these lines; the young man has died on the eve of his wedding; night has fallen. But apparently this is conveyed by comparing some funeral custom with something, possibly astronomical, seen in the sky; the mood of comparison is caught before it has worked itself out; instead of the sharp conceit at which Marvell excelled we are given the elements which were to have been fitted together, but flowing out, and associated only loosely into an impression of sorrow; something, perhaps something very apocalyptic and reassuring, seems to have been meant, but we cannot think of it; and a veil of tenderness is cast over the dissatisfaction of the mind.

This impression, that it is a Romantic Revival piece of writing, is given by regarding Marvell as one of the metaphysical poets, and then

failing to find their particular sort of precision in his methods. But
if you regard him as a disciple of Milton, there is nothing indefinite
about the image; *saffron* is merely the colour of a marriage, *purple* of
a mourning, robe; you are meant to see *Hymen*, an allegorical figure,
performing a simple symbolical movement, with all his stock epithets
about him. It is no longer necessary to *interpret* the first two lines, so
that they mean 'night fell and the stars came out,' the gods appear
as in a story about them. No doubt Milton or Spenser would have
intended the epithets to be beautiful for a variety of reasons, but such
extra meanings would be grouped loosely about an allegory to be
imagined in its own terms. It would not be necessary (as it is if you
expect a conceit) to wonder whether Hymen has any official standing
as a star, or whether he has become identified with the sun for a
moment, or how this could be justified; or to remember that Hymen,
even when unshadowed by the darkness of death, was beloved of
Vesper, and impatient for the nightfall. But then again, it is easier to
feel that Marvell is describing a sunset watched alone in the open than
the picture of a concretely imagined mythological figure; one feels,
for some reason, that he has observed intensely what he has described
only in this cursory and unplausible way, as yellow deepening into
purple, above a horizon of black with red isolated flares. The lines
have thus a curious and impalpable form of ambiguity, in that they
are drawing their energy from three different literary conventions at
once.

Only they drooping Hymeneus note,
Who for sad purple, tears his saffron coat,

Whatever he may be, he is considered in the puzzled and fanciful way
that one reserves for foreigners and the natural world; we must
watch patiently the strange pageant of his actions and force upon
them any interpretation we can imagine. *Only* means from the point
of view of the allegory 'the only thing that prevents their perfect
rejoicing,' but as a matter of nature-study only the brightest stars, and
they are not fully *unveiled*, can be there to *note* the solemn celebrations
of the nightfall. The next line contrasts its active and vehement verb
tears with the 'tears' of weeping, then pronounced the same way (and
the *coats* of a sunset are indeed formed of its *tears*), with the inactive
sorrow of *drooping*, with the ritual dignity of the mythological figure,

and with the slow far-reaching gradations of the colour-changes in the sky. If the *saffron* and *purple noted* by *stars* are indeed a sunset (we are not told so) there is another quieting influence from the sun's regularity; from a sense that he may safely *reverse* his operations (dangerous and extravagant as this seems with most sorts of *torch*) in that his setting is only the reversal of his rising; from a sense of order and perhaps of resurrection in the death of the hero.

And trails his torches through the starry hall
Reversed, at his darling's funeral.

Hymen may always *trail his torches,* and on this occasion be *trailing* them, with no less pomp, *reversed*; or he may at this painful news be *trailing* them in the sense of dragging them behind him, extinguished, not being used for anything, in his dejection. In either case the torches have to be interpreted as something to do with the sunset, something up in the sky, like the *stars*; they must be the same sort of thing, or why is it considered so striking that they should be different? *Torches* when *reversed* are liable to go out, smoke more, and are wasting themselves; never are they less like the perfect or eternal *stars*; and in that we find them up in the sky we are set free ourselves, with a sense of being made at home in the sunset, to float out into the upper air.[1]

I feel some word of apology or explanation is needed as to why such a particularly fantastic analysis has to be given to lines of so direct a beauty, which seem so little tortured by the intellect, which are, in fact, early work, and rather carelessly phrased. The fact is that it is precisely in such cases, when there is an elaborate and definite technique at the back of the author's mind but he is allowing it to fall into the disorders that come most easily, when he has various metaphors in mind which he means to fit in somewhere, when the effect is something rather unintelligible but with a strong poetical colour, when the mere act of wondering what it means allows it to sink, in an uncensored form, into the reader's mind; it is in just such cases that fifth type ambiguities are most likely to be found, and are most necessary as explanations.

1 I have cut nearly two pages of this analysis for the second edition, and indeed feel that the whole chapter is verbose. It seemed hard to make the points convincingly without evocative writing.

A very similar effect, again produced by blurring of the meta-physical conceit, comes in Marvell's poem on *Eyes and Tears*.[1] The funeral elegy on Lord Hastings moved rather in the world of Milton, whereas these verses are excellent and complete conceits, so that here there is no doubt the crux must be approached from the metaphysical point of view.

How wisely Nature did decree,
With the same eyes to weep and see.
That, having viewed the object vain,
They might be ready to complain.

And, since the self-deluding sight
In a false angle takes each height;
These tears that better measure all,
Like watery lines and plummets fall.

It is among such verses as these that one finds:

What in the world most fair appears,
Yea even laughter, turns to tears;
And all the jewels which we prize,
Melt in these pendants of the eyes.

The chief impression here surely is not one of neatness but of parts which do not quite fit; and since the verse 'carries it off' with such an air of gracious achievement the mind is blurred and puzzled into a reflective state, and the second couplet sticks in your head. *Jewels*, of course, are relevant as typical of *what appears most fair*, as a symbol of the lust of the eye; but why or how does a *jewel* melt in a *pendant*? The definiteness of the good conceit suddenly escapes us, and yet it is no use saying this produces a failure of the poetry; on the contrary, the lines seem suddenly to have become more serious and generalized.

Melt in may mean 'become of no account beside tears', or 'are made of no account by tears', or 'dissolve so that they themselves

1 I now think this example a mare's nest – not in the details of the analysis but in the claim that they amount to a blurring of the conceit. It is true, however, I think, that the lines would easily be enjoyed by nineteenth-century critics who thought conceits merely quaint.

become tears', or 'are dissolved by tears so that the value which was before genuinely their own has now been assumed by and resides in tears'. *Tears* from this become valuable in two ways, as containing the value of the *jewels* (as belonging to the world of Cleopatra and hectic luxury) and as being one of those regal solvents that are competent to *melt jewels* (as belonging to the world of alchemists and magical power). *Which* suggests, more than 'that' would have done, that not all *jewels* are *prized*, and only those prized *melt in*, or into, *pendants*. Eked out by this, but independent of it, there is a hint that it is *eyes*, especially a loved woman's, which shine and are *jewels*; why should *eyes* have *pendants*, the word prompts us, if they are not *jewels* themselves? *Eyes*, too, are brightest when suffused with *tears*, not for shedding, and of happiness; which yet, says the poet, shall *fall* from their *jewel*, turn to sorrow, and become *pendants*.

Thus we have now some more meanings for *melt in*: 'in the melting of these eyes into pendants, which is a type of the world, we see the melting of all jewels into nothing, or into lesser stones of no value', or 'in that these pendants coming from her eyes melt, and turn out to be water, we see that there is no permanence in those values that flow from the sources of the world', or 'her eyes have been jewels with tenderness, but such jewels melt; those tears shall fall and be despair'.

One may notice that the *jewels which we prize* are thought of as *eyes* all the more easily because, in so far as they are not, the most striking thing about the reflection made by the couplet is that it is so untrue:

> that jewel in your ear ...
> Shall last to be a precious stone
> When all your world of beauty's gone,
>   (Carew)[1]

represents not only the facts of the case but the more usual sentiment about it; and the couplet makes up for its lack of 'wit' by the claim on one's attention contained in its paradox. But the reason that this claim seems justified, as the verse enters the mind, is that it contains

[1] Actually Herrick, *To Dianeme*. [Ed.]

the materials of many true conceits, pruned into the background, left vague, and packed closely.

The reader may plausibly object that a poet cannot expect his readers to make up conceits for themselves, and that, in so far as I have been doing so, I have been making up a poem of my own. But no, I have been quoting; what is assumed by these verses is a wide acquaintance on the part of the reader with the conceits about tears that have been already made.

Perhaps I have overstated the extent to which the conceit has been dissolved in this example; the one about Lord Hastings, I think, has no simple point, but in this case the idea of a *jewel melting* in a *tear* is sharp enough, and carries most of the feeling. But, even if you regard it as a simple and successful conceit, there are yet crowding at its back this multitude of associations, taking effect in a different way, which are almost as strong as the main conceit and threaten to displace it in the mind or at least make it unnecessary. Marvell was admired both by his own generation and by the nineteenth century; one may suspect that this was because they were able to read him in different ways. If the previous example from Marvell was the bursting of the conceit, this is its final and most mellow ripeness, the skin thin and stretched to its utmost, the seeds ready to be scattered.

(167-73)

Joseph H. Summers

'Marvell's "Nature"', *Journal of English Literary History*, vol. 10 1953

The similarities between the verse of Marvell and that of many modern poets are seductive. A number of Marvell's poems have been cited as evidence to support the critical assumption, based largely on modern poetic practice, that the most mature and rich works of literature are necessarily ironical. One can disagree with the assumption and still recognize that irony, not of a paralysing variety, is central to most of Marvell's poems. Marvell's surfaces, moreover, are close to one modern ideal. The tones of the typical modern *personae* echo the sensuous richness of Marvell more often than the logical violence of Donne – that poet who wrote *To Mr Samuel Brooke*, boastfully yet accurately, 'I sing not siren-like to tempt; for I|Am harsh.' The 'speakers' of Marvell's poems are farther removed from immediate embroilment in action than are Donne's. They approach their situations from some distance, with a wider and a clearer view. Their speech is closer to that of meditation or of a quiet colloquy in a garden than to the raised voice, the immediate and passionate argument. And the verse which they speak shows a concern for euphony, a delicate manipulation of sound patterns suggesting Campion's songs – or much of the verse of Eliot and MacLeish and many younger poets.

The differences between Marvell and the moderns, however, are equally noteworthy, and failure to perceive them has resulted in strange readings of a number of Marvell's poems. To prevent misreadings, to define any specific poem, we need to achieve some sense of the body of Marvell's work. And here is the difficulty, for our sense of that work is likely to be an impression of dazzling fragments, each brilliant and disparate. The reader may feel that the sixth stanza of *The Gallery*, the poem in which the poet invites Chlora to view her portraits in his soul as 'an inhuman murderess', Aurora, 'an enchantress', Venus, and 'a tender shepherdess', applies more justly to the poet than to Chlora:

These pictures and a thousand more,
Of thee, my gallery do store;
In all the forms thou canst invent
Either to please me, or torment.

Yet the poem assures us that Chlora is one, however numerous her pictures; and the poet who could take various and even contradictory positions on the claims of the active and contemplative lives, of the body and the soul, of the time-honored plea to 'seize the day', of gardens ('These pictures and a thousand more') is equally one poet. The attempts to bring intellectual order out of the apparent confusion by means of a hypothetical biographical development of the poet have been unconvincing. The development or rather break in his poetic practice after 1660 is clear. Before that time, the single poem *Upon Appleton House* indicates that Marvell was an extraordinarily sophisticated poet, capable of employing numerous traditions and multiple attitudes as occasions or moments demanded. Among the few attitudes which I have been unable to discover in Marvell's poetry, however, are those expressed in two of the modern poems which owe most to Marvell. Archibald MacLeish's *You, Andrew Marvell* concludes with the lines,

And here face downward in the sun
To feel how swift how secretly
The shadow of the night comes on ...

Robert Penn Warren's *Bearded Oaks* includes the following stanza:

Upon the floor of light, and time,
Unmurmuring, of polyp made,
We rest; we are, as light withdraws,
Twin atolls on a shelf of shade.

In Marvell's verse man is neither an atoll nor an island, and if night is anticipated, so is light.

An examination of Marvell's uses of 'Nature,' the world of the flowers and fruits and the green grass, provides a sketch not only of the virtuosity and multiple intellectual and moral stances within the poems, but also of the central vision which occurs most frequently in the most successful poems. Occasionally Marvell used nature as an image of classical order, an artfully contrived realization of the mean which man is to imitate – or, more properly, which a specific man has imitated. Jonson had shown in his ode *To the Memory of Sir Lucius Cary and Sir Henry Morison* that nature conceived as an ordered mean was a most effective source of hyperbolical compliment. In *Upon the Hill and Grove at Billborow*, Fairfax too is at one with nature. After his active life (in which he had 'thunder'd' 'Through groves of pikes,' 'And mountains raised of dying men'), Fairfax has returned to the retirement of the hill and grove; the humanized landscape is both his ward and his image:

See how the arched earth does here
Rise in a perfect hemisphere!
The stiffest compass could not strike
A line more circular and like;

Nor softest pencil draw a brow
So equal as this hill does bow.
It seems as for a model laid,
And that the world by it was made.

(1–8)

See what a soft access and wide
Lies open to its grassy side;
Nor with the rugged path deters
The feet of breathless travellers.
See then how courteous it ascends,
And all the way it rises bends;
Nor for itself the height does gain,
But only strives to raise the plain.

(17–24)

After this delightfully artificial description of landscape as Republican
gentleman, we are not surprised that these Roman oaks should speak
oracles of praise for Fairfax. In the opening lines of *Upon Appleton
House*, an ordered and properly proportioned nature is again the
symbol for Fairfax and his dwelling, particularly in contrast to the
'unproportioned dwellings' which the ambitious have constructed
with the aid of 'foreign' architects: 'But all things are composed
here,| Like Nature, orderly and near.' Nature is also near and extra-
ordinarily 'orderly' when a natural object, 'A Drop of Dew' for
example, is examined as an emblem. Here we are close to Herbert,
but in Marvell we are chiefly compelled by the ingenuity with which
the natural is made to reflect the conceptual.

More often nature is nearer if not so orderly when it is conceived
as the lost garden, whether Eden or the Hesperides or England:

O thou, that dear and happy isle
The garden of the world erewhile,
Thou Paradise of four seas,
Which Heaven planted us to please,
But, to exclude the World, did guard
With watery if not flaming sword;

What luckless apple did we taste,
To make us mortal, and thee waste?
> (*Upon Appleton House*, 321–8)

The lost garden represents not measure but perfect fulfillment; its memory is an occasion for ecstasy:

And ivy, with familiar trails,
Me licks, and clasps, and curls, and hales.
Under this antic cope I move
Like some great prelate of the grove,
Then, languishing with ease, I toss
On pallets swoll'n of velvet moss.
> (*Upon Appleton House*, 589–94)

What wondrous life in this I lead!
Ripe apples drop about my head;
The luscious clusters of the vine
Upon my mouth do crush their wine;
The nectarine, and curious peach,
Into my hands themselves do reach;
Stumbling on melons, as I pass,
Ensnared with flowers, I fall on grass.
> (*The Garden*)

It is in this vein that Marvell occasionally gives a sensuous particularity to his descriptions of natural objects which may remind us of Vaughan's 'those faint beams in which this hill is dressed,|After the sun's remove' (*They are all gone into the world of light!*), and which has led some readers to consider him a romantic born too early. And yet the 'gelid strawberries' and 'The hatching throstle's shining eye' of *Upon Appleton House* contribute to a complicated vision of nature which is finally unlike the nineteenth century's; the 'hewel's wonders' (the activities of the woodpecker) teach the 'easy philosopher' who 'Hath read in Nature's mystic book' the just relationships between sin and death:

Who could have thought the tallest oak
Should fall by such a feeble stroke!

Nor would it, had the tree not fed
A traitor worm, within it bred.
(As first our flesh corrupt within
Tempts impotent and bashful sin.)
And yet that worm triumphs not long,
But serves to feed the hewel's young.
While the oak seems to fall content,
Viewing the treason's punishment.

(Upon Appleton House, 551–60)

In *The Garden*, too, identification with nature is neither complete
nor simple. The famous fifth stanza which I have quoted above,
expertly 'imitates' the bodily ecstasy, and the following stanzas
systematically portray the higher ecstasies of the mind and the soul;
all, moreover, are framed with witty and civilized reversals of the
ordinary civilized values, of classic myth, of the biblical account of
the creation of woman, and of the idea that sexual relations are
'natural'. To read *The Garden* and *The Mower Against Gardens* in
succession is to realize that in Marvell's poetry the man-made garden
and the 'natural' meadows are significant not intrinsically but in-
strumentally. Both poems are ultimately concerned with lost perfection. *The Garden* presents a fictional and momentary attempt to
recapture what has been lost. In *The Mower against Gardens*, the
garden itself is an image of the sophisticated corruption responsible
for the loss of 'A wild and fragrant innocence'. Marvell's image of
the lost garden is as much an occasion for the recognition of man's
alienation from nature as it is for remembered ecstasy.

The degree to which Marvell both followed and modified conventional practice can be seen most clearly in the 'pastoral' poems in
which he substituted the mower for the traditional shepherd. The
life of the shepherds had imaged the pre-agricultural golden age,
the paradisiacal simplicity ideally if not actually associated with the
simple country life, away from cities and civilizations, wars and cor-
ruptions. When love was concerned, the passion was usually direct,
uncontaminated by wordly considerations, and not much affected by
age, even if the lover was unhappy or the mistress proved untrue.
The good shepherd and his sheep could imply the ideal political
relation between the ruler and the ruled, and the Christian poets

explored the rich possibilities of the Good Shepherd and his flock and the large pastoral inheritance of the Psalms. Milton, who retained the shepherd image in *Lycidas*, kept the humanist emphasis on higher man (the poet, the pastor) as the guide of less perceptive humanity through the labyrinth of nature to an ultimate goal. The shepherd followed Christ, and he also led his own sheep into the true fold. Marvell used some of this material in a direct if not very distinguished fashion in *Clorinda and Damon*, and although the participants are oarsmen rather than shepherds, the spirit of the tradition is present in *Bermudas*. He gave up most of these associations, however, when he chose the figure of the mower as his central image. That figure, of course, had its own traditions. As *Damon the Mower* mentions, the mower's craft had long served to picture man's greatest mystery and fear:

Only for him no cure is found,
Whom Juliana's eyes do wound.
'Tis death alone that this must do:
For Death thou art a mower too.
(85–8)

The mower who cut down the living grass was a natural symbol for death. Because of the seasonal nature of his activities, he was also a symbol for time. Marvell's mower does not lead; he destroys. However simple his character or sincere his love, he cuts down for human ends what nature has produced. He symbolizes man's alienation from nature:

With whistling scythe, and elbow strong,
These massacre the grass along:
While one, unknowing, carves the rail,
Whose yet unfeathered quills her fail.
The edge all bloody from its breast
He draws, and does his stroke detest;
Fearing the flesh untimely mowed
To him a fate as black forebode.
(*Upon Appleton House*, 393–400)

The Mower's Song is a playful and elaborately artificial lament of a lover, but it is more than that. The refrain insists that the mower-lover's relation to nature exactly parallels his cruel mistress's relation to him:

> For Juliana comes, and she
> What I do to the grass, does to my thoughts and me.

Greenness in this poem, as so often in Marvell's verse, represents hope and vitality and virility, the fertile promise of life which man desires and destroys. The mower, angry that there is no true sympathy between man and nature, 'fictionally' determines to destroy nature to make the symbolism more complete:

> Unthankful meadows, could you so
> A fellowship so true forgo,
> And in your gaudy May-games meet,
> While I lay trodden under feet?
> When Juliana came, and she
> What I do to the grass, does to my thoughts and me.

> But what you in compassion ought,
> Shall now by my revenge be wrought:
> And flowers, and grass, and I and all,
> Will in one common ruin fall.
> For Juliana comes, and she
> What I do to the grass, does to my thoughts and me.

The Mower poems conveniently define the crucial terms of Marvell's most frequent poetic use of nature. Marvell did not discover an impulse from the vernal wood which spoke unambiguously to the human heart and which offered a possibility for man's at-oneness with all. Nor did he, like George Herbert, usually see in nature patterns of a distinguishable and logical divine will, the *paysage moralisé* which offered a way to the understanding and imitation of God. Human moral criteria do not apply to most of Marvell's landscapes. In his poems nature apart from man is usually 'green', vital, fecund, and triumphant. Since it affirms life it is, as part of the divine plan, 'good', but its goodness is neither available nor quite comprehensible to man. Man is barred from long or continuous spiritual communion, and his intellect cannot comprehend the natural language. Since his alienation with the departure from Eden. man can only live in nature either as its observer or its destroyer;

since he partially partakes of nature, he is, if he acts at all, also his own destroyer. His capacity for self-destruction is clearly implied by the contrast between nature's fecundity and man's harassed and frustrated attempts at love. Faced with unrequited love, man the mower only sharpens his scythe for the destruction of the grass and sharpens the 'woes' which destroy himself:

> How happy might I still have mowed,
> Had not love here his thistles sowed!
> But now I all the day complain,
> Joining my labour to my pain;
> And with my scythe cut down the grass,
> Yet still my grief is where it was:
> But, when the iron blunter grows,
> Sighing I whet my scythe and woes.
>
> *(Damon the Mower, 65–72)*

But man destroys the natural and dies not only because he is inferior but also because, suspended between the natural and divine, he is superior to the green world. In *A Dialogue between the Soul and the Body* each of the protagonists charges wittily and convincingly that the other is the source of human misery; of the first forty lines, each speaks twenty, and points are made and capped so expertly as to produce a forensic stalemate. But the Body wins and ironically resolves the argument with its final additional four lines:

> What but a soul could have the wit
> To build me up for sin so fit?
> So architects do square and hew
> Green trees that in the forest grew.

Without the soul the body would be truly a part of nature and could not sin. Yet architecture, whether external or internal, is the product and desire of a higher part of man, even though many 'Green trees' may be destroyed for it. Whether the building is used for good or ill, man's capacities for reason, for structure, for creation outside the carnal, are not natural but God-like. Man's distinctive gifts are as destructive within the post-Eden garden as are his weaknesses and his corruption.

It is, moreover, exactly man's superiority to the vegetative world which allows him to recognize his alienation. Nature does not possess the capacity for man's choices between the active and contemplative lives: it can only act. The rival claims of those two chief modes of man's life are ever present in Marvell's poetry, and they are closely related to his themes of nature and time. Man must act and he must contemplate, and he must do each in accordance with the demands of time. Yet the contemplative life is usually the more desirable way – at least for the poet. The poet surpasses most men in the degree and consistency of his recognition of man's alienation, for he is chiefly concerned with the contemplation of the condition of man. In Marvell's poetry, significantly, natural beauty is usually described and appreciated as if it were an imitation of the works of man. The fort and artillery of the garden in *Upon Appleton House* are not simply factual or fanciful. In *The Mower to the Glow-worms* nature is the gracious and kindly courtier to man, so lost in love 'That I shall never find my home'. In one of the most memorable descriptions in *Bermudas* God himself is the manlike decorator:

He hangs in shades the orange bright,
Like golden lamps in a green night.
And does in the pomegranates close,
Jewels more rich than Ormus shows.

It is the artifacts, the 'golden lamps' and the 'Jewels more rich than Ormus shows', which contribute most of the sensuous richness to the passage. In relation to the garden man is the judge and the measure as well as the accused.

Whatever the immediate resolutions, man is usually suspended between the greenness and God at the conclusions as well as at the beginnings of Marvell's poems. Within *A Dialogue between the Resolved Soul and Created Pleasure*, the Soul deftly propounds the orthodox thesis that the sensuous and worldly pleasures are only appearances, that the soul possesses the quintessence of all pleasures in his resolution. Yet the tensions are still felt, and the soul's conclusions, while 'true', are also partial. At the moment of death 'The rest' (both the ease and the remainder of all the pleasures) *does* 'lie beyond the pole,|And is thine everlasting store.' But before that moment, Marvell and most of his contemporaries believed that no man enjoyed fully and continuously either the flesh or the spirit, that the battle was constantly renewed so long as a living spirit inhabited a living body. This did not imply that the battle lacked interest nor that decisions and momentary achievements were impossible. Such decisions and such achievements were, in fact, the poet's subjects, not only in *A Dialogue* but also *To his Coy Mistress*. The speaker of the latter poem seems to resolve clearly for sensuality: *Carpe diem* appears to be all. The image of the 'birds of prey', however, makes us realize the costs of a resolution to 'devour' time, to choose destructive brevity of life since eternity cannot be sensually chosen.

The reader's awareness of Marvell's complex use of nature should cast light on almost any one of the poems. Within such light, the presentation of Cromwell in *An Horatian Ode* as a force of nature seems not perplexing but inevitable. *Upon Appleton House* is Marvell's most ambitious and in many respects his most interesting poem. A full consideration of it would require another essay, and I only wish to suggest here that it is a mistake to read it as an artificial 'public' poem interesting chiefly for a few 'personal' passages. Similarly, *The Picture of little T.C. in a Prospect of Flowers* is not a graceful trifle which somehow goes wrong. It is a fine poem, and it elucidates Marvell's central vision of man and nature: [quotes poem].

The opening stanza of the poem tells us of the child's alienation from and superiority to nature, as well as of her delight in it. Her apparently successful imposition of her own order and value on nature raises inevitably the question of the prospect of time, and we see prophetically in the second stanza her future triumph over 'wanton Love' – and over man. Not a combatant, the speaker of the poem resolves to observe the dazzling scene from the shade which allows vision, for the god-like glories cannot be viewed immediately by profane man. If he is to admire her triumph, it must be from a distance where there is no fear of its destructiveness. With the 'Meantime' of the fourth stanza we are back at the present prospect, and the observer from his advantageous point of view advises the present T.C. At the golden moment when 'every verdant thing' charms itself at her beauty, she is instructed to prepare for her future career by reforming the 'errors of the Spring'. At first it seems, or perhaps would seem to a child, an almost possible command. With the talismanic power of her 'fair aspect' she already 'tames|The wilder flowers, and gives them names,' and she tells the roses 'What colour best becomes them, and what smell.' At least within the circle of her immediate view she may, perhaps, by a judicious bouquet arrangement cause the tulips to share in sweetness, and it is possible to disarm roses of their thorns with assiduous labor. But the thing which should be 'most' procured is impossible for the human orderer even within his small area. And all of it is, of course, impossible if all the 'errors of the Spring' are in question. For, in comparison either with the triumph of T.C. or the vision of Eden, Spring is full of errors; the decorative details suggest exactly how far nature fails to sustain human visions of propriety, delight, and immortality. T.C. and the idealizing aspect of man wish delight and beauty and goodness to be single, but they cannot find such singleness within the promising verdancy of nature; if they desire it they must impose it on nature or must seek it in an 'unnatural' or supernatural world. The tulips show how improperly the delights of the senses are separated in this world; the roses with their thorns traditionally indicate the conjunction of pain and pleasure, the hidden hurts lying under the delights of the senses; and the transience of the violets is a perpetual reminder of the mortality of life and innocence and beauty. The description of the preceding triumph is placed in a doubtful light. If T.C.'s reformation of floral errors is so doomed, how much real hope or fear can there be of her reformation of the errors of that higher order, man? Is the former description a fantasy, ideal yet frightening, of what might happen if the superhuman power as well as the superhuman virtue were granted, a fantasy proceeding from the observer's sharing for one moment the simplicity of the nymph?

In the exclamatory warning of the final stanza the observer and the reader see the picture of little T.C. in the full prospect of time which the flowers have furnished. At the present moment 'Nature courts' her 'with fruits and flowers' as a superior being; she represents the promise of an order higher than we have known. But she is also the 'young beauty of the woods', and she is a 'bud'. The child of nature as well as its potential orderer, she shares the mortality as well as the beauty of the flowers; her own being, in the light of the absolute, is as 'improper' as are the tulips or the roses. The former vision of her triumph implied full recognition of only one half of her relationship to the fruits and flowers. The introduction of Flora reminds us more sharply than anything else in the poem of the entire relationship.

However lacking in the ideal, Flora has her own laws which man violates at the peril of self-destruction. Flora decrees that life shall continue: the infants shall not be killed 'in their prime' – either in their moment of ideal promise or in their first moment of conception. The sexual concerns which have been suggested throughout the poem are made explicit in the final stanza. The picture in the central stanzas of the complete triumph of T.C., the absolute rule of human notions of propriety, has inevitably meant that 'wanton Love's' bow will be broken, his ensigns torn: there will be no more marriages. With a recognition of mortality and of the power of Flora, we recognize also the doom of such a triumph, for both the ideal and the reality will soon die, and there is no prospect of renewal in future 'T.C.s'. The conclusion, however, is neither a Renaissance nor a modern 'naturalism.' Because perfect fulfillment is impossible, man is not therefore to abandon his attempts at perfection. T.C. is allowed and even commanded to 'Gather the flowers', to expend her present and her future energies in ordering the natural nearer to the ideal pattern – so long as she spares the buds. The qualification is all important. Man must beware of attempting to anticipate heaven by imposing the ideal absolutely on earth. The killing of the infants in their prime is not only a crime against Flora but against all the gods, for man is never free to commit either murder or suicide in the pursuit of the abstract ideal. The human triumph must function within and wait upon the fulness of time. It must recognize the real and individual as well as the ideal and the general or it becomes a horror. The ending of the poem revalues everything which has gone before. 'Ere we see' may mean something equivalent to 'in the twinkling of an eye'; it certainly means, 'Before we see what will become of you and the vision of a new and higher order.' What will be nipped 'in the blossom', in the first full flowering, unless the warning is heeded will be not only 'all our hopes' (our hopes of the idealized child and of a possible new order, our hopes of love and of a new generation), but also 'thee', the living child.

The Picture of little T.C. in a Prospect of Flowers is characteristic of Marvell's poetry both in its complexity and in its subtle use of superficially 'romantic' or decorative detail. It may remind us of modern poetry, but ultimately Marvell is both more complex and more assured of his meanings than are most of the moderns. Marvell does not present a *persona* simply and finally torn between this world and the next, distracted by the sensuous while attempting to achieve a spiritual vision. For Marvell, as for most Renaissance poets, the perception of a dilemma was not considered a sufficient occasion for a poem. Marvell made precise the differences between the values of time and of eternity. He recognized that man exists and discovers his values largely within time; he also believed that those values could be ultimately fulfilled only outside time. The recognition and the belief did not constitute a paralysing dilemma. Each of his early poems implies the realization that any action or decision costs something; yet each presents a precise stance, an unique position and a decision taken at one moment with a full consciousness of all the costs. The costs are counted, but not mourned; the position is taken, the poem is written, with gaiety.

When we have understood what the 'prospect of flowers' implies, *The Coronet* does not seem a churchly recantation of all that Marvell valued, but an artful recognition of the ultimate issues. Here the decision is taken in the full light of eternity, and, as in George Herbert's *A Wreath* (which Marvell probably remembered), the intricate and lovely form of the poem provides an index to the joy. The speaker of the poem describes his attempt to create a coronet for Christ. He dismantles 'all the fragrant towers|That once adorned my shepherdess's head' to gather the necessary flowers, but he discovers that the Serpent has entwined himself into the proposed offering, 'With wreaths of fame and interest'. The poet prays that Christ would untie the Serpent's 'slippery knots',

Or shatter too with him my curious frame:
And let these wither, so that he may die,
Though set with skill and chosen out with care.
That they, while thou on both their spoils dost tread,
May crown thy feet, that could not crown thy head.

The poem is moving as well as orthodox in its expression of willingness to sacrifice man's sensuous and aesthetic structures to a divine necessity. But Marvell's most Miltonic line, 'Though set with skill and chosen out with care', ruefully insists that, whatever his vision of ultimate value, the living poet also values the structures of time.

(121–35)

Robert Ellrodt

from *L'inspiration personelle et l'esprit du temps chez les poètes méta-physiques anglais* 1960 (translated by John Freeman)

The present is by far the most common tense in the poetry of Marvell, who introduces it even into the narrative of past events by giving direct speech to his characters.[1] Pure narrative is rare and always ends in an evocation of the present.[2] It is as though the past did not have an independent existence for this poet. He is without retrospection. He never traces the flow of time backwards. He inhabits the present instant, but it is a mobile instant. Behind him there is no expanse opening its perspectives to the memory; nothing but the menacing approach of death, before which he flies. The imminent chases him towards the future. There is no more gripping image of a man dispossessed of his past and encircled by his own future:

But at my back I always hear
Time's winged chariot hurrying near:
And yonder all before us lie
Deserts of vast eternity.
Thy beauty shall no more be found;
Nor, in thy marble vault shall sound
My echoing song ...

But here that future is 'desert', emptiness, absence: the only reality is this moving present. When what is to come is the remains of what is actual, the future is conceived as a 'presence'. It is not contemplated at a distance as Vaughan contemplates it: it is tasted in advance, 'antedated', and loses all its depth.

So we win of doubtful Fate;
And, if good she to us meant,
We that good shall antedate,
Or, if ill, that ill prevent.

(*Young Love*, 21-4)

1 See *Bermudas, Upon Appleton House* (st. 13 sq.).
2 See *Unfortunate Lover* (49 sqq.), *Daphnis and Chloe* (101 sq.), *Mower's Song.*

O sweet! O sweet! How I my future state
By silent thinking, antedate.

(Thyrsis and Dorinda, 27–8)

Like Donne and Herbert, Marvell, a poet of the present, likes to put himself into a dramatic situation. *The Garden* is not a simple description, nor an invocation to solitude. It is a scene in a particular context; 'What wondrous life in this I lead.' The poet portrays his feelings at the very moment he experiences them. Despite the exactness of place ('Fair quiet, have I found thee *here*?') the first stanzas still have that generality so common in the lyric poetry of the seventeenth century. But the fruit, the shade, the spring, the sundial have not only that typical or generic value which natural objects have in the pastorals of the time (or in Milton's *L'Allegro*): it is *this* fruit, *this* shadow, *this* spring, *this* sundial which the poet gathers or contemplates at a particular moment. It is not a universal sentiment, but a unique experience which is communicated to us. The particularity of the experience is brought out just as much in *To his Coy Mistress*. Nothing is more traditional than the hedonistic invitation to make the most of youth and the present moment. But the poem is not the illustration of a universal truth: it is a dramatic moment that owes all its intensity to its uniqueness in time and space. 'Mignonne, allons voir si la rose' is an unprompted apostrophe. Marvell's poem opens like a piece of theatrical dialogue: the demonstrative adjective refers to an anterior attitude, a pre-existent situation: 'Had we but world enough and time| *This* coyness, Lady, were no crime'. The interest attaches to the solution of a particular problem and not to the illustration of a universal truth. That thrice-repeated 'now' (lines 33, 37, 38) is more than the abstract 'today' of *les roses de la vie*: it is the most concrete, the most singular moment: it is the instant when the lovers are face to face and the consummation of their desire, it is the vivid intuition of a time felt and no longer merely conceived. . . .

Like Donne, Herbert and Crashaw, Marvell presents objects in the foreground without distance or perspective. He is at the foot of the tree, at the very side of the stream he describes, and always the fruit is within his reach, the melons at his feet. The absence of horizon, of the distant, is the secret of an incomparable clarity in the description. He excels in circumscribing. Sometimes he makes the single object

stand out against a uniform background, without distancing or depth:
'He hangs in shade the orange bright,|Like golden lamps in a green
night.' Sometimes he takes pleasure in enclosing a universe in a drop
of dew. If he wishes to describe a meadow of long grass, he does not
show us the tall stems waving in the wind as far as the eye can reach,
as would a poet of a vast field of vision. He plunges us *inside* this ocean
of verdure, gives us the immediate experience of depth, in preference
to the distant vision of height. Even when evoking immensity, he
puts a grasshopper or a flower in the foreground.[1] No space round the
objects; dark or pale, these green nights have a colour, an opacity
which excludes the impression of emptiness and of depth. If he must
depict a bare landscape, a mown field, he circumscribes it, shrinks
it in imagination by comparing it to a painter's still-virgin canvas or
to an arena, a circular figure taken in at a single glance.[2] Concern for
clarity and preference for near vision form an alliance: hence the
constant recourse to exact figures and geometric images in the
description. In Marvell's world the dimensions no longer have any
absolute value. Microscopic and cosmic vision are superimposed in
close up in the same field of vision without disconcerting us. Here are
some flocks in a meadow:

Such fleas, ere they approach the eye,
In multiplying glasses lie.
They feed so wide, so slowly move,
As constellations do above.

(*Upon Appleton House*, 461–4)

This world of definite objects is a world without fluidity. There is no
airy fancy. Music is 'the mosaic of the air'. The sky is a solid vault
where song rebounds and reverberates in echoes.[3] Marvell is never so
close to Donne as when he makes concrete the very ideas of extension
and interposition.[4] But the hard substances which he describes with
most imaginative intensity are cold ones: metal, alabaster, crystal.[5]

1 *Upon Appleton House*, 369–84.
2 *Upon Appleton House*, stanza 56. Marvell had travelled in Spain.
3 *Bermudas*, 34–6.
4 *Definition of Love.* Cf. *Valediction: forbidding mourning*, 21–36.
5 Metals: *Nymph*, 28–64, *Coy Mistress*, 44; *Definition*, 11, 17, etc. Alabaster:
Nymph, 120. Crystal: *Appleton*, 192, 636, 694.

Here is a first difference. The solid matter which attracts the imagination of George Herbert has the dryness and slight natural warmth of wood. Donne is fascinated by dry brilliant textures, most often without heat, like hair or bones.[1] Marvell is alone in showing preference for the cold and for cold materials. What is more, it is not solidity in itself but congealment which has most appeal for his imagination.

This poet takes pleasure in congealing the air and the wave, in vitrifying nature:

The viscous air, wheres'e'er she fly,
Follows and sucks her azure dye;
The jellying stream compacts below,
If it might fix her shadow so;
The stupid fishes hang, as plain
As flies in crystal overta'en;

   .   .   .   .

Nature is wholly vitrified.

There is no dew which is not 'congealed and chill'. The stream, like the strawberries, is 'gelid', an epithet which unites freshness with the impression of congelation.[2] One is not at all surprised that Marvell likes describing the making of jellies:[3] is not his liking for fruit of the same order?[4] Doesn't he taste in it the union of solid form and liquid substance when the fruit melts as it is enjoyed? Isn't what he likes in the grass its 'moister colour'?[5] Even the fluidity of the wave attracts him less than the 'seas' of verdure.[6] His sensibility craves freshness and humidity, but his mind demands the definite contours of the solid universe. Is it by chance that the predominance of liquids and the frequency of light vowels give his lines a damp gleam, at the same time as the vigour of the consonants and the rhythm assures their firmness, preventing those 'liquids' from flowing or melting? Steel,

1 Whether the poet is describing the sun or a torch, he usually has an impression of light and not of heat: cf. *First Anniversary*, 86-8, and *The Dream*, 11. *The Sun Rising* is an exception: 28.
2 *Damon the Mower*, 28; *Appleton*, 530.   3 *Appleton*, stanza 22.
4 Cf. *Bermudas*, *The Garden*.   5 *Appleton*, 627.
6 *Appleton*, stanza 48. When the meadow is flooded (lines 468-9), he turns from it and seeks refuge in the forest, that 'fifth element' (lines 481-4, 502).

that tempered metal, might be material expression of this quality of imagination which becomes a quality of style. A single line is enough to suggest it: 'And therefore her decrees of steel . . .' This poetic oeuvre, to borrow an image from Charles du Bos, 'partakes of two realms, the mineral and the liquid, but the latter can only be caught there in crystal ewers'.

(I, Chapter 2, 114–15, 120–22)

J. B. Broadbent

from 'The Metaphysical Decadence', *Poetic Love*   1964

Marvell is a glittering technician –

With whistling scythe, and elbow strong,
These massacre the grass along.

(*Appleton House*, 393–4)

– and his skill presents a quick refined intelligent sensibility. But his poems do not present anything else: they are vehicles for his sensibility, brilliant mosaics of language, but not otherwise than academically, as models for analysis, of interest.

When we inquire, we find even the perfection a cheat. The correspondence between manner and matter is achieved by writing always of what closely fits his mind. The expectations he so precisely fulfils have always been delimited by his own interest. His poems are as decorous as his tortoises:

The low-roofed tortoises do dwell
In cases fit of tortoise-shell.

(*Appleton House*, 13–14)

The syntax and rhyme click into place. He excludes all incompatibles from his verse. If there is conflict, it is conducted between toy-soldiers, like the 'sweet militia' of the formal garden at Appleton House, and the nuns who first lived there:

Nor is our order yet so nice
Delight to banish as a vice;
Here Pleasure Piety doth meet,
One pérfecting the other sweet.

(169–72)

Two forces are at work, crystallization and withdrawal. *The Mower against Gardens* combines them. It is a plea, like Perdita's, for nature against art, the wilderness against the formal garden, landscape as a retreat from the social place:

'Tis all enforced; the fountain and the grot;
   While the sweet fields do lie forgot:
Where willing Nature does to all dispense
   A wild and fragrant innocence,
And fauns and fairies do the meadows till,
   More by their presence than their skill.
Their statues polished by some ancient hand,
   May to adorn the gardens stand:
But howsoe'er the figures do excel,
   The gods themselves with us do dwell.

Marvell seeks the 'wild and fragrant innocence' of nature in *The Garden*; yet, finding it, he does not strip and plunge in but casts 'the body's vest aside' and flies in soul up to a tree. His paradise, there and in *Appleton House*, is solitary, and neat, unthreatened by Milton's 'enormous bliss'. He escapes from the urban artifice of 'the palm, the oak, or bays' into a 'wilderness of sweets'; but, 'Stumbling on melons', he withdraws further into the mind, 'the artifice of eternity'. In the same way, he abjures the artful polish of fountain and grot but, in style, is himself a crystallographer. Characteristically, he *hardens* the fluid:

But how should I avoid to be her slave,
Whose subtle art invisibly can wreathe
My fetters of the very air I breathe?
             (*Fair Singer*)

The music, the mosaic of the air . . .
             (*Music's Empire*)

Faced with the upheavals of civil war, regicide, the death of Cromwell, and feeling ambivalent about the issues –

'Tis not, what once it was, the world;
But a rude heap together hurled;
All negligently overthrown,
Gulfs, deserts, precipices, stone.

(*Appleton House*, 761-4)

– he really sought in gardens a 'more decent order tame': an ideal
which the Augustans, for the same reason, retrospectively pursued.

Marvell's poetry is not tame; but its excitements are surrealistic.
His typical distorting metaphor is a symptom of the same disorder as
his typical decency. The lenses of the *Weltanschauung* had been twisted
out of focus, the mirror of nature bent:

all things gaze themselves, and doubt
If they be in it or without.

(*Appleton House*, 637-8)

Marvell used this distortion of perspective as another means of
retreat and ease:

Thus I, easy philosopher,
Among the birds and trees confer

.   .   .   .

turn me but, and you shall see
I was but an inverted tree.

(561-8)

If you live in a topsy-turvy world, just turn yourself upside down and
you'll feel at one with it again:

But I, retiring from the flood,
Take sanctuary in the wood;
And, while it lasts, myself embark
In this yet green, yet growing ark.

(481-4)

The past history of the estate (in this case, flooding of the meadows)
shimmers in the present, mirroring political catastrophies, and Noah's

flood. But the synaesthetic eye can escape: a grove becomes, amid ecclesiastical strife, a sanctuary, an ark; its green is seasoned timber, and a vegetable womb, as well as youthful innocence before the Flood, the Fall.

Marvell has no connexion with Donne. His images are fanciful, not imaginative; and they are either sexless or anti-sexual. *The Garden* is doubly unfallen paradise because he is alone in it; the wood-ark is a retreat in which

> all creatures might have shares,
> Although in armies, not in pairs.
>
> (487–8)

To his Coy Mistress is an exquisite exercise in not making love. The careful metrics, the far allusions – Ganges, Humber – and the Biblicism (Samson's lion, Gideon's sun), distance the poem from man and woman. What is most striking in it, of an active kind, is an act of necrophilia: it celebrates rape by worms. Again, the hardening process is at work: her body is immured in a marble vault; their strength and sweetness (which, as 'lust' and 'quaint honour'[1] have already turned to ashes and dust) are rolled into a sweetmeat ball and then turned into a cannon-ball shot 'thorough the iron gates of life'. No poem could more lingeringly deny the love it pleads for.

Marvell links Herrick, and therefore Spenser, with Pope. Like Herrick, he is obsessed with the tiny. It is another way of with-drawing – turning the telescope the wrong way round:

> The flowers their drowsy eyelids raise,
> Their silken ensigns each displays,
> And dries its pan yet dank with dew,
> And fills its flask with odours new.
>
> (*Appleton House*, 293–6)

Marvell's micro-fantasies are usually a defence against war:

> Their leaves, that to the stalks are curled,
> Seem to their staves the ensigns furled.
> Then in some flower's belovèd hut
> Each bee as sentinel is shut.
>
> (315–18)

---

1 *Quaint* = pudendum, as in *Wife of Bath's Prologue*.

Herrick uses fairies to defend himself against the Church:

Hard by, i' the shell of half a nut,
The holy water there is put

. . . . . .

For sanctity they have, to these,
Their curious capes and surplices
Of cleanest cobweb, hanging by
In their religious vestiary.

(Fairy Temple)

and against sexuality: Oberon's bed is fringed with

those threads
Broke at the loss of maidenheads;
And all behung with those pure pearls
Dropped from the eyes of ravished girls.

(Oberon's Palace)

The link with Pope is the surrealism of satire:

Thanks for my rest ye mossy banks,
And unto you, cool zephyrs thanks,
Who, as my hair, my thoughts too shed,
And winnow from the chaff my head.

(Appleton House, 597–600)

Nonsense precipitate, like running lead,
That slipped through cracks and zigzags of the head.

(Dunciad, 1)

The emblematic fancy of Marvell and Herrick leads far more directly
than the Metaphysical wit of Donne, to the 'inverted nature' of
Swift and Pope:

The suffering eye inverted nature sees –
Trees cut to statues, statues thick as trees

. . . . . .

Here Amphitritë sails through myrtle bowers,
There gladiators fight or die in flowers;
Unwatered, see the drooping seahorse mourn,
And swallows roost in Nilus' dusty urn.

> (*Moral Essays*, IV,
> *Use of Riches, to Burlington*)

A more obvious example, from *Windsor Forest*, is when in the river

> the musing shepherd spies
> The headlong mountains and the downward skies;
> The watery landscape of the pendent woods,
> And absent trees that tremble in the floods;
> In the clear azure gleam the flock are seen
> And floating forests paint the waves with green.

This derives from *Appleton House*; but it is not Metaphysical – there is no reference beyond Newtonian physics.

(250–54)

S. L. Goldberg

'Marvell: Self and Art', *Melbourne Critical Review*, vol. 7   1965

Marvell's best work is continuously fascinating in the way it encompasses so many subtle, baffling complexities with such a light, easy simplicity. It seems indeed to baffle even the attempt to explain it to oneself. In an essay some years ago (*M.C.R.*, vol. 3, 1960) I tried to explore the how and why of this a little way; and concentrating on *Appleton House*, not as the best of Marvell but as probably the most accessible way into his work, offered some suggestions about why it is that we also feel in his other (and finer) poems what Eliot has called an 'inexhaustible and terrible nebula of emotion', and what this has to do with their 'wit'. That emotion doesn't come, I think, as Eliot's examples might seem to imply, from any specifically Christian insight, but rather (to put it summarily) from a wider, probably older and less answerable intuition that every activity in which life enhances and augments itself is also a step that inevitably restricts and in the end extinguishes it. But to recognize this, it seems to me now, leads to some further reflections about Marvell's quality, particularly in his major poems – and especially so when many critics still seem to miss how substantial, and how rare an achievement, Marvell's best work is.

The first reason why a good deal of his poetry should seem insubstantial isn't hard to see. *Appleton House* provides some clear enough examples. As the poem draws strength from Marvell's imaginative grasp on what is there in front of him to be seen and felt, so its weakest parts are those where he is most theoretical. The varied life of the Nunappleton estate – a life that involves the human and the natural in some highly problematical relationships – seems so moving partly because we see how delicate, almost fragile, its beauty is, and partly because we see it as the fruit of the 'whistling scythe, and elbow strong', of human minds and bodies working on real things to produce something correspondingly real. On the other hand, the emblematical ingenuities about the wood, for instance, seem only self-indulgence; the idealized view of Maria Fairfax at the end is a gesture in the right direction, but it does remain only a gesture. Where Marvell falls back on a merely ideal pattern or a merely ideal value, the poetry becomes thin and artificial. And this is true in all his work. Most of his poems are very skilful – much cleverer indeed than the general run of mid-seventeenth century lyrics – and their intentions at least are always intelligent. But apart from the dozen or so I named they lack body: it is as if they filter experience down almost to nothing. The *Definition of Love*, to take a much-discussed poem, is brilliantly 'Metaphysical' in style; but the interest is all in drawing a *diagram* of love. The emotion that needs so much elaborate intellection to express it remains little more than an idea. So with another test-case, the *Dialogue between the Resolved Soul and Created Pleasure*. This does show, as Dr Leavis has claimed, a wider range of interests and a maturer sense of their relative worth than *Comus*; it is, in parts, all that he claims for it. But at times the valuations seem to be rather distant from anything that insistently demands evaluation:

Soul

My gentler rest is on a thought,
Conscious of doing what I ought. . . .

Pleasure

Everything does seem to vie
Which should first attract thine eye:
But since none deserves that grace,
In this crystal view *thy* face.

Soul

When the creator's skill is prized
The rest is all but earth disguised. ....

Clearly, Marvell's other dialogue – *between the Soul and the Body* –
has consistently fuller life:

With bolts of bones, that fettered stands
In feet; and manacled in hands. ....

.   .   .   .   .

So architects do square and hew
Green trees that in the forest grew.

The bolting down is felt; the squaring and the hewing operate sharply
against the greenness, the growth. The force and value of physical
reality are evoked in the very way the Soul complains of its con-
striction; the strength and value of spiritual activity are evoked in the
very way the Body complains of its mutilation.

But if there are reasons why Marvell's work sometimes is rather
unsubstantial, there are other and less simple reasons why – even at
its best – it might still seem so: his constant concern with nature, and
(closely related to that) his self-consciousness. Thus the *Dialogue
between the Soul and the Body* seems able to crystallize its fuller imaginative life only by looking to man's relationships with nature; even
in the *Coy Mistress* and the *Horatian Ode*, love and politics are seen and
weighed in their relations with it.

The critic's first temptation is to oversimplify Marvell's concern
with nature, whether by trying to find some 'philosophy' of nature
behind the poetry to 'explain' it, or by attending only to those
attitudes that have a parallel in the formal philosophy of the seventeenth century. This is surely to look for the wrong thing in the
wrong place, and to miss the poetry in doing so. But a second
temptation is to underrate the poetry just because it is so concerned
with nature – as A. Alvarez does, for instance, in his book on *The*

School of Donne, or J. B. Broadbent in *Poetic Love*. Obviously Marvell's
range is limited. He can't deal directly with any wide variety of human
experience from the inside, as it were; his tone is always detached,
indeed self-consciously so; and for a man to maintain a cool 'wittiness'
about things, or to describe private ecstasies about vegetation, or to
concern himself with Damons and Julianas, when he is living in the
middle of a civil war, may well seem like stepping aside from reality
into a realm of delightful but impossible ideals.

And yet if this wouldn't be an unfair account of some of Marvell's
contemporaries – Lovelace or Cowley, for example – it really misses
everything that distinguishes him from them. For the crucial difference is not only the way Marvell experiences nature, nor merely
the reasons he is concerned with it, but the fact that he understands
his limitations himself. His response to nature is for him a way of
bringing to focus other kinds of experience, but as well as that other
potentialities of experience that, for one reason or another, he knows
he can neither act out nor envisage in their full human reality. Concentrating on nature is a way of discovering the living self and the
contexts in which it lives; he seems, in fact, to share something of
Shakespeare's dramatic insight that what a man sees *as* nature really
defines his physical, moral and spiritual being. But instead of Shakespeare's ability to show us this in a wide variety of human experience,
Marvell has a more apparent *intellectual* consciousness of it – a consciousness corresponding to his recognition that he can't command
that dramatic range and can't therefore explore it directly. Except,
that is, in himself. Self-consciousness is for him both a price and a
reward, since it does allow him to understand not only what he can't
do, but what he can and why it matters. He can't portray the world
of *Antony and Cleopatra*, for example; but realizing that, he can also
see how a mere walk in a garden, say, by its very limitations, can
sharply define insights that ripple out and apply in areas of experience
unavailable to him directly. His detachment becomes a subtle form
of action in and upon the world about him.

When we have run our passion's heat,
Love hither makes his best retreat.
The gods that mortal beauty chase,
Still in a tree did end their race.

Apollo hunted Daphne so,
Only that she might laurel grow.
And Pan did after Syrinx speed,
Not as a nymph, but for a reed.

What wondrous life in this I lead!
Ripe apples drop about my head;
The luscious clusters of the vine
Upon my mouth do crush their wine;
The nectarine, and curious peach,
Into my hands themselves do reach;
Stumbling on melons, as I pass,
Ensnared with flowers, I fall on grass.

The verse of *The Garden* is modest, but quite consciously so, and it is easy to miss how much it is doing in its own way, without fuss or pretension. Having moved from the delights of the quiet, innocence, and harmony offered by the garden, as against the struggle, competition, and limited successes available in society, it now begins to explore the deeper and more inclusive vitality man seems able to achieve here. Here, it seems, a man can fulfil *all* his needs, *all* his aspirations; even to fall is to fall without danger, 'on grass'. The verse itself demonstrates what such an inclusive, harmonious vitality is. It is delicately alive with every aspect of the garden's life and with the play of a mind that relates each aspect with every other: natural and moral life interfuse. The paradisal quality of the garden's life is all the more appealing just because it seems really available; the verse catches its physical reality: the trees are quietly present, the apples have weight, we feel the pressure of the grapes and the melons impeding us. Equally, the verse catches the ideals offered us here: detachment, harmony, passion quiet and sublimated, beauty and fertility wonderfully reaching out to us without our toiling to reach them. At the same time, however, the verse also responds to other aspects of this garden life, aspects that qualify its ideality (as the verse of Jonson's *To Penshurst*, for example, does not): as Marvell presents it, our 'retreat' may also be only a withdrawal from the race, merely compensation for impotence; the absence of effort, so delightful at first, eventually brings a feeling almost of embarrassment as the grapes press on us and the sprawling melons and flowers trip our feet. Again, the verse reaches out to those aspects of the garden that relate our life to other kinds of life: it catches something, but only a tantalizing touch, of the sheer energy of the natural gods, the out-pouring fruitfulness of the world, and its strange, quick self-baffling meta-morphoses. Even where it most enjoys its detachment from the 'busy companies of men', seems most absorbed in the garden state, the verse still retains its civil, 'social' tone (as in 'curious peach', for instance); and with that, its sense of what a genuinely transcendent life might cost: it reminds us, almost casually, of our relationship with the last of the 'race' of gods, whose Passion achieved a higher kind of life on a Tree, but in a very different way from this. All through these stanzas, one aspect of the garden-life somehow transforms itself into another, and at the same time it is made sharper and evaluated by all the others.

The result is that the almost trivial business of responding to a garden becomes a way of exploring the significance of responding at all; Marvell makes his experience of the garden into both a focus and a paradigm of all his experience. Can man achieve a wholly satisfying, wholly inclusive vitality? Is transcendence possible, and even if it were, is it even desirable? The non-human world reaches out for us to consume it and be consumed in it, and yet we come to feel an almost comic dismay at its ungoverned fertility; no sooner do we commit ourselves to it, feel welcome and at home in it, than we suddenly feel it slightly alien. Just so the mind can also transcend all its experience here; but to achieve 'a green thought in a green shade' is not actually to *experience* 'all that's made'. The same is true even at the very climax:

Here at the fountain's sliding foot,
Or at some fruit-tree's mossy root,
Casting the body's vest aside,
My soul into the boughs does glide;
There like a bird it sits, and sings,
Then whets, and combs its silver wings;
And, till prepared for longer flight,
Waves in its plumes the various light.

The lightness, the simplicity, the spontaneous ease and joy of the bird are real enough: to achieve all that – even perhaps to see life as this –

is freedom for the Soul. And yet will it quite do? The detached, slightly comic note in the verse, the slight comicality of the bird's fragile, self-absorbed, almost complacent little life, are real enough too. The verse already – well before the obvious jokes about the impossibility of sexual isolation in the following stanza – catches the irresponsibility of gaily casting the body's vest aside like that, and the inadequacy for the human Soul of sitting happily preening itself in the tree-tops. The life of Marvell's poetry is spontaneous, but it is also deliberated and courteously restrained; being so, it is as if it thoroughly understands itself.

Thus Eliot's description of Marvell's wit is certainly apt as far as it goes: 'a recognition, implicit in the expression of every experience, of other kinds of experience which are possible'. But at his best, I think, there is more to it than this. Marvell actively *searches* those possibilities of life for the larger inclusive life they seem to promise but which, he also comes to recognize, they also work inevitably to undermine.

Despite its weaknesses, *Appleton House* seems to me the most obvious example of this just because it searches so openly to discover what this paradox and our efforts to get free of it amount to in relation to each other. It discovers, in fact, that the poet's free 'witty' play of mind, and the various forms of life it plays upon, are in complex ways part of each other. The passages where Marvell is at his most lightly and fancifully detached, for example, find their significance in, and give significance to, the intensely engaged and intensely felt passages where he estimates the various 'bastions' of Nunappleton – where he judges, that is to say, the limits of even the most admirable decisions and activities open to men here and now.

What this means, however, is that since the poetry finds its life in the same conflicts it explores, it can never *resolve* them. And in the best of his work Marvell never pretends to resolve them. Responsive as he is to many kinds of possible experience, he offers no ultimate reconciliation of them, no *concors* emerging out of, and sanctifying, all *discordia*, no triumphant or prophetic vision, no assurance that everything can be harmonized by Faith or Reason or Symbols or graceful Indifference. The only resolution the poems offer is the one they achieve as poems. And he also recognizes what this implies: not only that as a man he has to maintain a difficult balance between equally possible but conflicting kinds of fulfilment, but that keeping such a balance is almost impossible – almost indeed, a kind of trick. (It is interesting to recall that, in his own life, he evidently had something of the character of a Trimmer about him.) This doesn't mean that his poems are politically or morally indecisive, however; his subtleties are not a way of evading choice and action. But they do delicately insist on the gap between the poet's activity and the activities he is writing about, between their own protean awareness and the limiting action forced on us in ordinary life. Usually, indeed, like *Appleton House*, though not so openly, they insist on the loss as well as the gain involved in their own imaginative creation.

In other words, although the poetry continually judges the experience it evokes, it never purports actually to settle anything. It claims no didactic or ideological usefulness. It offers itself only as an example – perhaps a unique one, but as limited as any – of living with irreconcilable conflicts easily, finely, and without losing one's head. We need, I would suggest, to add two riders to Eliot's description of his wit, for as it stands it rather under-rates Marvell's liveliness and his serene good-humour, and both are of the essence. Thus his 'recognitions' are the effect of a continual, vital, outgoing *activity* of imagination; but secondly, it is an activity always light and unfussed, its spontaneity never damaged by the most disturbing recognitions of human inadequacy – even its own. The particular effect of each of his best poems depends on the particular relations it creates between these two qualities.

We can see this in comparatively simple terms in the Mower poems. What seems only a 'slight lyric grace' is really a way both of grasping and of accepting the Mower's predicament. He sees Damon as something of a clown, for instance –

While thus he threw his elbow round,
Depopulating all the ground,
And, with his whistling scythe, does cut
Each stroke between the earth and root,
The edged steel by careless chance
Did into his own ankle glance;
And there among the grass fell down,
By his own scythe, the mower mown.

But *Marvell's* clownishness reaches out to other aspects of the situation which make us see how inadequate clownishness is: 'de-populating', for example, or the beautifully pointed last line of the poem: 'For Death thou art a mower too.' Or again, in *The Mower's Song*, where once again Marvell sees man's energy as part of nature, yet destroying it, and sexual passion as necessary to man's life, yet consuming it, the poetry avoids sentimentalizing man's predicament of course, but it also avoids chagrin. The sweeping, bitterly violent action of the scythe is felt as a real act – a man *working* and so making and destroying at once; a man worked upon, and so inevitably animated and consumed; but it is equally felt as a *lyrical* refrain:

... Juliana comes, and she
What I do to the grass, does to my thoughts and me.

In *The Mower to the Glow-worms*, the Mower's alienation from nature's 'dear light' caused by the equally natural force of sex is consciously recognized and accepted – for the recognition is a 'song' obviously 'meditated' (like the 'Nightingale's') and 'courteous' (like the lights). In other words, the poem consciously sees its own qualities as part of the material it is dealing with. Again, with characteristic integrity *The Coronet* comes to recognize that the sacrifice of its own integrity as a poem is the only 'coronet' it can offer Christ:

But thou who only couldst the serpent tame,
Either his slippery knots at once untie,
And disentangle all his winding snare:
Or shatter too with him my curious frame:
And let these wither, so that he may die,
Though set with skill and chosen out with care.
That they, while thou on both their spoils dost tread,
May crown thy feet, that could not crown thy head.

Something similar occurs in the *Dialogue between the Soul and the Body*. The whole texture of the language, in which each character in the debate needs the other even to state its case against it, insists on the inseparability of Soul and Body. The whole structure of the debate and the imaginative concreteness of the verse in each speech of it equally insist that the two characters *are* separate and irreconcilably opposed. (The last speech of the Body only brings us back again to the opening complaint of the Soul.) In other words, the sharp, neat form of the poem is continually seen as embodying a precarious, almost impossible, detachment, very different from the tangled struggles of soul and body as we ordinarily experience them. If Marvell catches the touch of absurdity in their situation here, he never forgets that we aren't usually in a position to stand off and appreciate it. He leaves the harmonious completeness of the poem and the baffling struggles it presents to comment on one another.

This may suggest one reason why *To his Coy Mistress* is a great love-poem even though at first sight it may seem to use 'love' as little more than an occasion. In fact, it makes the lover's emotion and his plight alive in his understanding of that emotion and that plight. His tender playfulness, his grace and ease of address, his bantering fancy, the intelligence and wit and mutual courtesy he so assuredly takes for granted in the love-relationship, the exactness with which he raises and measures every consideration – these are not simply vivid circumstantial details. They are part of the *content* of his love; they partly define it. But of course it would be unreal without one other quality; and in the elegant fantasy of the first section it does seem rather unreal. Here are the conditions of a highly 'Platonic' love – reduced to absurdity by being envisaged beside a real Ganges and a real Humber. The lovers' infinite wish is at once noble and silly, each to an extent precisely understood by the lover (and which he expects the lady to understand too):

My vegetable love should grow
Vaster than empires, and more slow. . . .
An age at least to every part,
And the last age should show your heart.
For Lady, you deserve this state;
Nor would I love at lower rate.

Ideally, his love would reach out to its slow, elaborate ritual of fulfilment (or is it fulfilment?); the real alternative is an even slower ritual:

. . . yonder all before us lie
Deserts of vast eternity.
Thy beauty shall no more be found,
Nor, in thy marble vault, shall sound

My echoing song: then worms shall try
That long preserved virginity:
And your quaint honour turn to dust;
And into ashes all my lust. . . .

Once again the alternatives are measured against each other because
they are evoked in terms of each other: the lover's active 'lust' and
the worm's, for example, or the present love-song and the silent
tomb. In fact we hear the song most vividly when it makes us most
vividly feel its absence. The 'virginity' will be 'tried'; like the
'fineness' and the 'privacy' of the grave, it is given its due weight:
there is no sneer in the tone. He is even willing to call his own feeling
'lust'. But the energy of that 'lust', the vitality in it, can be unmistakably felt giving reality to the whole poem. For all its syllogistic
structure, this is what impels the lover to understand his own case,
measure it, and argue it – argue, finally, the necessity for *enacting*
'lust'. It is surely a rather odd predicament: that a lover should
deliberately, in full consciousness even that the energies of life destroy
themselves in fulfilling themselves (the youthful dew is evaporated as
much by inner fires as by the temporal sun) *argue* with all the resources
of conscious logic, for the intense, impulsive, wholly *blinding* act of
love?

. . . tear our pleasures with rough strife,
Thorough the iron gates of life.
Thus, though we cannot make our sun
Stand still, yet we will make him run.

We are made to feel, in the lover's own sense of it, the natural force
that animates even beings so highly self-aware and civilized that they
are aware they must give themselves to that force, which is highly
uncivilized and which demands the price of everything else their
love consists in. And yet the 'thus' in the penultimate line is as much
to the point as the self-mocking absurdity of the final image. It is
characteristic that as the poem drives forward to the consuming act of
love, it should still keep undiminished all its tenderness, courtesy,
understanding, passion, and lightness of touch. These values and the
act in which they (ironically) seek fulfilment are brought face to face,
as it were, but the force of neither kind of vitality is lessened. Once

again it is as if the poem, expressing all the values of a subtle, refined consciousness, and its subject – or rather, its conclusion – in which those values are necessarily obliterated, were left to measure and complete each other.

With the *Horatian Ode*, there is no need to elaborate on the way it balances the conflicting forces that made the tragedy of the Civil War. Marvell does more than sympathize with both Cromwell and Charles of course; protagonist and antagonist represent opposing values – opposing forces, in fact – in Marvell himself and in the very substance of human society. Viewing them with the detachment of a poet, Marvell manages to balance them; viewing them also as a member of society, he equally recognizes that such a balance is impossible on the political stage. What makes Cromwell so hard to reckon with, for instance, is that he is at once a great man who chose to act as he did, and a divine instrument, and a bolt of the same natural energies that also nourish life. The poetry actually embodies something of his driving force (and something of his austere reserve): the formalized measures would be vapid if they didn't evoke the fierce energies that they measure with such difficulty. At the same time the poetry also embodies something of Charles's graceful (perhaps too graceful) moral dignity: Marvell's eye is even 'keener' than Charles's, but he too avoids any hint of 'vulgar spite'. The implications of all this have been worked out before, of course (e.g. by Cleanth Brooks in *English Institute Essays 1946*; L. D. Lerner, in *Interpretations*, ed. John Wain; and Robin Grove in *M.C.R.*, 1963); clearly this is largely why the *Ode* is so magnificent an achievement and, indeed, Marvell's finest work.

And yet there is a further aspect of it that seems to me to help make it so peculiarly *moving* a poem: I mean Marvell's view of his own position in it. He raises the question himself in the way he begins and ends it:

The forward youth that would appear
Must now forsake his Muses dear.
   Nor in the shadows sing
   His numbers languishing.
'Tis time to leave the books in dust
And oil th' unused armour's rust,

> Removing from the wall
> The corslet of the hall.
> So restless Cromwell could not cease
> In the inglorious arts of peace . . .
>
> . . . . . .
>
> The same arts that did gain
> A power must it maintain.

Up to a point we can read the opening as a declaration not simply that men now must, and ought to, abandon poetry for action, but perhaps that poetry must, and ought to, now become heroic, politically engaged, a kind of action itself. Even so, there is still the undercurrent in 'restless Cromwell', the obvious fact that this is a poem (a highly formal and detached one at that), and the point made at the end: that the political 'arts' are not only, as Marvell has suggested, pretty dubious morally, but in themselves, without the backing of God and Nature, of doubtful efficacy anyway. Again, if Marvell's eye is keener than Charles's, so he also clearly 'knows' more than Cromwell, the man who, like the ideal Renaissance hero, 'does both act and know'. Marvell's wisdom, embracing the universal and tragic dimension of events, is larger than Cromwell's prudential 'wiser art' and even his moral 'goodness' and 'justice'. For Marvell himself, the struggle between action and contemplation, nature and 'art', is an urgent reality. The art of the poet may be useless; at most it can celebrate heroic victory; in the end, he seems conscious enough that for himself (and for us as we share his vision of life) it is really impossible to 'know' as deeply as this and to act. Is there not a touch of self-recognition in the phrase about Charles's helplessness

> While round the armed bands
> Did clap their bloody hands?
>
> (55–6)

One of the things I find so moving here is Marvell's characteristic humility. He isn't tempted – as a nineteenth- or twentieth-century poet might be – to regard his imaginative integrity as more important than heroic action, necessarily limited as that is. On the contrary, if he decides between them, he backs, with all qualifications recognized, Cromwell's activity, not his own artistic detachment:

But thou the wars' and Fortune's son
March indefatigably on . . .

That powerful rhythm is not overcome even by the irony of the last
few lines that follow it. As in other poems, his self-consciousness
doesn't lead him to persuade himself that writing poetry – Art – is
somehow grander or more valuable than anything else. However
deeply poetry engages the self, however much it seems the only way
in which one can fulfil all of one's opposing needs and values, however complete its *imaginative* engagement may be – and Marvell
clearly appreciates all this – he always places it with delicate humility
at the feet of, in the service of, actual living: of casting the Kingdom
into another mould, for example, even if it does mean ruining the
great work of Time, or of actually consummating one's love, or
experiencing more fully the demands of one's soul and body, or
working in the fields of Nature, or really sacrificing one's self to God.
Recognizing all the difficulties, he nevertheless gets the priorities
right – not just in theory, but in the actual life of his poetry.

The strength of this artistic humility is not just a matter of Marvell's
having lived in the mid-seventeenth century, however – an age that
encouraged such humility by allotting poetry definable modes and a
definable status within a coherent 'world-picture'. This has some
relevance, obviously. Marvell does respect the objective existence of
the modes he uses (Pastoral, the public Ode, the traditional invitation
of the lover, and so on); his poems are not openly *personal explorations*.
His assumptions are rooted in the Christian-Humanist Renaissance,
even though they aren't reducible to 'philosophical' generalities any
more than real poetry ever is. He is certainly not a Romantic or post-
Romantic. But when this obvious fact has been noted, there is another
worth noting as well: he is very different from other poets of his own
day too. There is, for example, a crucial difference between the self-
consciousness of his art and that of, say, *Comus*. For all his distance
from Shakespeare, Marvell has more of his sharpness and spontaneity
than of Milton's touch of idealizing and straining *will*. In fact he
avoids both kinds of will to be found in seventeenth-century poetry:
the anxious spirituality, in which the will drives to cut free of the
physical world or to grind it into some kind of spiritual fodder; and
the equally anxious libertinism, in which the will drives towards a

natural sensuality but clogs it by needing to justify itself or by a self-conscious bravado. In all his best work, Marvell is concerned, almost explicitly, with the nature of human vitality and its contradictory but necessary manifestations. The remarkable thing is how much of it he retains while being so conscious of the problems and what he is doing with them. He doesn't lapse into mere slightness or fragmentation (like much of Cleveland or of Cowley, for example) or merely graceful sensuality (like much of Lovelace) or a rather self-flattering idealism (like much of Milton). Being conscious of his 'art' involves for him no subtle aggrandisement of the ego; it is instead a way of placing his sensitive and subtle intelligence, aware as it is of so much more than he can answer to in action, in the service of his full living being as a man. The result is – to apply a phrase Leavis has used of Wordsworth – 'a spontaneity engaging an advanced and delicate organization'. The word to emphasize, I think, is 'engaging': the spontaneity is manifest *in* Marvell's complex self-awareness.

And perhaps this is why he is such a fascinating figure. One aspect of our plight over the last century or so is indeed to be 'too much conscious and conscious of too much', and to have to seek a 'new naturalness on the far side of the experience of disharmony': these phrases are Leavis's too, but the problem is familiar enough in writers as diverse as Wordsworth, Yeats, Joyce, and Lawrence, to name only a few. And for many writers, unable to find any solid relationship between their art, the self, and the world about them, their consciousness of themselves has seemed the only possible way, not only of exploring their plight, but of answering it. Aestheticism has been an endemic temptation, most formidable in fact not when it seems to justify our despising or evading a hostile reality, but when it seems the only way of giving it the only meaning it seems able to sustain. The pride of Art has subtler and more insidious temptations than the nineteenth-century Aesthete's. (Lawrence is right, of course, when he remarks, that 'the glory of mankind has been to produce lives, to produce vivid, independent, individual men, not buildings or engineering works or even art . . .'; yet how many of us, I wonder, would assent instantly, without at least hesitating over the last phrase ?) The truth Lawrence is pointing to perhaps suggests why Marvell's best poetry, born as it is out of a similar plight to ours, is so attractive. With all his self-consciousness, he manages to remain a man vividly, independently as alive as he can be. The example is a telling one since the plight was so acute for him, and even despite the fact that we are conscious of so much more – conscious, indeed, as Eliot reminds us, that the writers of the past are that which we know.

(32-44)

Yvor Winters

from *Forms of Discovery*   1967

The best poems by Andrew Marvell (1621–78) are *To his Coy Mistress*, *The Garden*, and *An Horatian Ode upon Cromwell's Return from Ireland*. There are others which are important in connexion with his thought, and there are others which contain passages of interesting poetry, but these three are the best, just as they are the most famous. The *Horatian Ode* is on the most serious subject of the three, but it is perhaps the least successful in execution. The first twenty-six lines are stereotyped and of no interest in themselves; they may be the sort of dead rhetoric which is expected in this kind of ode, but if this is so, then this kind of ode is intrinsically defective. There is a great deal of the same kind of language in the remainder of the poem, but there are good passages: lines twenty-seven through thirty-six, and fifty-seven through sixty in particular. Fifty-seven, however, introduces a mild structural weakness: up to this point the pronoun *he* has referred to Cromwell; in fifty-seven it refers to Charles. There is no transition, and we have to remember the historical fact of the beheading after we have read two or three lines in order to understand the new reference. The poem may well have the structure which is expected of this kind of ode but the virtue of any structural principle lies in the results produced: the general effect of the ode is that of a kind of news-letter for the year. Here as in *Lycidas* and as in much of Vaughan the close organization of Renaissance poetry can be seen in the initial stages of its disintegration.

To his Coy Mistress is an elaborate treatment of a trivial and stereo-typed subject. The best discussion of the poem with which I am acquainted is that of J.V. Cunningham. The structure is that of close rational argument: Had we but time ... But we have not time ...

Therefore let me seduce you now. Each stage of the argument is expanded by a great deal of ingenious detail. The poem might fairly be described as an exceptionally brilliant academic exercise on a set theme, but it is no more than that.

The best poem is *The Garden*. The poem is famous and has often been explained. The best discussion – a very fine discussion – is by Frank Kermode. The essay is too long to summarize; it deals with the poem partly in terms of the philosophical ideas involved, mainly in terms of the literary tradition which had used these ideas and from which Marvell's poem emerges. The poem deals with a longing which at times appears almost mystical, although it is probably literary for the most part, for a return to Eden, an Eden in which man had not yet been corrupted by women or civilization. Instead of sexual love we have a 'pure' love for the vegetation of the garden. Yet the sources of Marvell's ideas and tradition are also remote sources of Romanticism, and the poem seems to be a precursor as well as a result. The love for the vegetation is 'pure', yet in the fifth stanza it is very sensual, and the last lines suggest – no doubt remotely – Whitman's illicit love-affair with Mother Nature early in the *Song of Myself*. Whitman is gross and grotesque, and Marvell is extremely civilized, but the suggestion is there. As Kermode tells us, the sixth stanza is Platonic yet it verges on pantheism. Green, Kermode tells us, signifies innocence, and this, I suppose, should eliminate all traces of pantheism from the last couplet, but it does not:

Annihilating all that's made
To an innocent thought in an innocent shade.

If anything, this reading is more pantheistic than the lines in the poem. For the pantheist this would be satisfactory, but I cannot understand pantheism and consequently I cannot grasp the idea by which I am supposed to be moved. For most scholars, it is sufficient merely to understand the poet's intention, but this understanding brings us only to the brink of the poem, to the brink of the critical judgement. Unless we go beyond the scholar's mere elucidation, we have not even tried to experience the poem; the poem is an interesting puzzle, no more. In the seventh stanza, the soul becomes a bird and sings in the branches; it is a charming bird, but it casts little light on the experience of the soul. That is, we have ornament at the expense of meaning, a great deal of vehicle and very little tenor. Kermode provides us with a good deal of the literary background of Marvell's bird-soul, but the background does not help us. The writing of the poem is beautiful throughout if we can be satisfied with a meaning which seems to escape us at the crucial moments. The theme is not profoundly serious; the poem is witty in the sense in which Marvell would have used this term, and it is charming, but it is far from great.

(103-5)

An Horatian Ode

Cleanth Brooks

'Marvell's *Horatian Ode*', *English Institute Essays* 1947

The easiest error into which we may fall in defining the relationship between historical and critical studies is illustrated by the preface of Maurice Kelley's interesting book on Milton, *This Great Argument*. For Kelley, the problem of exegesis is almost amusingly simple: we will read Milton's *Christian Doctrine* to find out what Milton's ideas are, and then we shall be able to understand his *Paradise Lost*, explaining the tangled and difficult poetic document by means of the explicit prose statement. But Kelley's argument rests not only upon the assumption that the Milton who wrote the *Christian Doctrine* was precisely and at all points the same man who composed *Paradise Lost* – a matter which, for all practical purposes, may well be true; it rests upon the further and much more dangerous assumption that Milton was able to *say* in *Paradise Lost* exactly what he intended to say; and that what he supposed he had put into that poem is actually to be found there. in short, Mr Kelley tends to make the assumption about poetry which most of us constantly make; namely, that a poem is essentially a decorated and beautified piece of prose.

But I propose to deal here with a more modest example than Milton's epic. I propose to illustrate from Marvell's *Horatian Ode*. If we follow the orthodox procedure, the obvious way to understand the *Ode* is to ascertain by historical evidence – by letters and documents of all kinds – what Marvell really thought of Cromwell, or, since Marvell apparently thought different things of Cromwell at different times, to ascertain the date of the *Ode*, and then neatly fit it into the particular stage of Marvell's developing opinion of Cromwell. But this is at best a relatively coarse method which can hope to give no more than a rough approximation of the poem; and there lurk in it some positive perils. For to ascertain what Marvell the man thought of Cromwell, and even to ascertain what Marvell as poet consciously intended to say in his poem, will not prove that the poem actually says this, or all this, or merely this. This last remark, in my opinion, does not imply too metaphysical a notion of the structure of a poem. There is surely a sense in which any one must agree that a poem has a life of its own, and a sense in which it provides in itself the only criterion by which what it says can be judged. It is a commonplace that the poet sometimes writes better than he knows, and, alas, on occasion, writes worse than he knows. The history of English literature will furnish plenty of examples of both cases.

As a matter of fact, Marvell's *Ode* is not a shockingly special case. Indeed, I have chosen it for my example, not because it is special – not because I hope to reveal triumphantly that what it really says is something quite opposed to what we have supposed it to be saying – but because it seems to me a good instance of the normal state of affairs. Yet, even so, the *Ode* will provide us with problems enough. To the scholar who relies upon the conventional approach, the problems become rather distressingly complicated.

Let us review the situation briefly. Hard upon his composition of the *Ode* in 1650, Marvell had published in 1649 a poem *To his Noble Friend, Mr Richard Lovelace*, and a poem *Upon the Death of the Lord Hastings*. Both Margoliouth and Legouis find these poems rather pro-Royalist in sentiment and certainly it is difficult to read them otherwise. If we add to these poems the *Elegy upon the Death of My Lord Francis Villiers*, a Cavalier who was killed fighting for the King in 1649, the Royalist bias becomes perfectly explicit. As Margoliouth puts it: 'If [the elegy on Villiers] is Marvell's, it is his one unequivocal royalist utterance; it throws into strong relief the transitional character of *An Horatian Ode* where royalist principles and admiration for Cromwell the Great Man exist side by side. . . .'

A transition in views there must have been, but the transition certainly cannot be graphed as a steadily rising curve, when we take into account Marvell's next poem, *Tom May's Death*. May died in November, 1650. Thus we have the *Horatian Ode*, which was almost certainly written in the summer of 1650, preceding by only a few months a poem in which Marvell seems to slur at the Commander of the Parliamentary armies – either Essex or Fairfax – as 'Spartacus', and to reprehend May himself as a renegade poet who has prostituted the mystery of the true poets. The curve of Marvell's political development shows still another surprising quirk when we recall that only a few months after his attack on May, Marvell was to be living under Spartacus Fairfax's roof, acting as tutor to his little daughter Mary.

Let me interrupt this summary to say that I am not forcing the evidence so as to crowd the historian into the narrowest and most uncomfortable corner possible. On the contrary, whatever forcing of the evidence has been done has been done by the editors and the historians. If we limit ourselves to historical evidence, it is possible to suppose that *Tom May's Death* was actually written on the Hill at Billborrow; and Margoliouth chooses early 1651 as the probable date for Marvell's arrival at Appleton House only because, as he says, '*Tom May's Death* is not the sort of poem Marvell would have written under Fairfax's roof.'

There is no need, in view of our purposes, to extend the review of Marvell's political development through the late 1650s with their Cromwellian poems or through the Restoration period with its vexed problems concerning which of the anti-court satires are truly, and which are falsely, ascribed to Marvell. The problem of Marvell's attitude through the years 1649–51 will provide sufficient scope for this examination of some of the relations and interrelations of the historical approach and the critical approach. For there is still another complication, which has received less attention than it deserves. It is the curious fact that the *Horatian Ode* in which Marvell seems to affirm the ancient rights of the monarchy –

Though Justice against Fate complain,
And plead the ancient rights in vain –
$$(37-8)$$

is full of echoes of the poetry of Tom May, the poet whom Marvell was, a few months later, to denounce for having failed poetry in the hour of crisis:

When the sword glitters o'er the judges' head,
And fear has coward churchmen silenced,
Then is the poet's time, 'tis then he draws,
And single fights forsaken virtue's cause.
He, when the wheel of empire, whirleth back,
And though the world's disjointed axle crack,
Sings still of *ancient rights* and better times,
Seeks wretched good, arraigns successful crimes.
$$(63-70)$$

The echoes of May's poetry, of course, may well have been unconscious: to me it is significant that they are from May's translation of Lucan's poem on the Roman civil wars. I must say that I find the parallels quite convincing and that I am a little surprised at Margoliouth's restraint in not pushing his commentary further. For one is tempted to suppose that in the year or so that followed the execution of Charles, Marvell was obsessed with the problem of the poet's function in such a crisis; that the poet May was frequently in his mind through a double connexion – through the parallels between the English and the Roman civil war, Lucan's poem on which May had translated, and through May's conduct as a partisan of the Commonwealth; and that the *Horatian Ode* and *Tom May's Death*, though so different in tone, are closely related and come out of the same general state of mind. But to hazard all this is to guess at the circumstances of Marvell's composition of these poems. It can be only a guess, and, in any case, it takes us into a consideration of what must finally be a distinct problem: how the poem came to be; whereas our elected problem is rather: what the poem is. I am, by the way, in entire sympathy with the essay 'The Intentional Fallacy', by W. K. Wimsatt and M. C. Beardsley, recently published in the *Sewanee Review*. We had best not try to telescope the separate problems of 'the psychology of composition' and that of 'objective evaluation'. I have no intention of trying to collapse them here.

Well, what is said in the *Horatian Ode*? What is the speaker's attitude toward Cromwell and toward Charles? M. Legouis sees in the *Ode* a complete impartiality, an impartiality which is the product of Marvell's nonparticipation in the wars. Legouis can even speak of the poem as 'ce monument d'indifférence en matière de régime politique.' But the *Ode*, though it may be a monument of impartiality, is not a monument of indifference. To read it in this fashion is to miss what seems to me to be a passionate interest in the issues, an interest which is manifested everywhere in the poem. It is true that we have no evidence that Marvell ever served in the civil war, but we had better not leap to conclusions of his indifference from that. My own guess is that some young Cavaliers who shed their blood for the King thought and felt less deeply about the issues than does the speaker of this poem. The tone is not that of a 'plague o' both your houses' nor is it that of 'the conflict provided glory enough to be shared by both sides.'

Mr Margoliouth comes much closer to the point. He sums up as follows: 'The ode is the utterance of a constitutional monarchist, whose sympathies have been with the King, but who yet believes more in men than in parties or principles, and whose hopes are fixed now on Cromwell, seeing in him both the civic ideal of a ruler without personal ambition, and the man of destiny moved by and yet himself driving a power which is above justice.' This statement is plausible, and for its purposes, perhaps just. But does it take us very far – even on the level of understanding Marvell the man? What sort of constitutional monarchist is it who 'believes more in men than in ... principles'? Or who can accept a 'power which is above justice'? I do not say that such a monarchist cannot exist. My point is that Margoliouth's statement raises more problems than it solves. Furthermore, in what sense are the speaker's hopes 'fixed ... on Cromwell'? And how confident is he that Cromwell is 'without personal ambition'? I have quoted earlier Margoliouth's characterization of the Ode as a poem 'where royalist principles and admiration for Cromwell the Great Man exist side by side.' I think that they do exist side by side, but if so, how are they related? Do they exist in separate layers, or are they somehow unified? Unified, in some sense, they must be if the Ode is a poem and not a heap of fragments.

I hope that my last statement indicates the kind of question which we finally have to face and answer. It is a problem of poetic organization. As such, it addresses itself properly to the critic. The historical scholars have not answered it, for it is a question which cannot be answered in terms of historical evidence. (This is not to say, of course, that the same man may not be both historical scholar and critic.) Moreover, I have already taken some pains to indicate how heavily the critic, on his part, may need to lean upon the historian. To put the matter into its simplest terms: the critic obviously must know what the words of the poem mean, something which immediately puts him in debt to the linguist; and since many of the words in this poem are proper nouns, in debt to the historian as well. I am not concerned to exalt the critic at the expense of specialists in other disciplines: on the contrary, I am only concerned to show that he has a significant function, and to indicate what the nature of that function is.

But I am not so presumptuous as to promise a solution to the problem. Instead, the reader will have to be content with suggestions – as

to what the *Ode* is not saying, as to what the *Ode* may be saying
– in short, with explorations of further problems. Many critical problems, of course, I shall have to pass over and some important ones
I shall only touch upon. To illustrate: there is the general Roman cast
given to the *Ode*. Marvell has taken care to make no specifically
Christian references in the poem. Charles is Caesar; Cromwell is a
Hannibal; on the scaffold, Charles refuses to call with 'vulgar spite,'
not on God, but on 'the gods', and so on. Or to point to another
problem, metaphors drawn from hunting pervade the poem. Charles
chases himself to Carisbrooke; Cromwell is like the falcon; Cromwell
will soon put his dogs in 'near|The Caledonian deer'. Or, to take up
the general organization of the poem: Marvell seems to have used the
celebrated stanzas on Charles's execution to divide the poem into two
rather distinct parts: first, Cromwell's rise to power; and second,
Cromwell's wielding of the supreme power. This scheme of division,
by the way, I intend to make use of in the discussion that follows.
But I shall try, in general, to limit it to the specific problem of the
speaker's attitude toward Cromwell, subordinating other critical
problems to this one, which is, I maintain, essentially a critical problem
too.

From historical evidence alone we would suppose that the attitude
toward Cromwell in this poem would have to be a complex one. And
this complexity is reflected in the ambiguity of the compliments paid
to him. The ambiguity reveals itself as early as the second word of
the poem. It is the 'forward' youth whose attention the speaker
directs to the example of Cromwell. 'Forward' may mean no more
than 'high-spirited', 'ardent', 'properly ambitious'; but the *New
English Dictionary* sanctions the possibility that there lurks in the
word the sense of 'presumptuous', 'pushing'. The forward youth can
no longer now

> in the shadows sing
> His numbers languishing.
>
> (3–4)

In the light of Cromwell's career, he must forsake the shadows and
his 'Muses dear' and become the man of action.

The speaker, one observes, does not identify Cromwell himself as
the 'forward youth', or say directly that Cromwell's career has been

motivated by a striving for fame. But the implications of the first two stanzas do carry over to him. There is, for example, the important word 'so' to relate Cromwell to these stanzas:

So restless Cromwell could not cease. . . .
(9)

And 'restless' is as ambiguous in its meanings as 'forward', and in its darker connotations even more damning. For, though 'restless' can mean 'scorning indolence', 'willing to forego ease', it can also suggest the man with a maggot in the brain. 'To cease', used intransitively, is 'to take rest, to be or remain at rest', and the *New English Dictionary* gives instances as late as 1701. Cromwell's 'courage high' will not allow him to rest 'in the inglorious arts of peace'. And this thirst for glory, merely hinted at here by negatives, is developed further in the ninth stanza:

Could by industrious valour climb
To ruin the great work of Time.
(33-4)

'Climb' certainly connotes a kind of aggressiveness. In saying this we need not be afraid that we are reading into the word some smack of such modern phrases as 'social climber'. Marvell's translation of the second chorus of Seneca's *Thyestes* sufficiently attests that the word could have such associations for him:

Climb at Court for me that will
Tottering favour's pinnacle;
All I seek is to lie still.

Cromwell, on the other hand, does not seek to lie still – has sought something quite other than this. His valor is called – strange collocation – an 'industrious valour', and his courage is too high to brook a rival:

For 'tis all one to courage high
The emulous or enemy;
   And with such to enclose,
   Is more than to oppose.
(17-20)

The implied metaphor is that of some explosive which does more violence to that which encloses it, the powder to its magazine, for instance, than to some wall which merely opposes it – against which the charge is fired.

But the speaker has been careful to indicate that Cromwell's motivation has to be conceived of as more complex than any mere thirst for glory. He has even pointed this up. The forward youth is referred to as one who 'would appear' – that is, as one who wills to leave the shadows of obscurity. But restless Cromwell 'could not cease' – for Cromwell it is not a question of will at all, but of a deeper compulsion. Restless Cromwell could not cease, if he would.

Indeed, the lines that follow extend the suggestion that Cromwell is like an elemental force – with as little will as the lightning bolt, and with as little conscience:

And, like the three-forked lightning, first
Breaking the clouds where it was nursed,
   Did thorough his own side
   His fiery way divide.

(13–16)

We are told that the last two lines refer to Cromwell's struggle after Marston Moor with the leaders of the Parliamentary party. Doubtless they do, and the point is important for our knowledge of the poem. But what is more important is that we be fully alive to the force of the metaphor. The clouds have bred the lightning bolt, but the bolt tears its way through the clouds, and goes on to blast the head of Caesar himself. As Margoliouth puts it: 'The lightning is conceived as tearing through the side of his own body the cloud.' In terms of the metaphor, then, Cromwell has not spared his own body: there is no reason therefore to be surprised that he has not spared the body of Charles.

I do not believe that I overemphasized the speaker's implication that Cromwell is a natural force. A few lines later the point is reinforced with another naturalistic figure, an analogy taken from physics:

Nature that hateth emptiness,
Allows of penetration less:
   And therefore must make room
   Where greater spirits come . . .

(41–4)

The question of right, the imagery insists, is beside the point. If nature will not tolerate a power vacuum, no more will it allow two bodies to occupy the same space. (It is amusing, by the way, that Marvell has boldly introduced into his analogy borrowed from physics the nonphysical term 'spirits'; yet I do not think that the clash destroys the figure. Since twenty thousand angels can dance on the point of a needle, two spirits, even though one of them is a greater spirit, ought to be able to occupy the same room. But two spirits, as Marvell conceives of spirits here, will jostle one another, and one must give way. True, the greater spirit is immaterial, but he is no pale abstraction – he is all air and fire, the 'force of angry Heaven's flame'. The metaphor ought to give less trouble to the reader of our day than it conceivably gave to readers bred up on Newtonian physics.)

What are the implications for Charles? Does the poet mean to imply that Charles has angered heaven – that he has merited his destruction? There is no suggestion that Cromwell is a thunderbolt hurled by an angry Jehovah – or even by an angry Jove. The general emphasis on Cromwell as an elemental force is thoroughly relevant here to counter this possible misreading. Certainly, in the lines that follow there is nothing to suggest that Charles has angered heaven, or that the Justice which complains against his fate is anything less than justice.

I began this examination of the imagery with the question, 'What is the speaker's attitude toward Cromwell?' We have seen that the speaker more than once hints at his thirst for glory:

So restless Cromwell could not cease . . .
Could by industrious valour climb . . .

But we have also seen that the imagery tends to view Cromwell as a natural phenomenon, the bolt bred in the cloud. Is there a contradiction? I think not. Cromwell's is no vulgar ambition. If his valor is an 'industrious valour', it contains plain valor too of a kind perfectly capable of being recognized by any Cavalier:

What field of all the Civil Wars,
Where his were not the deepest scars?
(45-6)

If the driving force has been a desire for glory, it is a glory of that kind which allows a man to become dedicated and, in a sense, even selfless in his pursuit of it. Moreover, the desire for such glory can become so much a compulsive force that the man does not appear to act by an exercise of his personal will but seems to become the very will of something else. There is in the poem, it seems to me, at least one specific suggestion of this sort:

> But through advent'rous war
> Urged his active star. . . .
>
> (11–12)

Cromwell is the marked man, the man of destiny, but he is not merely the man governed by his star. Active though it be, he cannot remain passive, even in relation to it: he is not merely urged by it, but himself urges it on.

Yet, if thus far Cromwell has been treated as naked force, something almost too awesome to be considered as a man, the poet does not forget that after all he is a man too – that 'the force of angry Heaven's flame' is embodied in a human being:

> And, if we would speak true,
> Much to the man is due.
>
> (27–8)

The stanzas that follow proceed to define and praise that manliness – the strength, the industrious valor, the cunning. (You will notice that I reject the interpretation which would paraphrase 'Much to the man is due' as 'After all, Cromwell has accomplished much that is good.' Such an interpretation could sort well enough with Legouis's picture of Marvell as the cold and detached honest broker between the factions: unfortunately it will not survive a close scrutiny of the grammar and the general context in which the passage is placed.)

One notices that among the virtues comprising Cromwell's manliness, the speaker mentions his possession of the 'wiser art':

> Where, twining subtle fears with hope,
> He wove a net of such a scope,
>> That Charles himself might chase
>> To Carisbrooke's narrow case.
>>
>> (49–52)

On this point Cromwell has been cleared by all the modern historians (except perhaps Mr Hilaire Belloc). Charles's flight to Carisbrooke Castle, as it turned out, aided Cromwell, but Cromwell could have hardly known that it would; and there is no evidence that he cunningly induced the King to flee to Carisbrooke. Royalist pamphleteers, of course, believed that Cromwell did, and used the item in their general bill of damnation against Cromwell. How does the speaker use it here – to damn or to praise? We tend to answer, 'To praise.' But then it behoves us to notice what is being praised. The things praised are Cromwell's talents as such – the tremendous disciplined powers which Cromwell brought to bear against the King.

For the end served by those powers, the speaker has no praise at all. Rather he has gone out of his way to insist that Cromwell was deaf to the complaint of Justice and its pleading of the 'ancient rights'. The power achieved by Cromwell is a 'forced power' – a usurped power. On this point the speaker is unequivocal. I must question therefore Margoliouth's statement that Marvell sees in Cromwell 'the man of destiny moved by ... a power that is above justice.' Above justice, yes, in the sense that power is power and justice is not power. The one does not insure the presence of the other. Charles has no way to vindicate his 'helpless right', but it is no less right because it is helpless. But the speaker, though he is not a cynic, is a realist. A kingdom cannot be held by mere pleading of the 'ancient rights':

> But those do hold or break
> As men are strong or weak.
>
> (39–40)

In short, the more closely we look at the *Ode*, the more clearly apparent it becomes that the speaker has chosen to emphasize Cromwell's virtues as a man, and likewise, those of Charles as a man. The poem does not debate which of the two was right, for that issue is not even in question. In his treatment of Charles, then, the speaker no more than Charles himself attempts to vindicate his 'helpless right'. Instead, he emphasizes his dignity, his fortitude, and what has finally to be called his consummate good taste. The portraits of the two men beautifully supplement each other. Cromwell is – to use Aristotle's distinction – the man of character, the man of action, who 'does both act and know.' Charles, on the other hand, is the man of passion, the man who is acted upon, the man who knows how to suffer. The contrast is pointed up in half a dozen different ways.

Cromwell, acted upon by his star, is not passive but actually urges his star. Charles in 'acting' – in chasing away to Carisbrooke – actually is passive – performs the part assigned to him by Cromwell. True, we can read 'chase' as an intransitive verb (the *New English Dictionary* sanctions this use for the period): 'that Charles himself might hurry to Carisbrooke.' But the primary meaning asserts itself in the context: 'that Charles might chase himself to Carisbrooke's narrow case.' For this hunter, now preparing to lay his dogs in 'near|The Caledonian deer', the royal quarry has dutifully chased itself.

Even in the celebrated stanzas on the execution, there is ironic realism as well as admiration. In this fullest presentation of Charles as king, he is the player king, the king acting in a play. He is the 'Royal Actor' who knows his assigned part and performs it with dignity. He truly adorned the 'tragic scaffold'

> While round the armed bands
> Did clap their bloody hands.

(55–6)

The generally received account is that the soldiers clapped their hands so as to make it impossible for Charles's speech to be heard. But in the context this reference to hand-clapping supports the stage metaphor. What is being applauded? Cromwell's resolution in bringing the King to a deserved death? Or Charles's resolution on the scaffold as he suffered that death? Marvell was too good a poet to resolve the ambiguity. It is enough that he makes the armed bands applaud.

It has not been pointed out, I believe, that Robert Wild, in his poem on *The Death of Mr Christopher Love*, has echoed a pair of Marvell's finest lines. Love was beheaded by Cromwell on 22 August 1651. In Wild's poem, Marvell's lines

> But with his keener eye
> The axe's edge did try

(59–60)

become: 'His keener words did their sharp axe exceed.' The point is of no especial importance except that it indicates, since Wild's poem was evidently written shortly after Love's execution, that in 1651 the

Horatian Ode was being handed about among the Royalists. For
Wild was that strange combination, an English Presbyterian Royalist.

I have pointed out earlier that the second half of the poem begins
here with the reference to

> that memorable hour
> Which first assured the forced power.
>
> (65–6)

Cromwell is now the *de facto* head of the state, and the speaker, as a
realist, recognizes that fact. Cromwell is seen henceforth, not primarily
in his character as the destroyer of the monarchy, but as the agent of
the new state that has been erected upon the dead body of the King.
The thunderbolt simile, of the first part of the poem, gives way here
to the falcon simile in this second part of the poem. The latter figure
revises and qualifies the former: it repeats the suggestion of ruthless
energy and power, but Cromwell falls from the sky now, not as the
thunderbolt, but as the hunting hawk. The trained falcon is not a
wanton destroyer, nor an irresponsible one. It knows its master: it is
perfectly disciplined:

> She, having killed, no more does search,
> But on the next green bough to perch . . .
>
> (93–4)

The speaker's admiration for Cromwell the man culminates, it
seems to me, here. Cromwell might make the Fame his own; he *need*
not present kingdoms to the state. He might assume the crown rather
than crowning each year. Yet he forbears:

> Nor yet grown stiffer with command,
> But still in the Republic's hand . . .
>
> (81–2)

Does the emphasis on 'still' mean that the speaker is surprised that
Cromwell has continued to pay homage to the republic? Does he
imply that Cromwell may not always do so? Perhaps not: the emphasis is upon the fact that he need not obey and yet does. Yet the compliment derives its full force from the fact that the homage is not forced,
but voluntary and even somewhat unexpected. And a recognition of

this point implies the recognition of the possibility that Cromwell will not always so defer to the commonwealth.

And now what of the republic which Cromwell so ruthlessly and efficiently serves? What is the speaker's attitude toward it? To begin with, the speaker recognizes that its foundations rest upon the bleeding head of Charles. The speaker is aware, it is true, of the Roman analogy, and the English state is allowed the benefit of that analogy. But it is well to notice that the speaker does not commit himself to the opinion that the bleeding head is a happy augury:

> And yet in that the state
> Foresaw its happy fate.
>
> (71–2)

The Roman state was able to take it as a favorable omen, and was justified by the event. With regard to the speaker himself, it seems to me more to the point to notice what prophecy he is willing to commit himself to. He does not prophesy peace. He is willing to predict that England, under Cromwell's leadership, will be powerful in war, and will strike fear into the surrounding states:

> What may not then our isle presume
> While victory his crest does plume!
>   What may not others fear
>   If thus he crown each year!
>
> (97–100)

Specifically, he predicts a smashing victory over the Scots.

But what of the compliments to Cromwell on his ruthlessly effective campaign against the Irish? Does not the speaker succumb, for once, to a bitter and biased patriotism, and does this not constitute a blemish upon the poem?

> And now the Irish are ashamed
> To see themselves in one year tamed:
>   So much one man can do,
>   That does both act and know.
> They can affirm his praises best,
> And have, though overcome, confessed
>   How good he is, how just. . . .
>
> (73–9)

Margoliouth glosses the word 'confessed' as follows: 'Irish testimony in favor of Cromwell at this moment is highly improbable. Possibly there is a reference to the voluntary submission of part of Munster with its English colony.' But surely Margoliouth indulges in understatement. The most intense partisan of Cromwell would have had some difficulty in taking the lines without some inflection of grim irony. The final appeal in this matter, however, is not to what Marvell the Englishman must have thought, or even to what Marvell the author must have intended, but rather to the full context of the poem itself. In that context, the lines in question can be read ironically, and the earlier stanzas sanction that reading. Cromwell's energy, activity, bravery, resolution – even what may be called his efficiency – are the qualities that have come in for praise, not his gentleness or his mercy. The Irish, indeed, are best able to affirm such praise as has been accorded to Cromwell; and they know from experience 'how good he is, how just,' for they have been blasted by the force of angry Heaven's flame, even as Charles has been. But I do not mean to turn the passage into sarcasm. The third quality which the speaker couples with goodness and justice is fitness 'for highest trust', and the goodness and justice of Cromwell culminate in this fitness. But the recommendation to trust has reference not to the Irish, but to the English state. The Irish are quite proper authorities on Cromwell's trustworthiness in this regard, for they have come to know him as the completely dedicated instrument of that state whose devotion to the purpose in hand is unrelenting and unswerving.

To say all this is not to suggest that Marvell shed any unnecessary tears over the plight of the Irish, or even to imply that he was not happy, as one assumes most Englishmen were, to have the Irish rebellion crushed promptly and efficiently. It is to say that the passage fits into the poem – a poem which reveals itself to be no panegyric on Cromwell but an unflinching analysis of the Cromwellian character.

The wild Irish have been tamed, and now the Pict will no longer be able to shelter under his particolored mind. It is the hour of decision, and the particolored mind affords no protection against the man who 'does both act and know'. In Cromwell's mind there are no conflicts, no teasing mixture of judgements. Cromwell's is not only an 'industrious valour', but a 'sad valour'. Margoliouth glosses 'sad' as 'steadfast', and no doubt he is right. But sad can mean 'sober' also, and I suspect that in this context, with its implied references to Scottish plaids, it means also drab of hue. It is also possible that the poet here glances at one of Virgil's transferred epithets, *maestum timorem*, sad fear, the fear that made the Trojans sad. Cromwell's valor is *sad* in that the Scots will have occasion to rue it.

Thus far the speaker has been content to view Cromwell from a distance, as it were, against the background of recent history. He has referred to him consistently in the third person. But in the last two stanzas, he addresses Cromwell directly. He salutes him as 'the wars' and Fortune's son'. It is a great compliment: Cromwell is the son of the wars in that he is the master of battle, and he seems fortune's own son in the success that has constantly waited upon him. But we do not wrench the lines if we take them to say also that Cromwell is the creature of the wars and the product of fortune. The imagery of the early stanzas which treats Cromwell as a natural phenomenon certainly lends support to this reading. Cromwell can claim no sanction for his power in 'ancient rights'. His power has come out of the wars and the troubled times. I call attention to the fact that we do not have to choose between readings: the readings do not mutually exclude each other: they support each other, and this double interpretation has the whole poem behind it.

Cromwell is urged to march 'indefatigably on'. The advice is good advice; but it is good advice because any other course of action is positively unthinkable. Indeed, to call it advice at all is perhaps to distort it: though addressed to Cromwell, it partakes of quiet commentary as much as of exhortation. After all, it is restless Cromwell who is being addressed. If he could not cease 'in the inglorious arts of peace' when his 'highest plot' was 'to plant the bergamot', one cannot conceive of his ceasing now in the hour of danger.

> And for the last effect
> Still keep thy sword erect.

(115–16)

Once more the advice (or commentary) is seriously intended, but it carries with it as much of warning as it does of approval. Those who take up the sword shall perish by the sword: those who have achieved their power on contravention of ancient rights by the sword can only expect to maintain their power by the sword.

What kind of sword is it that is able to 'fright the spirits of the shady night'? Margoliouth writes: 'The cross hilt of the sword would avert the spirits. . . .' But the speaker makes it quite plain that it is not merely the spirits of the shady night that Cromwell will have to fight as he marches indefatigably on. It will not be enough to hold the sword aloft as a ritual sword, an emblematic sword. The naked steel will still have to be used against bodies less diaphanous than spirits. If there is any doubt as to this last point, Marvell's concluding lines put it as powerfully and explicitly as it can be put:

> The same arts that did gain
> A power must it maintain.
>
> (119–20)

But, I can imagine someone asking, What is the final attitude toward Cromwell? Is it ultimately one of approval or disapproval? Does admiration overbalance condemnation? Or, is the *Ode*, after all, merely a varied Scottish plaid, the reflection of Marvell's own parti-colored mind – a mind which had not been finally 'made up' with regard to Cromwell? I think that enough has been said to make it plain that there is no easy, pat answer to such questions. There is a unified total attitude, it seems to me; but it is so complex that we may oversimplify and distort its complexity by the way in which we put the question. The request for some kind of summing up is a natural one, and I have no wish to try to evade it. For a really full answer, of course, one must refer the questioner to the poem itself; but one can at least try to suggest some aspects of the total attitude.

I would begin by re-emphasizing the dramatic character of the poem. It is not a statement – an essay on 'Why I cannot support Cromwell' or on 'Why I am now ready to support Cromwell.' It is a poem essentially dramatic in its presentation, which means that it is diagnostic rather than remedial, and eventuates, not in a course of action, but in contemplation. Perhaps the best way therefore in which to approach it is to conceive of it as, say, one conceives of a Shakespearean tragedy. Cromwell is the usurper who demands and commands admiration. What, for example, is our attitude toward Macbeth? We assume his guilt, but there are qualities which emerge from his guilt which properly excite admiration. I do not mean that the qualities palliate his guilt or that they compensate for his guilt.

They actually come into being through his guilt, but they force us
to exalt him even as we condemn him. I have chosen an extreme
example. I certainly do not mean to imply that in writing the *Ode*
Marvell had Shakespeare's tragedy in mind. What I am trying to
point to is this: that the kind of honesty and insight and whole-
mindedness which we associate with tragedy is to be found to some
degree in all great poetry and is to be found in this poem.

R.P. Warren once remarked to me that Marvell has constantly
behind him in his poetry the achievement of Elizabethan drama with
its treatment of the human will as seen in the perspective of history.
He had in mind some of the lyrics, but the remark certainly applies
fully to the *Ode*. The poet is thoroughly conscious of the drama,
and consciously makes use of dramatic perspective. Charles, as we
have seen, becomes the 'Royal Actor', playing his part on the 'tragic
scaffold'. But the tragedy of Charles is merely glanced at. The poem
is Cromwell's – Cromwell's tragedy, the first three acts of it, as it
were, which is not a tragedy of failure but of success.

Cromwell is the truly kingly man who is *not* king – whose very virtues conduce to kingly power and almost force kingly power upon
him. It is not any fumbling on the poet's part which causes him to call
Cromwell 'a Caesar' before the poem ends, even though he has earlier
appropriated that name to Charles. *Both* men are Caesar, Charles the
wearer of the purple, and Cromwell, the invincible general, the in-
veterate campaigner, the man 'that does both act and know'. Cromwell is the Caesar who must refuse the crown – whose glory it is that
he is willing to refuse the crown – but who cannot enjoy the reward
and the security that a crown affords. The tension between the speaker's admiration for the kingliness which has won Cromwell the power
and his awareness that the power can be maintained only by a continual exertion of these talents for kingship – this tension is never relaxed. Cromwell is not of royal blood – he boasts a higher and a baser
pedigree: he is the 'wars' and Fortune's son'. He cannot rest because
he is restless Cromwell. He must march indefatigably on, for he cannot afford to become fatigued. These implications enrich and qualify
an insight into Cromwell which is as heavily freighted with admiration as it is with a great condemnation. But the admiration and the
condemnation do not cancel each other. They define each other; and
because there is responsible definition, they reinforce each other.

Was this, then, the attitude of Andrew Marvell, born 1621, some-time student at Cambridge, returned traveler and prospective tutor, toward Oliver Cromwell in the summer of 1650? The honest answer must be: I do not know. I have tried to read the poem, the *Horatian Ode*, not Andrew Marvell's mind. That seems sensible to me in view of the fact that we have the poem, whereas the attitude held by Marvell at any particular time must be a matter of inference – even though I grant that the poem may be put in as part of the evidence from which we draw inferences. True, we do know that Marvell was capable of composing the *Ode* and I must concede that that fact may tell us a great deal about Marvell's attitude toward Cromwell. I think it probably does. I am not sure, for reasons given earlier in this paper, that it tells us everything: there is the problem of the role of the un-conscious in the process of composition, there is the possibility of the poet's having written better than he knew, there is even the matter of the happy accident. I do not mean to overemphasize these matters. I do think, however, that it is wise to maintain the distinction between what total attitude is manifested in the poem and the attitude of the author as citizen.

Yet, though I wish to maintain this distinction, I do not mean to hide behind it. The total attitude realized in the *Ode* does not seem to me monstrously inhuman in its complexity. It could be held by human beings, in my opinion. Something very like it apparently was. Listen, for example, to the Earl of Clarendon's judgement on Cromwell:

He was one of those men, quos vitupare ne inimici quidem possunt, nisi ut simul laudent [whom not even their enemies can inveigh against without at the same time praising them], for he could never have done half that mischief, without great parts of courage and industry and judgement, and he must have had a wonderful understanding in the nature and humours of men, and as great a dexterity in the applying them, who from a private and obscure birth (though of a good family), without interest of estate, alliance or friendships, could raise himself to such a height, and compound and knead such opposite and contradictory humours and interests, into a consistence, that contributed to his designs and to their own destruction, whilst himself grew insensibly powerful enough, to cut off those by whom he had climbed, in the instant, that they projected to demolish their own building. . . .

He was not a man of blood, and totally declined Machiavell's method . . . it was more than once proposed, that there might be a general massacre of all the royal party, as the only expedient to secure the government, but Cromwell would never consent to it, it may be out of too much contempt of his enemies; In a word, as he had all the wickednesses against which damnation is denounced and for which Hell fire is prepared, so he had some virtues, which have caused the memory of some men in all ages to be celebrated, and he will be looked upon by posterity, as a brave, bad man.

The resemblance between Clarendon's judgement and that reflected in the *Ode* is at some points so remarkable that one wonders whether Clarendon had not seen and been impressed by some now lost manuscript of the *Ode*: 'Who from a private and obscure birth' – 'Who, from his private gardens, where|He lived reserved and austere' – 'could raise himself to such a height . . . by whom he had climbed' – 'Could by industrious valour climb', and so on and so forth. But I do not want to press the suggestion of influence of Marvell on Clarendon. Indeed, it makes for my general point to discount the possibility. For what I am anxious to emphasize is that the attitude of the *Ode* is not inhuman in its Olympian detachment, that something like it could be held by a human being, and by a human being of pronounced Royalist sympathies.

I have argued that the critic needs the help of the historian – all the help that he can get – but I have insisted that the poem has to be read as a poem – that what it 'says' is a question for the critic to answer, and that no amount of historical evidence as such can finally determine what the poem says. But if we do read the poem successfully, the critic may on occasion be able to make a return on his debt to the historian. If we have read the *Ode* successfully – *if*, I say, for I am far from confident – it may be easier for us to understand how the man capable of writing the *Ode* was also able to write *Tom May's Death* and *On Appleton House* and indeed, years later, after the Restoration, the statement: 'Men ought to have trusted God; they ought and might have trusted the King.'

(127-58)

Douglas Bush

'Marvell's *Horatian Ode*', *Sewanee Review*, vol. 60   1952[1]

The *Horatian Ode* is commonly regarded not only as one of Marvell's finest poems but as an embodiment of two usually distinct poetic modes, the classical and the 'metaphysical'. For all its metaphysical texture and originality, it is the nearest approach in English to the form and the *gravitas* of Horace's patriotic odes. There is the further fact that the poem is not a conventional eulogy but a subtle portrait of its subject, warts and all. At a time when Cromwell aroused violently conflicting passions among Englishmen (as indeed he has ever since), Marvell was able to contemplate both him and King Charles with a mixture of warm admiration and cool, analytical detachment. To read the poem as poetry is also to read it as an historical document, for we must ask what Marvell is saying, in and between the lines, about Cromwell

In *English Institute Essays, 1946*, Professor Cleanth Brooks, attacking 'the specific problem of the speaker's attitude toward Cromwell', gives an elaborate and acute analysis of the ode which is intended to illustrate, in contrast to the 'coarse' method of historical criticism, the critic's obligation to interpret the poem as it stands, to bring out all the conscious and unconscious hints and complexities that it contains, and thereby to define Marvell's view of Cromwell from the inside. One might stop to quarrel with such an arbitrary doctrine of criticism, since the critic's obligation is surely to use all helpful evidence of any kind (and Mr Brooks himself, when he wishes, goes outside the poem), but in this case one may be quite willing to suspend disbelief and consider the ode on Mr Brooks's terms. Accepting the judgement of Marvell's editor, Mr Margoliouth, that 'royalist principles and admiration for Cromwell the Great Man exist side by side', Mr Brooks holds that the problem is a subtle one of poetic organization and therefore addresses itself properly to the critic.

But the moment we enter upon Mr Brooks's exegesis we see that, far from making a disinterested inquiry into the evidence provided by the poem, he is forcing the evidence to fit an unspoken assumption

1 Cleanth Brooks's reply, 'A Note on the Limits of "History" and the Limits of "Criticism"', is in *Sewanee Review*, vol. 61, 1953, pp. 129–35. [Ed.]

– namely, that a sensitive, penetrating, and well-balanced mind like Marvell could not really have admired a crude, single-minded, and ruthless man of action like Cromwell. This is a prejudice natural enough in a good modern liberal, who is bound to see Cromwell, even the Cromwell of 1650, as a sort of Puritan Stalin, but it is a prejudice; and it leads, as I have said, to frequent straining or distortion of what Marvell says and to the supplying of things he does not say. Indeed, if people in 1681 would have read the poem with Mr Brooks's eyes, as in the main a condemnation of Cromwell, there would not have been much reason for the poem's being cut out of the first edition of Marvell, since such a view of Cromwell would have been welcome enough to the Restoration. But that is irrelevant historical speculation, and we must look at the poem.

Mr Brooks's special pleading begins with his gloss on the first lines:

The forward youth that would appear
Must now forsake his Muses dear,
   Nor in the shadows sing
   His numbers languishing.
'Tis time to leave the books in dust,
And oil th' unused armour's rust:
   Removing from the wall
   The corslet of the hall.

To the unprejudiced reader, the lines say that, in these troubled times, the young man of spirit must leave bookish and poetical pursuits for military action. Says Mr Brooks: '"Forward" may mean no more than "high-spirited", "ardent", "properly ambitious"; but the New English Dictionary sanctions the possibility that there lurks in the word the sense of "presumptuous", "pushing",' and 'It is the "forward" youth whose attention the speaker directs to the example of Cromwell.' Thus the critic has already made up his mind about the poet's view of Cromwell, and, instead of taking 'forward' in its common and natural sense, must grasp at a pejorative possibility (the meaning 'presumptuous', to judge from the New English Dictionary, has been commoner in modern times than it was in Marvell's).

After the prelude, Marvell shifts to Cromwell, stressing his tremendous, superhuman energy, with the aid of a violent and elaborate simile:

So restless Cromwell could not cease
In the inglorious arts of peace,
 But through advent'rous war
 Urged his active star.
And, like the three-forked lightning, first
Breaking the clouds where it was nursed,
 Did thorough his own side
 His fiery way divide.
For 'tis all one to courage high
The emulous or enemy;
 And with such to enclose
 Is more than to oppose.
Then burning through the air he went,
And palaces and temples rent:
 And Caesar's head at last
 Did through his laurels blast.

(9-24)

Here, as before, Mr Brooks makes a pejorative choice among 'ambiguous' possibilities. '"Restless" is as ambiguous in its meanings as "forward", and in its darker connotations even more damning.' The critic finds Cromwell's thirst for glory hinted at in many phrases – 'could not cease', 'the inglorious arts of peace', in the fact that, instead of being led by his star, Cromwell 'Urged' his. Mr Brooks may, theoretically, or ultimately, be correct, but has Marvell, so far, given warrant for these 'darker connotations'? At any rate Mr Brooks is consistent in always loading the dice against Cromwell.

The simile, says Mr Brooks, makes Cromwell 'like an elemental force – with as little will as the lightning bolt, and with as little conscience.' Cromwell manifestly is likened to an elemental force, but, again, has Marvell given any warrant for the interpretative phrases, or are they a prejudiced addition? Does a lightning bolt have 'courage high'? But comment on the full meaning of the simile must wait for a moment. The nature of Mr Brooks's special pleading becomes conspicuous in his treatment of the next two lines, which are, for his problem, perhaps the most significant lines in the whole poem:

'Tis madness to resist or blame
The force of angry Heaven's flame.

                    (25–6)

Mr Brooks writes:

> Does the poet mean to imply that Charles has angered heaven – that
> he has merited his destruction? There is no suggestion that
> Cromwell is a thunderbolt hurled by an angry Jehovah – or even
> by an angry Jove. The general emphasis on Cromwell as an
> elemental force is thoroughly relevant here to counter this possible
> misreading. Certainly, in the lines that follow there is nothing to
> suggest that Charles has angered heaven, or that the Justice which
> complains against his fate is anything less than justice.

I do not know what to make of such a statement as 'There is no suggestion that Cromwell is a thunderbolt hurled by an angry Jehovah –
or even by an angry Jove,' since that is what Marvell unmistakably
says. In keeping with the pagan tone of a Horatian ode, of course, he
nowhere permits a Christian allusion, but the poem is not a period
piece of artificial classicism and the reader makes an obvious transfer
from pagan Rome to Christian England. Even if Cromwell be conceived only as a traditional 'Scourge of God', he is the agent of the
Providence whose will, in the common view of history, has worked in
human affairs. Mr Brooks seems to be merely rejecting evidence that
is signally inconvenient for his reading of the poem.

Since, as we observed, Mr Brooks himself, in spite of his premise,
goes outside the poem for desired data, one may venture to do likewise – although the poem itself is sufficiently clear and emphatic in
presenting Cromwell as the agent of angry heaven. We need not assume that Marvell's view of men and events remained quite unaltered
up to the time, between four and five years later, when he wrote so
wholly eulogistic a poem as *The First Anniversary of the Government
under O.C.*, but it is altogether unlikely either that he had made a
volte-face or that he had become a mere time-server. We might take
a few bits from the later poem as glosses on 'angry Heaven's flame'
which – however inferior the poetry – are not less reliable than a
modern critic's inferences:

> While indefatigable Cromwell hies,
> And cuts his way still nearer to the skies,
> Learning a music in the region clear,
> To tune this lower to that higher sphere.
> $(45-8)$

> Hence oft I think, if in some happy hour
> High grace should meet in one with highest power,
> And then a seasonable people still
> Should bend to his, as he to Heaven's will,
> What we might hope, what wonderful effect
> From such a wished conjuncture might reflect.
> $(131-6)$

> What since he did, an higher force him pushed
> Still from behind, and it before him rushed,
> Though undiscerned among the tumult blind,
> Who think those high degrees by man designed.
> 'Twas Heav'n would not that his power should cease,
> But walk still middle betwixt war and peace;
> Choosing each stone, and poising every weight,
> Trying the measures of the breadth and height;
> Here pulling down, and there erecting new,
> Founding a firm state by proportions true.
> $(239-48)$

And, especially for the sake of one phrase, we might add a couplet from the opening of Marvell's *Poem upon the Death of O.C.*:

> And he whom Nature all for peace had made,
> But angry Heaven unto war had swayed. . . .
> $(15-16)$

In these later poems Cromwell is unquestionably the instrument of God, and if in the earlier one the lines about 'angry Heaven's flame' do not say the same thing, one does not know what they do say. The modern liberal – who normally reacts against Toynbee and Butterfield – can seldom fully understand the providential conception of history which was traditional in Marvell's age (witness Raleigh's *History of*

the World) and which was indeed a necessary part of Christian belief;
and Marvell, however liberal and emancipated from common prejudices, was a Christian. All this is not to say that he takes, here or
elsewhere, a simple, one-sided view of either Cromwell or Charles,
but one must emphasize the central importance of Cromwell's being
a divine agent and hence endowed with the power of a force of nature.

In the next few lines Cromwell is associated with peaceful rural
nature:

> And, if we would speak true,
> Much to the man is due.
> Who, from his private gardens, where
> He lived reserved and austere,
>   As if his highest plot
>   To plant the bergamot. . . .

> (27-32)

The first two lines are something more than a transition. 'Much to
the man is due', in focusing on the actual person in himself, helps to
define the previous conception of the being who was an instrument of
Providence. The next quatrain is clearly intended to link Cromwell
the man with the simple, frugal heroes of Roman tradition, like Cin-
cinnatus, called from the plough to rule the state. In what they say,
and in the affinity they imply, the lines are a quiet refutation of some
of Mr Brooks's darker inferences.

Then we come to a passage where the warts may seem to protrude.
The man who lived as if only to plant the bergamot

> Could by industrious valour climb
> To ruin the great work of time,
>   And cast the kingdom old
>   Into another mould.
> Though Justice against Fate complain,
> And plead the ancient rights in vain:
>   But those do hold or break
>   As men are strong or weak.
> Nature that hateth emptiness
> Allows of penetration less:

And therefore must make room
Where greater spirits come.
What field of all the Civil Wars
Where his were not the deepest scars? . . .

(33–46)

Mr Brooks thinks that 'climb' 'certainly connotes a kind of aggressiveness' and a thirst for glory, and that, in the lines on 'Nature',
'The question of right, the imagery insists, is beside the point,' since
the question of power alone is being weighed. He admits that Marvell
recognizes Cromwell's martial valor, even a dedicated rather than a
merely selfish sense of glory, and the role of a man of destiny; and he
points out, following Margoliouth and Firth, that there is no ground
for the contemporary charge, which Marvell repeats, that Cromwell
had engineered Charles's flight to Carisbrooke Castle. But the critic
maintains nevertheless that Cromwell has 'thus far . . . been treated
as naked force'; he has been praised for 'the tremendous disciplined
powers' he has brought to bear against the king. However, Mr
Brooks proceeds,

For the end served by those powers, the speaker has no praise at
all. Rather he has gone out of his way to insist that Cromwell was
deaf to the complaint of justice and its pleading of the 'ancient
rights'. The power achieved by Cromwell is a 'forced power' – a
usurped power. On this point the speaker is unequivocal. I must
question therefore Margoliouth's statement that Marvell sees in
Cromwell 'the man of destiny moved by . . . a power that is above
'ustice.' Above justice, yes, in the sense that power is power and
justice is not power. The one does not insure the presence of the
other. Charles has no way to vindicate his 'helpless right', but it is
no less right because it is helpless. But the speaker, though he is not
a cynic, is a realist. A kingdom cannot be held by mere pleading of
the 'ancient rights':

But those do hold or break
As men are strong or weak.

(39–40)

In short the more closely we look at the *Ode*, the more clearly
apparent it becomes that the speaker has chosen to emphasize

Cromwell's virtues as a man, and likewise, those of Charles as a man. The poem does not debate which of the two was right, for that issue is not even in question.

This may be the right, or a tenable view of the central passage we have arrived at, and of the whole poem, yet it seems open to query. In the first place, if the issue of 'right' is not even in question, how can anyone be concerned, as Mr Brooks is all along, with distinguishing right from power, with sifting moral praise and blame, and, in short, making the strongest possible case for the prosecution? In the second place, although elsewhere he is on the watch for sinister ambiguities, even in words that appear innocent, here words of at least equal ambiguity have become moral absolutes that condemn Cromwell. The word 'right' ('the ancient rights', 'his helpless right') may mean not only abstract rightness but traditional claims which may or may not be wholly right. 'Justice' may be absolute justice, or it may be the limited vision of human law that must give way before the divine will ('Fate', in Roman terms). The 'great work of time' that Cromwell has ruined is not necessarily or wholly the good work of time; a great nation may have nourished wrongs that must, at whatever cost, be righted. Marvell was assuredly not of 'Machiavellian' outlook, but in his view of Cromwell he may – with some important differences – have somewhat resembled Machiavelli: while Machiavelli's ideal was the old Roman republic, a republic could not bring order out of chaos, and the strong man who could must be welcomed. Though Marvell does not go into the causes of the civil war but concentrates on Cromwell and his royal opponent, he indicates that he sees 'the kingdom old' as undergoing the pangs of both death and rebirth, and, with all his admiration for the royal actor, he bows to the man of action who can, however violently, establish order. And, as we have seen, he bows not only to the heroic individual but to the Providence who has raised him up.

After the account of Charles's execution – which for too many readers disturbs the center of gravity of the poem – the poet turns, as Mr Brooks says, from Cromwell the destroyer of the monarchy to 'the agent of the new state that has been erected upon the dead body of the King.' The execution was 'that memorable hour Which first assured the forced power.' But while Cromwell has been an

illegal regicide, the effect of 'forced power' is partly countered by
what follows, the incident from Roman history in which 'the state
Foresaw its happy fate'. If the execution was evil, it can bring forth
good. As Mr Brooks sees it, Marvell 'does not commit himself to the
opinion that the bleeding head is a happy augury', but makes this the
popular opinion. I doubt if Marvell – whatever he privately felt – is
here consciously disassociating himself from 'the state'. If he were,
would he go so far elsewhere in the poem in celebrating Cromwell
with his own voice?

There follows at once a passage that is probably more embarrassing
than any other part of the ode to anyone intent upon proving that
Marvell's main attitude toward Cromwell is hostility or at most unwilling respect for unscrupulous strength and courage:

And now the Irish are ashamed
To see themselves in one year tamed:
  So much one man can do,
  That does both act and know.
They can affirm his praises best,
And have, though overcome, confessed
  How good he is, how Just,
  And fit for highest trust.

(73–80)

Mr Margoliouth remarks that 'Irish testimony in favour of Cromwell
at this moment is highly improbable' (though he sees a possible
reference to the voluntary submission of part of Munster), and we
may, with Mr Brooks, take the remark as an understatement. For Mr
Brooks the appeal 'is not to what Marvell the Englishman must have
thought, or even to what Marvell the author must have intended, but
rather to the full context of the poem itself'. One may not quite
understand these several possibilities, since the poem did not get itself
written by some agency outside of Marvell. However, Mr Brooks is
driven to what may be thought the desperate solution of finding the
lines ironical, a view he thinks sanctioned by the earlier stanzas
because the Irish have learned of the qualities in Cromwell that Marvell had praised, energy, activity, and the like. 'The Irish, indeed, are
best able to affirm such praise as has been accorded to Cromwell; and

they know from experience "how good he is, how just", for they have been blasted by the force of angry Heaven's flame, even as Charles has been.'

Since I cannot follow much of Mr Brooks's reading of the earlier stanzas, I cannot follow such an explanation. Nothing in the wording seems to me to carry the faintest trace of irony; it is as straightforward a statement as we could have, however little we like it. Nor do I see how irony could pass at once into what Mr Brooks accepts as eulogy without the slightest hint of a change of tone. Although, as he says, the recommendation of trust has reference to the English state, it is the Irish who have 'confessed' it, and I see nothing in the text to support Mr Brooks's oblique interpretation of Marvell's account of Irish feelings: 'The Irish are quite proper authorities on Cromwell's trustworthiness in this regard, for they have come to know him as the completely dedicated instrument of that state whose devotion to the purpose in hand is unrelenting and unswerving.' But, instead of twisting Marvell's plain words into irony, and thereby molding him into the likeness of a modern liberal, we really must accept the unpalatable fact that he wrote as an Englishman of 1650; and, in regard to what seems to us a strange assertion, we must say that he is indulging in some wishful thinking – Cromwell is so great a conqueror that even the Irish must share English sentiment and accept the course of history. In the poem on Cromwell's death, it may be added, Marvell glanced at his Irish campaign with nothing but admiration for his religious zeal and martial prowess (lines 179 ff.). It may be added further that Milton was far closer to Marvell than any modern reader can be (and Milton was bold enough, a few years later when Cromwell was at the height of his power, to rebuke him for turning a republic into a dictatorship), and we have only to look at Milton's *Observations on the Articles of Peace*, 1649, to see what the English attitude was. That is not to say that Marvell thought just as Milton thought; it is to say that the text of Marvell's poem means what it says, and that the suggestion of irony raises a much more difficult problem, within the poem, than the one it seeks to explain.

Early in his essay Mr Brooks observed that 'the critic obviously must know what the words of the poem mean, something which immediately puts him in debt to the linguist', but he neglects this sound precept in his comment on the next lines:

Nor yet grown stiffer with command,
But still in the Republic's hand.

(81–2)

Says Mr Brooks:.

Does the emphasis on 'still' mean that the speaker is surprised that
Cromwell has continued to pay homage to the republic? Does he
imply that Cromwell may not always do so? Perhaps not: the emphasis is upon the fact that he need not obey and yet does. Yet the
compliment derives its full force from the fact that the homage is
not forced but voluntary and even somewhat unexpected. And a
recognition of this point implies the recognition of the possibility
that Cromwell will not always so defer to the commonwealth.

But such 'darker connotations' are quite gratuitous. 'Still' here – as
later in 'Still keep thy sword erect' – has its normal seventeenth-
century meaning, 'always', and Marvell's words afford no ground for
an ominous hint of a possible change of heart in Cromwell.

We need not concern ourselves with the rest of the ode, in which
Marvell sees Cromwell as the obedient servant of Parliament, the
prospective conqueror of the Scots, and a leader to be feared by
Europe. But we may notice the last lines, where Mr Brooks again
finds sinister implications:

But thou the wars' and Fortune's son
March indefatigably on;
    And for the last effect
    Still keep thy sword erect:
Besides the force it has to fright
The spirits of the shady night,
    The same arts that did gain
    A power must it maintain.

(113–20)

The salutation in the first line means, as Mr Brooks says, that 'Cromwell is the son of the wars in that he is the master of battle, and he
seems fortune's own son in the success that has constantly waited
upon him.' But he goes on to say that 'we do not wrench the lines
if we take them to say also that Cromwell is the creature of the wars
and the product of fortune.' I think this is a very decided wrenching

of the lines; we must remember that Marvell has seen Cromwell as the agent of heaven. And there is some further wrenching in Mr Brooks's comment on 'Still keep thy sword erect': 'Those who take up the sword shall perish by the sword: those who have achieved their power on contravention of ancient rights by the sword can only expect to maintain their power by the sword.' Does Marvell give any hint toward such an interpretation?

Mr Brooks always offers general and particular insights that sharpen our perceptions, and this essay, like his others, is precise and provocative. His readers, if they came to it with the notion that Marvell's ode is a simple poem, could never again be misled in that way. But they could be misled into finding a greater degree of complexity than the text warrants. There is surely a line between legitimate and illegitimate ambiguity, a line to be respected by both poet and critic, and Mr Brooks seems continually to overstep that line. He sees the poem as expressing a 'unified total attitude', though a very complex one, yet it would be hard to merge his findings into any total unity unless Marvell is more or less lifted out of his age into ours. As we have seen, the result, if not the aim, of Mr Brooks's inquiry is, in large measure, to turn a seventeenth-century liberal into a modern one. That is one reason why historical conditioning has a corrective as well as a positive value, although in this case we do not need to go outside the poem to recognize fallacies and distortions in what purports to be a purely critical and unprejudiced analysis.

(363-76)

To his Coy Mistress

John Crowe Ransom

from *The New Criticism* 1941

Returning to rhymed verse, there is this passage from a poem which deserves its great fame, but whose fabulous 'perfections' consist with indeterminacies that would be condemned in the prose of scientists, and also of college freshmen; though I think in the prose of college seniors they might have a different consideration:

Had we but world enough, and time,
This coyness, lady, were no crime.
We would sit down, and think which way
To walk, and pass our long love's day.
Thou by the Indian Ganges' side
Should'st rubies find: I by the tide
Of Humber would complain. I would
Love you ten years before the flood:
And you should, if you please, refuse
Till the conversion of the Jews.
My vegetable love should grow
Vaster than empires and more slow.

I will use the pedagogical red pencil, though I am loath. World, as distinguished from time, is not space, for the lovers already have all the space in the world, and long tenure would not increase it. It is a violent condensation meaning, I think, 'the whole history of the world before us', and combining with the supposal of their having the time to live through it; it supports the historical references which follow. *We would, thou should'st, my love should*: the use of the auxiliaries is precise, varying according to rule from person to person, and uniformly denoting determination or command; 'we would arrange it so.' But it is remarkable that in so firm a set of locutions, which attests the poet's logical delicacy, the *thou should'st* is interchangeable with *you should*; the meter is responsible for the latter version, since otherwise we should have the line, *And thou should'st, if thou pleased'st, refuse*, or, taking the same liberty with tenses which we find actually taken (again for metrical reasons), *And thou should'st, if thou pleas'st, refuse*; but either line clogs the meter. *Which way* is one phrase, but language is an ambiguous thing, and it has two meanings: *in which direction* as applied to *walk*, and *in what manner* as applied to *pass our day*. The parallel series in lines 5–7 is in three respects not uniform: *Ganges* has little need of a defining adjective, except the metrical one, but when once it has become *Indian Ganges* there is every right on the part of its analogue to be styled *English Humber*; and *Ganges' side* calls for *Humber's side*, or for merely *Humber's*, with *side* understood but rhyme produces for Humber a *tide*; and the possessive case in the first member would call for the same in the second member, but is replaced there actually by an *of*-phrase. *Refuse* brings out of the rhyming dictionary the *Jews*, which it will tax the poet's invention to supply with a context; but for our present purposes the poet has too much invention, for it gives him the historical period from the Flood to the conversion of the Jews, which is a useless way of saying ten thousand years, or some other length of time, and which seems disproportionate to the mere ten years of the same context, the only other period mentioned. *Vegetable* is a grotesque qualification of love, and on the whole decidedly more unsuitable than suitable, though there are features in which it is suitable. *Vaster* would correlate with *slower*, not with *more slow*, but they would not be correlatives at all after *grow*, for *vaster* is its factitive complement and *slower* can only be for *more slowly*, its adverb. Finally, there is the question of how the vastness of the poet's love can resemble the vastness of empires; the elegance of the terms seems to go along with the logic of a child.

(311–13)

J. V. Cunningham

from *Tradition and Poetic Structure* 1960 (first printed in *Modern Philology*, vol. 51, 1953, pp. 33–41)

May the principal structure of a poem be of a logical rather than an alogical sort? For example, to confine ourselves to the Old Logic, may a lyric be solely or predominantly the exposition of a syllogism? and may the propositions of the lyric, one by one, be of the sort to be found in a logical syllogism?

The incautious romantic will deny the possibility, and with a repugnance of feeling that would preclude any further discussion. For logic and lyric are generally regarded as opposites, if not as contradictory terms. 'It is a commonplace,' says a recent writer on logic, 'that poetry and logic have nothing to do with each other, that they are even opposed to one another.'[1] You will find this explicitly stated, sometimes with the substitution of 'science' for 'logic', in most of the school handbooks on the study of literature, in most of the introductions to poetry. 'The peculiar quality of poetry,' we read in one of these:

can be distinguished from that of prose if one thinks of the creative mind as normally expressing itself in a variety of literary forms ranged along a graduated scale between the two contrasted extremes of scientific exposition and lyrical verse.

And, a little later:

[Poetry] strives for a conviction begotten of the emotions rather than of reason.

Consequently, we are told:

The approach of poetry is indirect. It proceeds by means of suggestion, implication, reflection. Its method is largely symbolical. It is more interested in connotations than in denotations.[2]

This is common doctrine. Poetry is in some way concerned with emotion rather than reason, and its method is imaginative, indirect, implicit rather than explicit, symbolical rather than discursive, concerned with what its terms suggest rather than with what they state. The kind of poetry which most fully possesses and exhibits these concerns, methods, and qualities is generally thought to be the lyric, and hence it, of all poetry, is regarded as the most antithetical to reason, logic and science.

This was not always the case. In the eighth century, for example, a scholiast of the school of Alcuin regarded not only grammar and rhetoric but dialectic or logic also as the disciplines that nourish and

1 Richard von Mises, *Positivism*, Cambridge, Mass, 1951, p. 289.
2 Harold R. Walley and J. Harold Wilson, *The Anatomy of Literature*, New York, 1934, pp. 143 and 144.

form a poet. In the medieval and renaissance traditions of commentary on Aristotle's logic, poetic is sometimes regarded as a part, a sub-division, of logic – as, indeed, I consider it myself. So late as the eighteenth century David Hume writes in an essay *Of the Standard of Taste*:

Besides, every kind of composition, even the most poetical, is nothing but a chain of propositions and reasonings; not always indeed the justest and most exact, but still plausible and specious, however disguised by the colouring of the imagination.

And even today the writer whom I quoted earlier asserts, in denial of the commonplace: 'Every poem, except in rare extreme cases, contains judgements and implicit propositions, and thus becomes subject to logical analysis.'[1]

But may the chain of propositions and reasonings be not merely plausible and specious but even sufficiently just and exact? May the poem be not merely subject to logical analysis but logical in form? May, in return to our point, the subject and structure of a poem be conceived and expressed syllogistically? Anyone at all acquainted with modern criticism and the poems that are currently in fashion will think in this connexion of Marvell's *To his Coy Mistress*. The apparent structure of that poem is an argumentative syllogism, explicitly stated. 'Had we but world enough and time,' the poet says,

This coyness, lady, were no crime ...

But at my back I always hear
Time's winged chariot hurrying near ...

Now, therefore ...
... let us sport us while we may ...

If we had all the time and space in the world we could delay consummation. But we do not. Therefore. The structure is formal. The poet offers to the lady a practical syllogism, and if she assents to it the

1 Scholiast cited in Otto Bird, 'The Seven Liberal Arts', in Joseph T. Shipley (ed.), *Dictionary of World Literature*, New York, 1943, p. 55; J. E. Spingarn, *A History of Literary Criticism in the Renaissance*, 2nd edn, New York, 1908, pp. 24–7; David Hume, *Philosophical Works*, Boston and Edinburgh, 1854, vol. 3, p. 264; von Mises, loc. cit.

appropriate consequence, he hopes, will follow: [quotes *To his Coy Mistress*].

The logical nature of the argument here has been generally recognized, though often with a certain timidity. Mr Eliot hazards: 'the three strophes of Marvell's poem have something like a syllo-gistic relation to each other.' And in a recent scholarly work we read: 'The dialectic of the poem lies not only or chiefly in the formal demonstration explicit in its three stanzas, but in all the contrasts evoked by its images and in the play between the immediately sensed and the intellectually apprehended.'[1] That is, the logic is recognized, but minimized, and our attention is quickly distracted to something more reputable in a poem, the images or the characteristic tension of metaphysical poetry. For Mr Eliot the more important element in this case is a principle of order common in modern poetry and often employed in his own poems. He points out that the theme of Marvell's poem is 'one of the great traditional commonplaces of European literature . . . the theme of . . . *Gather ye rosebuds*, of *Go, lovely rose.*' 'Where the wit of Marvell,' he continues, 'renews the theme is in the variety and order of the images.' The dominant principle of order in the poem, then, is an implicit one rather than the explicit principle of the syllogism, and implicit in the succession of images.

Mr Eliot explains the implicit principle of order in this fashion:

In the first of the three paragraphs Marvell plays with a fancy that begins by pleasing and leads to astonishment. . . . We notice the high speed, the succession of concentrated images, each magnifying the original fancy. When this process has been carried to the end and summed up, the poem turns suddenly with that surprise which has been one of the most important means of poetic effect since Homer:

But at my back I always hear
Time's winged chariot hurrying near:
And yonder all before us lie
Deserts of vast eternity.

A whole civilization resides in these lines:

1 T. S. Eliot, *Selected Essays*, new edn, New York, 1950, p. 254; Helen C. White, Ruth C. Wallerstein and Ricardo Quintana (eds.), *Seventeenth Century Verse and Prose*, New York, 1951, vol. I, p. 454.

Pallida Mors aequo pulsat pede pauperum tabernas
Regumque turres . . .

A modern poet, had he reached the height, would very likely have
closed on this moral reflection.

What is meant by this last observation becomes clear a little later
where it is said that the wit of the poem 'forms the crescendo and
diminuendo of a scale of great imaginative power'. The structure of
the poem, then, is this: it consists of a succession of images increasing
in imaginative power to the sudden turn and surprise of the image of
time, and then decreasing to the conclusion. But is there any sudden
turn and surprise in the image of time? and does the poem consist of
a succession of images?

   This talk of images is a little odd since there seem to be relatively
few in the poem if one means by image what people usually do – a
descriptive phrase that invites the reader to project a sensory construction. The looming imminence of Time's winged chariot is, no
doubt, an image, though not a full-blown one since there is nothing
in the phrasing that properly invites any elaboration of sensory detail.
But when Mr Eliot refers to 'successive images' and cites 'my
vegetable love', with vegetable italicized, and 'Till the conversion of
the Jews', one suspects that he is provoking images where they do not
textually exist. There is about as much of an image in 'Till the conversion of the Jews' as there would be in 'till the cows come home',
and it would be a psychiatrically sensitive reader who would immediately visualize the lowing herd winding slowly o'er the lea. But
'my vegetable love' will make the point. I have no doubt that Mr
Eliot and subsequent readers do find an image here. They envisage
some monstrous and expanding cabbage, but they do so in mere
ignorance. Vegetable is no vegetable but an abstract and philosophical
term, known as such to every educated man of Marvell's day. Its
context is the doctrine of the three souls: the rational, which in man
subsumes the other two; the sensitive, which men and animals have
in common and which is the principle of motion and perception; and,
finally, the lowest of the three, the vegetable soul, which is the only
one that plants possess, and which is the principle of generation and
corruption, of augmentation and decay. Marvell says, then, my love,
denied the exercise of sense, but possessing the power of augmenta-

tion, will increase 'Vaster than empires'. It is an intellectual image, and hence no image at all but a conceit. For if one calls any sort of particularity or detail in a poem an image, the use of the wrong word will invite the reader to misconstrue his experience in terms of images, to invent sensory constructions and to project them on the poem.

A conceit is not an image. It is a piece of wit. It is in the tradition in which Marvell was writing, among other possibilities, the discovery of a proposition referring to one field of experience in terms of an intellectual structure derived from another field, and often enough a field of learning, as is the case in 'my vegetable love'. This tradition, though it goes back to the poetry of John Donne, and years before that, was current in Marvell's day. The fashionable poetry at the time he was writing this poem, the poetry comparable to that of Eliot or of Auden in the past two decades, was the poetry of John Cleveland, and the fashionable manner was generally known as Clevelandizing. It consisted in the invention of a series of witty hyperbolical conceits, sometimes interspersed with images, and containing a certain amount of roughage in the form of conventional erotic statements:

Thy beauty shall no more be found,
Nor in thy marble vault shall sound
My echoing song ...

It was commonly expressed in the octosyllabic couplet. Cleveland, for example, writes *Upon Phillis Walking in a Morning before Sun-rising*:

The trees, like yeomen of the guard,
Serving her more for pomp than ward ...

The comparison here does not invite visualization. It would be inappropriate to summon up the colors and serried ranks of the guard. The comparison is made solely with respect to the idea: the trees like the guard serve more for pomp than ward. Again:

The flowers, called out of their beds,
Start and raise up their drowsy heads,
And he that for their colour seeks
May see it vaulting to her cheeks,
Where roses mix – no civil war
Divides her York, and Lancaster.[1]

1 John M. Berdan (ed.), *The Poems*, New Haven, 1911, pp. 80–81.

One does not here picture in panorama the Wars of the Roses. One sees rather the aptness and the wit of York and Lancaster, the white rose and the red, reconciled in her cheeks, or one rejects it as forced and far-fetched. This is a matter of taste.

But if the poem is not a succession of images, does it exhibit that other principle which Mr Eliot ascribes to it, the turn and surprise which he finds in the abrupt introduction of time's chariot and which forms a sort of fulcrum on which the poem turns. Subsequent critics have certainly felt that it has. In a current textbook we read:

The poem begins as a conventional love poem in which the lover tries to persuade his mistress to give in to his entreaties. But with the introduction of the image of the chariot in line 21, the poet becomes obsessed by the terrible onrush of time, and the love theme becomes scarcely more than an illustration of the effect which time has upon human life.

And the leading scholar in the field, a man who is generally quite unhappy with Mr Eliot's criticism, nevertheless says:

the poet sees the whole world of space and time as the setting for two lovers. But wit cannot sustain the pretence that youth and beauty and love are immortal, and with a quick change of tone – like Catullus' *nobis cum semel occidit brevis lux* or Horace's *sed Timor et Minae* – the theme of time and death is developed with serious and soaring directness . . .[1]

These, I believe are not so much accounts of the poem as accounts of Mr Eliot's reading of the poem. Let us question the fact. Does the idea of time and death come as any surprise in this context? The poem began, 'Had we but world enough and time.' That is, it began with an explicit condition contrary to fact, which by all grammatical rules amounts to the assertion that we do not have world enough and time. There is no surprise whatever when the proposition is explicitly made in line 21. It would rather have been surprising if it had not been made. Indeed, the only question we have in this respect, after we have read the first line, is, how many couplets will the poet expend

1 Wright Thomas and Stuart Gerry Brown (eds.), *Reading Poems*, New York, 1941, p. 702; Douglas Bush, *English Literature in the Earlier Seventeenth Century*, Oxford, 1945, p. 163.

on the ornamental re-iteration of the initial proposition before he comes to the expected *but*. The only turn in the poem is the turn which the structure of the syllogism had led us to await.

Mr Eliot compares the turn and surprise which he finds in this poem to a similar turn in an ode of Horace's, and the scholars seem to corroborate the comparison. This is the fourth ode of the first book:

Solvitur acris hiems grata vice veris et Favoni,
    trahuntque siccas machinae carinas ...

The poem begins with a picture of spring and proceeds by a succession of images, images of the external world and mythological images:

Sharp winter relaxes with the welcome change to Spring and the west wind, and the cables haul the dry keels of ships. The herd no longer takes pleasure in its stalls or the farmer in his fire, and the pastures no longer whiten with hoar frost. Cytherean Venus leads her dancers beneath the overhanging moon, and the beautiful graces and nymphs strike the ground with alternate foot, while blazing Vulcan visits the grim forges of the Cyclops. Now is the time to wind your bright hair with green myrtle or with the flowers that the thawed earth yields. Now is the time to sacrifice to Faunus in the shadowed woods, whether it be a lamb he asks or a kid:

Pallida mors aequo pulsat pede pauperum tabernas
    regumque turres.

Pallid death with indifferent foot strikes the poor man's hut and the palaces of kings. Now, fortunate Sestius, the brief sum of life forbids our opening a long account with hope. Night will soon hem you in, and the fabled ghosts, and Pluto's meagre house.[1]

Death occurs in this poem with that suddenness and lack of preparation with which it sometimes occurs in life. The structure of the poem is an imitation of the structure of such experiences in life. And as we draw from such experiences often a generalization, so

1 My translation, except for 'the brief sum of life forbids our opening a long account with hope', which is in Basil L. Gildersleeve's; see Paul Shorey and Gordon J. Laing, *Odes and Epodes*, rev. edn, Chicago, 1910, ad loc.

Horace from the sudden realization of the abruptness and impartiality of death, reflects

vitae summa brevis spem nos vetat incohare longam.

The brief sum of life forbids our opening a long account with hope.

But the proposition is subsequent to the experience; it does not rule and direct the poem from the outset. And the experience in Horace *is* surprising and furnishes the fulcrum on which the poem turns. It has, in fact, the characteristics which are ascribed to Marvell's poem but which Marvell's poem does not have. The two are two distinct kinds of poetry, located in distinct and almost antithetical traditions; both are valuable and valid methods, but one is not to be construed in terms of the other.

In brief, the general structure of Marvell's poem is syllogistic, and it is located in the Renaissance tradition of formal logic and of rhetoric. The structure exists in its own right and as a kind of expandable filing system. It is a way of disposing of, of making a place for, elements of a different order: in this case, Clevelandizing conceits and erotic propositions in the tradition of Jonson and Herrick. These reiterate the propositions of the syllogism. They do not develop the syllogism, and they are not required by the syllogism; they are free and extra. There could be more or less of them since there is nothing in the structure that determines the number of interpolated couplets. It is a matter of tact, and a matter of the appetite of the writer and the reader.

(40–49)

Barbara Herrnstein Smith

from *Poetic Closure* 1968

We might observe, however, that although the conclusion is indeed appropriate, it is not, strictly speaking, logical. The same is true of one of the most famous of lyrical arguments, Marvell's *To his Coy Mistress*, where it has been observed that the three divisions of the poem correspond exactly to the major and minor premises and conclusion of a formal syllogism.

Had we but world enough and time
This coyness, lady, were no crime . . .

But at my back I always hear
Time's winged chariot hurrying near . . .

Now therefore, . . .
. . . let us sport us while we may . . .

The syllogism, however, is an excellent example of a textbook
fallacy known as 'denying the antecedent': if P, then not Q; not P;
therefore Q. 'It does not follow', the lady might have replied. In
each of these poems [the other being Daniel's *Look, Delia*] a principle
of logical sequence is pursued to a conclusion which, though logically
invalid, is nevertheless experienced by the reader as appropriate and
stable. It might be urged that the feebleness or falseness of the logic
has been obscured by rhetorical luxuriance. I think that it would be
more accurate to say that logical validity has become irrelevant to the
reader's experience – or not relevant in the same way that it would
be to his experience of non-literary logical discourse.

We might recall at this point the observation made in chapter 1,
namely that poems imitate not only the structure but also the circumstances and motives of everyday speech. In each of these poems,
very particular (though conventional) circumstances and motives are
suggested: the speaker's relationship to his presumed audience, the
quality of his feeling for her, and, of course, his desire to persuade her
to yield to him. We may, moreover, think of the circumstances and
motives of an utterance as including not merely the gross features of
the attendant situation or the speaker's most apparent intentions, but
everything that presumably gave his speech its individual form.
Particular details of Marvell's poem for example, reveal the speaker's
acute and unfeigned consciousness of mutability, and a quality of
playful tenderness in his feeling for the lady. These too may be
regarded as motives of his speech. Taken together, all the particular
circumstances and motives thus suggested will create for the reader
the poem's implied context. Returning to the question of the stability
of an illogical conclusion, we may now suggest that such a conclusion
may nevertheless be entirely appropriate to the context of the poem,
indeed *more* appropriate in this sense than a logically respectable

conclusion. The argumentative lover is ostensibly concerned only with the response of his mistress, and she, perhaps, will be suspicious of the persuasive resources of rhetoric. But any other reader will respond to the argument, including its conclusion, with regard not to its ultimate persuasiveness but to its ultimate expressiveness.

(133–5)

René Wellek and Austin Warren

from *Theory of Literature* 1963 (first published 1949)

Stylistics, of course, cannot be pursued successfully without a thorough grounding in general linguistics, since precisely one of its central concerns is the contrast of the language system of a literary work of art with the general usage of the time. Without knowledge of what is common speech, even unliterary speech, and what are the different social languages of a time, stylistics can scarcely transcend impressionism. The assumption that, especially for past periods, we know the distinction between common speech and artistic deviation is, regrettably, quite unfounded. Much closer study must be given to the diversely stratified speech of remote times before we shall possess the proper background for judgement of the diction of an author or of a literary movement.

In practice we simply apply instinctively the standards we derive from our present-day usage. But such standards may be largely misleading. On occasion, in the reading of older poetry, we need to shut out our modern linguistic consciousness. We must forget the modern meaning even in such lines as Tennyson's

    And this is well
To have a dame indoors, who trims us up
And keeps us tight.

But if we admit the necessity of historical reconstruction in such obvious cases, can we stipulate its possibility in all cases? Can we ever learn Anglo-Saxon or Middle English, not to speak of ancient Greek, well enough to forget our own current language? And if we could, are we necessarily better critics by constituting ourselves linguistic contemporaries of the author? Could not the retention of the modern association in verses like Marvell's

My vegetable love should grow
Vaster than empires, and more slow

be defended as an enrichment of its meanings? Louis Teeter comments:

> The grotesque conception of an erotic cabbage outlasting the pyramids and overshadowing them seems the result of studied artistry. We may be sure, however, that Marvell himself had no such precise effect in mind. To the seventeenth century, *vegetable* meant *vegetative*, and the poet probably was using it in the sense of the life-giving principle. He could scarcely have had in mind the truckgarden connotation that it bears today.[1]

One may ask, with Teeter, whether it is desirable to get rid of the modern connotation and whether, at least, in extreme cases, it is possible. We are again at the question of historical 'reconstructionism', its possibility and desirability.

(177-8)

Harold E. Toliver

from *Marvell's Ironic Vision* 1965

In the context of this inversion of customary Marvellian patterns, the vegetable love image is especially resonant, not only because it is an ironic version of dendro-eroticism but also because of the strategic equation within the poem of vegetation and ceremony, which the speaker uses finally to overthrow ceremony for naturalism. Defining 'vegetable love' as an 'abstract philosophical' term rather than a reference to 'erotic cabbages' will not free it entirely of vegetable connotations, I think (even truck garden ones), unless separating the various levels of a phrase will somehow enable us to suppress one or the

1 'Scholarship and the Art of Criticism', *J.E.L.H.*, vol. 5, 1938, p. 183.

other of them. E. D. Hirsch, in discussing a proposal to retain them, suggests that it might:

No doubt, the associated meaning *is* here desirable (since it supports the mood of the poem), but Wellek could not even make his point unless we could distinguish between what 'vegetable' probably means as used in the text, and what it commonly means to us. Simply to discuss the issue is to admit that Marvell's poem probably does not imply the modern connotation, since if we could not separate the sense of 'vegetative' from the notion of an 'erotic cabbage', we could not talk about the difficulty of making the separation.[1]

But distinguishing in this case does not necessarily mean separating, any more than philosophers when distinguishing among rational, sensitive and vegetative souls mean that man can separate one from the other and remain man. (Man shares with the vegetables, Aquinas writes, growth, generation, and need for nutrition.) Anyway, the poetry of Marvell has enough amorous green stuff in it to make the argument largely beside the point: the difference between curious peaches and cabbages is very fine. The irony has purchase against the mistress's ceremonies because she wishes to generate slowly and innocently like the plants. But the speaker, too, conceives of love as growing in the sun and growing faster as the sun runs hotter – and unable to grow in the marble vault or in the vast desert. The worm has the last word with man as with vegetation, and time chews on both with its 'slow-chapped power,' unless they devour it first.

(159–60)

R. S. Crane

from 'Criticism and Literary History', *The Idea of the Humanities* 1967

I want to emphasize especially, however, the other main way of establishing first principles in this criticism. It is essentially a method of dialectical analysis, in which you begin by laying down some gen-

1 'Objective Interpretation,' *P.M.L.A.*, vol. 75, 1960, p. 465.

eral postulate – as, for example, that 'poetry' is the polar opposite of
science – and then proceed to work out logically all the implications
of this; the nature and attributes of poetry, you assume, will be contained exhaustively in the rational scheme of definitions and distinctions you thus arrive at. There are good examples of this 'abstract'
method, as David Hume called it, in John Crowe Ransom's discussions of poetry in relation to science in various parts of *The World's
Body*, in Cleanth Brooks's proof in *The Well Wrought Urn* that the
language of poetry is 'the language of paradox', in Charles Feidelson's
argument in *Symbolism and American Literature* that metaphor in
poetry is something quite distinct from metaphor in prose, and, most
recently in Philip Wheelwright's discussion of 'plurisignation' (or
multiple verbal meaning) as an essential principle of poetry or 'depth
language' in *The Burning Fountain*.

The way the method operates can be seen in Feidelson's treatment
of metaphor. His conclusion is that, whereas metaphor in prose
undoubtedly consists in using words in such a way as to analogize
one thing to another, metaphor in poetry, despite most earlier writers
on the subject, obeys a wholly different principle, which he calls the
principle of creative interaction. In setting forth this doctrine, he
discusses, among other texts, Andrew Marvell's phrase 'the iron
gates of life' in *To his Coy Mistress* ('And tear our pleasures with
rough strife|Thorough the iron gates of life'). The phrase does not,
he insists, 'point out' or 'play on' a 'preexisting similarity between
the logical elements, life and iron gates'. What the phrase really does
is to establish 'the idea of life *under the aspect of* iron gates, and of iron
gates under the aspect of life'. The tenor of the metaphor 'is at once
the special kind of life that we can entertain under the aspect of iron
gates, and the special kind of iron gates that are capable of being
thought under the aspect of life'. It is a case, in other words, not of
analogy, as it would be in prose, but of 'creative interaction'.

Now we can, of course, read Marvell's metaphor and all other
metaphors we encounter in poems in this way, if we want to; the
difficulty is that we can do the same thing, if we want to, for all
metaphors in prose. But it is equally possible to continue to read all
metaphors, in both poems and prose works, as most people have
always read them. Why, then, must we accept Feidelson's revolutionary distinction? The problem, as he states it, is a problem of fact, and

his conclusions about both Marvell's metaphor and poetic metaphors in general are advanced as conclusions of fact, with practical implications for literary exegesis. The chain of argument by which he arrives at them, however, is purely *a priori* and dialectical. What he is saying is that we *must* read Marvell's metaphor and all other metaphors in poetry (but not in prose) in the way he indicates because this follows from the essential nature of poetry. And he knows what the essential nature of poetry must be simply by inferring it from the nature of what he calls 'poetic language'; and he knows what the nature of 'poetic language' must be because he has begun by dividing all language into two opposing and incommensurable kinds – the language of 'logic' and the language of 'symbolism' – and has then deduced from this initial assumption that the 'symbolic' language of poetry must necessarily possess the contraries of all qualities commonly asserted of 'logical discourse'. No matter what poets may have done, therefore, or other readers and critics thought, he can be confident that metaphor in poetry cannot possibly involve, as in 'logical' prose, a transference of names based on some resemblance between the things they signify. For he knows from his dialectic that the concepts of 'transference' and 'resemblance', since they are essentially 'logical' concepts, are incompatible with the concept of 'poetry', not merely, as he explains, 'because logic is unpoetic, but even more fundamentally, because poetic structure is not logical'. As far as I can see, that is all the warrant he has for saying what he does about metaphor in poetry.

You can perhaps gather from this example what the method is. It is the old method of bipartite division, in which a subject matter is explored, and its elements defined and related to one another, simply by applying to it a more or less elaborate pattern of logically contrary terms unified by a single principle of classification. You start, that is, with a very large concept such as 'language' or 'discourse' in general; you then move down from this by setting up dialectical oppositions, major and subordinate, within it (as, for instance, poetic discourse versus logical discourse, the symbolic versus the realistic, the ironical versus the simple); and you end by supposing, after the manner of Feidelson on metaphor, that the essential characteristics of poetry are necessarily what this scheme of antithetical distinctions determines them to be.

In order to be quite fair to these critics, I think we must distinguish between what they have been trying to get at in their dialectical theorizing and what they have actually accomplished. There is undoubtedly something in poetic literature – in its peculiar manipulations of language, in its techniques for implying or suggesting more than it explicitly says, in its special preoccupation with concrete experiences rather than with general ideas – to which their speculations point. When Wheelwright, for example, writes a book on what he calls 'depth language', he is not talking about nothing; he has his eye on genuine problems well worth exploring. And so too with most of the others. What disturbs me in these theorists is not their lack of real and important problems but their choice of a method for dealing with them, a method which I think is, in the first place, inappropriate to literature and, in the second place, incompatible with inquiry.

It is inappropriate to literature for two reasons (among others). First of all, it disregards the most obvious and fundamental fact about literature – namely, that it is not a natural phenomenon but a product of human invention and art. It is something, therefore, that exists in history and has had its character molded in countless unpredictable ways by it. You can know what its nature is, consequently, only by finding out *a posteriori* what the men and women who have created it, through the ages, have made that nature to be; and there is no presumption that this can ever be reduced to a single set of logically symmetrical and necessary principles, such as these critics have attempted to formulate. There are indeed necessities in literature, since literature is an art and hence partakes of reason; but, these necessities are always relative to the specific tasks which writers set themselves in writing individual works, and they vary according to the widely variant characters of these tasks. If you are writing a lyric poem, for instance, in which the speaker is conceived as being in a very despondent mood, and if you want to elicit the reader's sympathy with his feelings, it is clearly necessary that you show somehow in the poem some humanly significant causes for his state of mind. In this sense of necessity, literature may be said to involve an element of predictability, but only in this sense. For the history of literature shows unmistakably that literature does not have to be, *in general* – as one scholar has put it – 'anything determinate at all'. To attempt, therefore, to derive its nature *a priori* from general postulates, to geometrize about it – for that is what these theorists in effect have been doing – is wholly to miss the point.

The other respect in which the method is inappropriate appears when you consider what it does to the concrete natures of particular literary works. A simple example may make clear what I mean. *The Origin of Species* is admittedly a scientific treatise, and *The Ring and the Book* is admittedly a poem; and the two can undoubtedly be contrasted meaningfully with one another in a good many particular respects. But each exists in itself as an individual production, which has come to be what it is as a result of innumerable decisions, by Darwin and Browning respectively, that can be understood sufficiently for each work by itself without reference to the other. It would be absurd, therefore, to base our examination of them on the notion that there is some kind of significant polar opposition between them. They are merely different human productions, which require to be analysed and judged, accordingly, in different terms; and we only obscure and distort the facts on which our analysis and judgement ought to rest, when we imitate the theorists I have been discussing and reduce the relation between the poem and the treatise to an abstract contrariety between something called 'poetry' and something called 'science' or 'logic'. This is to turn poetry and science into hypostatized qualities, with natures determined not by variable human choices and actions – as we know is actually the case – but merely by the logic of the critic's divisions and definitions.

It is futile to try to determine by dialectical analysis of concepts like 'language', 'discourse', 'logic', 'science', 'symbol', 'poetry', etc., any of the actually operative principles of construction, meaning, or value in literature. Literature is just not suited to such a quasi-mathematical treatment.

Furthermore – and this is the second main objection – all theorizing of this kind, in so far as it is taken seriously, is bound to bring inquiry in practical criticism to a stop before it is well begun, or at least to reduce it to a mere application of pre-established dogmas. For you already know from your theory, in some determinate sense, what you ought to look for and what you will be likely to find in literary works before you read them. You know that there will almost certainly be 'ambiguity' in the next poem you look at, or that its structure will probably be 'some kind of paradoxical tension', or that it will be based on one or another of the currently talked-of ritualistic or mythical 'archetypes', or that, if certain objects are mentioned in it, they will necessarily have such and such symbolic meanings, and so on: you put your money into the dialectical machine and, behold, you get the same money back. And there is another and equally serious consequence, following from the fact that theories of this kind are necessarily developed from a single principle by a method of dichotomous division, one thing paired against another at different levels of generality throughout, with nothing left over and no loose ends. You will tend to think about all your problems in practical criticism in simple *either-or* disjunctions: if the work is not 'logical discourse', it must be 'poetry' and hence have characteristics contrary to those of 'logical discourse'; if it is not simple, it must be 'ironical'; if it is not realistic, it must be 'symbolic'; and so on. You can indeed frame alternative hypotheses for individual works or passages, but only those provided for in the dichotomies of your system. You will know, that is, before you examine a work what all the significantly different possibilities of meaning and structure in literature are; and beyond these you will have no warrant or inducement, in your theory, for venturing to look. There will be, in short, no *X*s, as I have called them, in your practical criticism that might lead to fresh discoveries, but at best only a narrowed-down choice between *A* and *B*. It is hard to see what research in criticism can amount to under these conditions.

What it actually has amounted to in the dealings of these critics with particular works and writers – under the direct or indirect influence of the fashionable theorizing – I can speak of only briefly. I shall concentrate on a single point; and since it is the style now to talk about 'fallacies' in criticism, I shall call what I have in mind the 'dialectical fallacy'. Let me give an example from my own experience. I once thought for a short time, when I was still more or less a 'new critic', that the essential structure of poetic works, as contrasted with prose arguments, consisted in a hierarchy of proportions or metaphors, running upward from lines and stanzas to the poem as a whole. I derived this principle, as my statement of it may suggest, by positing a dialectical opposition between poetry and syllogistic argument, and then merely drawing out one of the logical consequences of this. I took for granted, on the strength of this logic, that the principle was applicable universally; that is, to all poems and indeed to all works of the imagination. And, curiously enough, that proved to be in fact the case. I can take my oath that I never had any trouble, for as long as I clung to my theory, in making any poem, drama, or novel I examined in detail conform most beautifully to its specifications. All I had to do – and this was not hard – was to arrange the words, thoughts, and incidents of the work into proportional relationships with one another. (I did a very neat job of this sort, I recall, on Fielding's *Joseph Andrews* and equally neat ones on the odes of William Collins.) There was no need to trouble myself about biographical or historical probabilities or to raise the question whether the same textual details I had brought into harmony with my hypothesis might not admit of another or simpler explanation. Hypothesis, backed by dialectic, was enough.

I cannot see any difference between this method of mine (of which I now blush to speak) and the procedure by which Wheelwright, in *The Burning Fountain*, establishes the presence of 'plurisignation' in Marvell's couplet,

The grave's a fine and private place,
But none, I think, do there embrace.

What Marvell is saying in the first of these lines, Wheelwright tells us, is 'that in one of its aspects, its privacy, the grave would be a welcome refuge for lovers; that the grave marks an end, in that it deprives lovers of the joy of mutual embrace; and that the grave is very cramping.' And he supports this interpretation by attributing multiple meanings to the words 'fine' and 'private'.

On the surface, he says, the word 'fine' expresses approval of a place so 'private' (also in the most obvious sense) where lovers might embrace without interruption, if only they were any longer capable of embracing at all. But the grave is 'fine' also in marking the *finis*, the end of all earthly joys, the end of all embracing: an attentive reader thus gets a preview of the counteractive idea even before the second line of the couplet makes it explicit. And thirdly, 'fine' carries the added meaning of narrow, constricted: as when

232 R. S. Crane

we say 'a fine line'. Meanings 2 and 3 of 'fine' stir up a second
meaning of 'private', from the Latin *privatus*, 'deprived'.

I shall not discuss whether or not this somewhat complex reading
of the line is a probable one – that is to say, whether or not we have to
apprehend in the line the three meanings of 'fine' and the two
meanings of 'private' which Wheelwright finds there if we want to
do justice to the effect Marvell was trying to get. I am concerned
merely with the question of proof. What warrant has Wheelwright
for asserting that the line means the various things he says it does?
His hypothesis clearly states a possibility. We all know that poets do
sometimes – and very often in modern poetry – seek effects by means
of diction that has to be analysed much as he analyses the two words
in Marvell. As a recurring device in poetry, 'plurisignation' cannot
be denied; but why must we conclude that there is actually 'plurisignation' here? There is no compelling obviousness in his reading, such
as we find in the statement, for instance, that in Hart Crane's line in
Lachrymae Christi, 'Thy Nazarene and tinder eyes', the word 'tinder'
has a double meaning. Wheelwright may be right, but if so, he should
have argued the case, and he should have done this by giving some
reasons, from the character of the poem as a whole or from Marvell's
habits of diction, why it is not just as likely, or more likely, that the
poet would have wanted his readers to get from 'fine' and 'private'
only what Wheelwright calls their 'obvious' senses, without dwelling
on the words too closely, in order that the sudden turn in the second
line ('But none, I think, do there embrace') might produce its full
effect of witty surprise. It is no argument to say that the multiple
meanings attributed to 'fine' and 'private' here are authorized
historically by the *O.E.D.*, except on the absurd assumption that
particular words in poetry always mean in any given use of them all
the different things they *may* mean in the language of the time (this
is merely early William Empsonism). The only warrant Wheelwright
has, therefore, for asking us to accept his interpretation is that given
him by his general theory, in which 'plurisignation' is shown to be
one of the essential principles of 'poetry' merely by logical deduction
from the basic antithesis set up in his book between the idea of 'poetry'
and the idea of 'logical discourse'.

The 'dialectical fallacy' then is simply the tacit assumption that what is true in your theory as a dialectical consequence must also be, or tend to be, true in actuality – that if you can so read a literary work as to reveal in it the particular kind of meaning or structure that is entailed by your definition of literature, poetry, poetic language or the like, or by your formula for the author or his age, you have sufficiently demonstrated that it has that kind of meaning or structure. The fallacy lies in the circumstance that, with a little interpretative ingenuity these conditions can almost always be fulfilled. I have said before how incompatible all this is with the spirit of inquiry. Our theory may tell us, for instance, that poetry is or tends to be symbolic; but there is nothing in this proposition, whatever its dialectical guarantees, that warrants us, as scholars, in saying more than that there may perhaps be symbols in the poem before us. But, by the same token, there also may not be; and so we have no business to conclude that there are unless we are forced so to conclude by the poem itself when we look at it, independent of theory, as the work of a given poet at a given time, and examine it with the other possibility actively in mind. If a non-symbolic interpretation makes adequate sense of the text and, all other things considered, is relatively more probable, then anything we may believe about symbolism and poetry in general is beside the point. And the same would be true of a symbolic interpretation that satisfied the same requirements.

(II 33–40)

The Garden

William Empson

from 'Marvell's Garden', *Some Versions of Pastoral* 1966 (first published 1935)

The chief point of the poem is to contrast and reconcile conscious and unconscious states, intuitive and intellectual modes of apprehension; and yet that distinction is never made, perhaps could not have been made; his thought is implied by his metaphors. There is something very Far-Eastern about this; I was set to work on the poem by I. A. Richards' discussion of the philosophical arguments in Mencius. The Oxford edition notes bring out a crucial double meaning (so that this at least is not my own fancy) in the most analytical statement of the poem, about the Mind –

Annihilating all that's made
To a green thought in a green shade.

(47–8)

'Either "reducing the whole material world to nothing material, *i.e.* to a green thought", or "considering the material world as of no value compared to a green thought"'; either contemplating everything or shutting everything out. This combines the idea of the conscious mind, including everything because understanding it, and that of the unconscious animal nature, including everything because in harmony with it. Evidently the object of such a fundamental contradiction (seen in the etymology: turning all *ad nihil*, to nothing, and *to* a thought) is to deny its reality; the point is not that these two are essentially different but that they must cease to be different so far as either is to be known. So far as he has achieved his state of ecstasy he combines them, he is 'neither conscious nor not conscious', like the seventh Buddhist state of enlightenment. This gives its point, I think, to the other ambiguity, clear from the context, as to whether the *all* considered was *made* in the mind of the author or the Creator; to so peculiarly 'creative' a knower there is little difference between the two. Here as usual with 'profound' remarks the strength of the thing is to combine unusually intellectual with unusually primitive ideas; thought about the conditions of knowledge with a magical idea that the adept controls the external world by thought.

The vehemence of the couplet, and this hint of physical power in thought itself (in the same way as the next line gives it colour), may hint at an idea that one would like to feel was present, as otherwise it is the only main idea about Nature that the poem leaves out; that of the *Hymn to David* and *The Ancient Mariner*, the Orpheus idea, that by delight in Nature when terrible man gains strength to control it. This grand theme too has a root in magic; it is an important version of the idea of the man powerful because he has included everything in himself, is still strong, one would think, among the mountain climbers and often the scientists, and deserves a few examples here. I call it the idea of the *Hymn to David*, though being hidden behind the religious one it is nowhere overtly stated, except perhaps in the line

Praise above all, for praise prevails.

David is a case of Orpheus-like behaviour because his music restrained the madness of Saul.

His furious foes no more maligned
When he such melody divined,
    And sense and soul detained;

By *divining* – intuiting – the harmony behind the universe he 'makes it divine', rather as to discover a law of nature is to 'give nature laws', and this restrains the madman who embodies the unruled forces of nature from killing him. The main argument of the verses describing nature (or nature as described by David) is that the violence of Nature is an expression of her adoration of God, and therefore that the man of prayer who also adores God delights in it and can control it.

Strong the gier eagle on his sail;
Strong against tide, th' enormous whale
Emerges, as he goes.

But stronger still, in earth or air
Or in the sea, the man of prayer,
And far beneath the tide.

The feeling is chiefly carried by the sound; long Latin words are packed into the short lines against a short one-syllable rhyming word

full of consonants; it is like dancing in heavy skirts; he juggles with
the whole cumbrous complexity of the world. The *Mariner* makes a
more conscious and direct use of the theme, but in some degree runs
away from it at the end. The reason it was a magical crime for a
sailor to kill the albatross is that it both occurs among terrible scenes
of Nature and symbolizes man's power to extract life from them, so
ought doubly to be delighted in. So long as the Mariner is horrified
by the creatures of the calm he is their slave; he is set free to act, in
the supreme verses of the poem, as soon as he delights in them. The
final moral is

He prayeth best, that loveth best
    All things both great and small.

But that copybook maxim is fine only if you can hold it firmly
together with such verses as this:

The very deeps did rot; oh Christ
    That such a thing could be;
Yea, slimy things did crawl with legs
    Upon the slimy sea.

And it was these creatures, as he insisted in the margin by giving the
same name to both, that the Mariner blessed unaware when he discovered their beauty. This is what Coleridge meant by alternately
saying that the poem has too much of the moral and too little;
knowing what the conventional phrases of modern Christianity
ought to mean he thought he could shift to a conventional moral
that needs to be based upon the real one. Byron's nature-poetry gives
more obvious examples of the theme; he likes to compare a storm on
the Jura or what not to a woman whom, we are to feel, only Byron
could dominate. Poe was startled and liberated by it into a symbol of
his own achievement; the sailor in *The Maelstrom* is so horrified as to
be frozen, through a trick of neurosis, into idle curiosity, and this
becomes a scientific interest in the portent which shows him the way
to escape from it.

    Nature when terrible is no theme of Marvell's, and he gets this note
of triumph rather from using nature when peaceful to control the
world of man.

How safe, methinks, and strong, behind
These trees have I encamped my mind;
Where beauty, aiming at the heart,
Bends in some tree its useless dart;
And where the world no certain shot
Can make, or me it toucheth not.
But I on it securely play,
And gall its horsemen all the day.

(Upon Appleton House, 601–8)

The masculine energy of the last couplet is balanced immediately
by an acceptance of Nature more masochist than passive, in which
he becomes Christ with both the nails and the thorns.

Bind me ye woodbines in your twines,
Curl me about ye gadding vines,
And O so close your circles lace,
That I may never leave this place:
But, lest your fetters prove too weak,
Ere I your silken bondage break,
Do you, O brambles chain me too,
And courteous briars nail me through.

(Upon Appleton House, 609–16)

He does not deify himself more actively, and in any case the theme
of *The Garden* is a repose.

How vainly men themselves amaze
To win the palm, the oak, or bays;
And their uncessant labours see
Crowned from some single herb or tree.
Whose short and narrow verged shade
Does prudently their toils upbraid;
While all flowers and all trees do close
To weave the garlands of repose.

This first verse comes nearest to stating what seems the essential
distinction, with that between powers inherent and powers worked
out in practice, being a general and feeling one could be; in this ideal
case, so the wit of the thing claims, the power to have been a general

is already satisfied in the garden. 'Unemployment' is too painful and normal even in the fullest life for such a theme to be trivial. But self-knowledge is possible in such a state so far as the unruly impulses are digested, ordered, made transparent, not by their being known, at the time, as unruly. Consciousness no longer makes an important distinction; the impulses, since they must be balanced already, neither need it to put them right nor are put wrong by the way it forces across their boundaries. They let themselves be known because they are not altered by being known, because their principle of indeterminacy no longer acts. This idea is important for all the versions of pastoral, for the pastoral figure is always ready to be the critic; he not only includes everything but may in some unexpected way know it.

Another range of his knowledge might be mentioned here. I am not sure what arrangement of flower-beds is described in the last verse, but it seems clear that the sun goes through the 'zodiac' of flowers in one day, and that the bees too, in going from one bed to another, reminding us of the labours of the first verse, pass all summer in a day. They compute their time as well as we in that though their lives are shorter they too contract all experience into it, and this makes the poet watch over large periods of time as well as space. So far as he becomes Nature, he becomes permanent. It is a graceful finale to the all-in-one theme, but not, I think, very important; the crisis of the poem is in the middle.

Once you accept the Oxford edition's note you may as well apply it to the whole verse.

Meanwhile the mind, from pleasure less,
Withdraws into its happiness;
The mind, that ocean where each kind
Does straight its own resemblance find;
Yet it creates, transcending these,
Far other worlds, and other seas,
Annihilating . . .

From pleasure less. Either 'from the lessening of pleasure' – 'we are quiet in the country, but our dullness gives a sober and self-knowing happiness, more intellectual than that of the over-stimulated pleasures of the town' or 'made less by this pleasure' – 'The pleasures of the country give a repose and intellectual release which make me less intellectual, make my mind less worrying and introspective.' This is the same puzzle as to the consciousness of the thought; the ambiguity gives two meanings to pleasure, corresponding to his Puritan ambivalence about it, and to the opposition between pleasure and happiness. *Happiness*, again, names a conscious state, and yet involves the idea of things falling right, happening so, not being ordered by an anxiety of the conscious reason. (So that as a rule it is a weak word; it is by seeming to look at it hard and bring out its implications that the verse here makes it act as a strong one.)

The same doubt gives all their grandeur to the next lines. The sea if calm reflects everything near it; the mind as knower is a conscious mirror. Somewhere in the sea are sea-lions and -horses and everything else, though they are different from land ones; the unconsciousness is unplumbed and pathless, and there is no instinct so strange among the beasts that it lacks its fantastic echo in the mind. In the first version thoughts are shadows, in the second (like the *green thought*) they are as solid as what they image; and yet they still correspond to something in the outer world, so that the poet's intuition is comparable to pure knowledge. This metaphor may reflect back so that *withdraws* means the tide going down; the *mind* is *less* now, but will return, and it is now that one can see the rock-pools. On the Freudian view of an Ocean, *withdraws* would make this repose in Nature a return to the womb; anyway it may mean either 'withdraws into self-contemplation' or 'withdraws altogether, into its mysterious processes of digestion'. *Straight* may mean 'packed together', in the microcosm, or 'at once'; the beasts see their reflection (perhaps the root idea of the metaphor) as soon as they look for it; the calm of Nature gives the poet an immediate self-knowledge. But we have already had two entrancingly witty verses about the sublimation of sexual desire into a taste for Nature (I should not say that this theme was the main emotional drive behind the poem, but it takes up a large part of its overt thought), and the *kinds* look for their *resemblance*, in practice, out of a desire for *creation*; in the mind, at this fertile time for the poet, they can *find* it 'at once', being 'packed together'. The transition from the beast and its reflection to the two pairing beasts implies a transition from the correspondences of thought with fact to those of thought with thought, to find which is to be creative; there is necessarily here a suggestion of rising from one 'level' of thought to another; and in the next couplet not only does the mind transcend the world it mirrors, but a sea, to which it is parallel, transcends both land and sea too, which implies self-consciousness and all the antinomies of philosophy. Whether or not you give *transcendent* the technical sense 'predictable of all categories' makes no great difference; by including everything in itself the mind includes as a detail itself and all its inclusions. And it is true that the sea reflects the *other worlds* of the stars; Donne's metaphor of the globe is in the background. Yet even here the double meaning is not lost; all land-beasts have their sea-beasts, but the sea also has the kraken; in the depths as well as the transcendence of the mind are things stranger than all the kinds of the world.

Miss M.C. Bradbrook has pointed out to me that the next verse, while less triumphant, gives the process a more firmly religious interpretation.

Here at the fountain's sliding foot,
Or by some fruit tree's mossy root,
Casting the body's vest aside,
My soul into the boughs does glide;
There like a bird it sits, and sings,
Then whets, and combs its silver wings;
And, till prepared for longer flight,
Waves in its plumes the various light.

The bird is the dove of the Holy Spirit and carries a suggestion of the rainbow of the covenant. By becoming inherent in everything he becomes a soul not pantheist but clearly above and apart from the world even while still living in it. Yet the paradoxes are still firmly maintained here, and the soul is as solid as the green thought. The next verse returns naturally and still with exultation to the jokes in favour of solitude against women.

Green takes on great weight here, as Miss Sackville-West pointed out, because it has been a pet word of Marvell's before. To list the uses before the satires may seem an affectation of pedantry, but shows how often the word was used; and they are pleasant things to look up. In the Oxford text: pages 12, l. 23; 17, l. 18; 25, l. 11; 27, l. 4; 38, l. 3; 45, l. 3; 46, l. 25; 48, l. 18; 49, l. 48; 70, l. 376; 71, l. 390; 74,

l. 510; 122, l. 2. Less rich uses: 15, l. 18; 21, l. 44; 30, l. 55; 42, l. 14; 69, l. 339; 74, ll. 484, 496; 78, l. 628; 85, l. 82; 89, l. 94; 108, l. 196. It is connected here with grass, buds, children, an as yet virginal prospect of sexuality, and the peasant stock from which the great families emerge. The 'unfathomable' grass makes the soil fertile and shows it to be so; it is the humble, permanent, undeveloped nature which sustains everything, and to which everything must return. No doubt D. H. Lawrence was right when he spoke up for Leaves of Grass against Whitman and said they felt themselves to be very aristocratic, but that too is eminently a pastoral fancy. Children are connected with this both as buds, and because of their contact with Nature (as in Wordsworth), and unique fitness for Heaven (as in the Gospels).

The tawny mowers enter next,
Who seem like Israelites to be,
Walking on foot through a green sea . . .

(*Upon Appleton House*, 388–90)

connects greenness with oceans and gives it a magical security;

And in the greenness of the grass
Did see its hopes as in a glass . . .

(*The Mower's Song*)

connects greenness with mirrors and the partial knowledge of the mind. The complex of ideas he concentrates into this passage, in fact, had been worked out already, and in a context that shows how firmly these ideas about Nature were connected with direct pastoral. The poem indeed comes immediately after a pastoral series about the mower of grass.

I am the mower Damon, known
Through all the meadows I have mown;
On me the morn her dew distils
Before her darling daffodils.

(*Damon the Mower*, 41–4)

In these meadows he feels he has left his mark on a great territory, if not on everything, and as a typical figure he has mown all the meadows of the world; in either case Nature gives him regal and magical honours, and I suppose he is not only the ruler but the executioner of the daffodils – the Clown as Death.

> Only for him no cure is found,
> Whom Juliana's eyes do wound.
> 'Tis death alone that this must do:
> For Death thou art a mower too.
>
> *(Damon the Mower, 85–8)*

He provides indeed more conscious and comic mixtures of heroic and pastoral:

> every mower's wholesome heat
> Smells like an Alexander's sweat.
>
> *(Upon Appleton House, 427–8)*

It is his grand attack on gardens which introduces both the connexion through wit between the love of woman and of nature, which is handled so firmly in *The Garden*:

> No white nor red was ever seen
> So am'rous as this lovely green:

– and the belief that the fruitful attitude to Nature is the passive one:

> His [the gardener's] green seraglio has its eunuchs too;
>   Lest any tyrant him outdo.
> And in the cherry he does Nature vex,
>   To procreate without a sex.
> 'Tis all enforced; the fountain and the grot;
>   While the sweet fields do lie forgot;
> Where willing Nature does to all dispense
>   A wild and fragrant innocence:
> And fauns and fairies do the meadows till,
>   More by their presence than their skill.
>
> *(The Mower against Gardens)*

It is Marvell himself who tills the Garden by these magical and contemplative powers.

Grass indeed comes to be taken for granted as the symbol of pastoral humility:

Unhappy birds! what does it boot
To build below the grasses' root;
When lowness is unsafe as height,
And chance o'ertakes what scapeth spite?

(Upon Appleton House, 409-12)

It is a humility of Nature from which she is still higher than man,
so that the grasshoppers preach to him from their pinnacles:

And now to the abyss I pass
Of that unfathomable grass,
Where men like grasshoppers appear,
But grasshoppers are giants there;
They, in their squeaking laugh, contemn
Us as we walk more low than them:
And, from the precipices tall
Of the green spires, to us do call.

(Upon Appleton House, 369-76)

It seems also to be an obscure merit of grass that it produces 'hay',
which was the name of a country dance, so that the humility is
gaiety.

With this the golden fleece I shear
Of all these closes ev'ry year,
And though in wool more poor than they,
Yet am I richer far in hay.

(Damon the Mower, 53-6)

To nineteenth-century taste the only really poetical verse of the
poem is the central fifth of the nine; I have been discussing the sixth,
whose dramatic position is an illustration of its very penetrating
theory. The first four are a crescendo of wit, on the themes 'success
or failure is not important, only the repose that follows the exercise
of one's powers' and 'women, I am pleased to say, are no longer
interesting to me, because nature is more beautiful'. One effect of
the wit is to admit, and so make charming, the impertinence of the
second of these, which indeed the first puts in its place; it is only for
a time, and after effort among human beings, that he can enjoy
solitude. The value of these moments made it fitting to pretend they

were eternal; and yet the lightness of his expression of their sense of power is more intelligent, and so more convincing than Wordsworth's solemnity on the same theme, because it does not forget the opposing forces.

> When we have run our passion's heat,
> Love hither makes his best retreat.
> The gods, that mortal beauty chase,
> Still in a tree did end their race.
> Apollo hunted Daphne so,
> Only that she might laurel grow;
> And Pan did after Syrinx speed,
> Not as a nymph, but for a reed.
>
> (*The Garden*)

The energy and delight of the conceit has been sharpened or keyed up here till it seems to burst and transform itself; it dissolves in the next verse into the style of Keats. So his observation of the garden might mount to an ecstasy which disregarded it; he seems in this next verse to imitate the process he has described, to enjoy in a receptive state the exhilaration which an exercise of wit has achieved. But striking as the change of style is, it is unfair to empty the verse of thought and treat it as random description; what happens is that he steps back from overt classical conceits to a rich and intuitive use of Christian imagery. When people treat it as the one good 'bit' of the poem one does not know whether they have recognized that the Alpha and Omega of the verse are the Apple and the Fall.

> What wondrous life in this I lead!
> Ripe apples drop about my head;
> The luscious clusters of the vine
> Upon my mouth do crush their wine;
> The nectarine, and curious peach,
> Into my hands themselves do reach;
> Stumbling on melons, as I pass,
> Ensnared with flowers, I fall on grass.

Melon, again, is the Greek for apple; 'all flesh is *grass*', and its own *flowers* here are the snakes in it that stopped Eurydice. Mere grapes are at once the primitive and the innocent wine; the *nectar* of Eden, and yet the blood of sacrifice. *Curious* could mean 'rich and strange' (nature), 'improved by care' (art), or 'inquisitive' (feeling towards me, since nature is a mirror, as I do towards her). All these eatable beauties give themselves so as to lose themselves, like a lover, with a forceful generosity; like a lover they *ensnare* him. It is a triumph for the attempt to impose a sexual interest upon nature; there need be no more Puritanism in this use of sacrificial ideas than is already inherent in the praise of solitude; and it is because his repose in the orchard hints at such a variety of emotions that he is contemplating *all that's made.* Sensibility here repeats what wit said in the verse before; he tosses into the fantastic treasure-chest of the poem's thought all the pathos and dignity that Milton was to feel in his more celebrated Garden; and it is while this is going on, we are told in the next verse, that the mind performs its ambiguous and memorable *withdrawal.* For each of the three central verses he gives a twist to the screw of the microscope and is living in another world.

(99–109)

William Empson

from 'Rhythm and Imagery in English Poetry', *British Journal of Aesthetics*, vol. 2   1962

The trouble about Imagism and all its connexions, which are still crawling about underfoot in the contemporary jungle and tripping up the innocent reader of poetry, is that it is determinedly anti-intellectual, and tells us that we ought to try to be very stupid. I was having a small controversy some while ago about *The Garden* by Andrew Marvell, and the opponent said it was inept of me to have said that the word *straight* could mean 'tightly together' as well as 'at once'; because, he said, the poet was writing about the sea, which is big, so the image of being crowded into a small space would be inept.

Meanwhile the mind, from pleasure less,
Withdraws into its happiness,
The mind, that ocean where each kind
Does straight its own resemblance find;

Yet it creates, transcending these,
Far other worlds, and other seas;
Annihilating all that's made
To a green thought in a green shade.

The poet is comparing his own mind to the sea, and though the sea is big his head is small. Such would be the position for any poet, but a mystic might feel himself entitled to large claims. Marvell does echo the claims of mystics, but he knows very well that he is being impudent and can only rely upon the humour of a logical analogy. If one of my sons said he needn't hold down a pay packet because he could get as much experience by sitting in Appleton House garden as by learning any skill, I would think it a bit much. Literary critics nowadays I think lose the impact of the poem because they refuse to look at it in this real way. Actually the war had finished in England and gone to Scotland when Marvell was at Appleton House, but he still felt the great estate as an enchanted peace. He had been directed into a very quiet staff job with frightfully useful contacts; and it wasn't his fault, though he knew he ought to be fighting the King. You understand, I am puzzling about what was at the back of his mind when he wrote these few extremely magical poems. There is something about the tone of them, as many critics have felt, which though so deliciously relaxed feels like a challenge. But an Imagist reader is not allowed to understand anything. If the poet says the mind is like the sea, then the Imagist reader must have a picture of the sea, in his head, and he must make a unique kind of muscular effort so as never to think of what is being talked about, the other half of the comparison, at all. The belief that poetry positively ought not to mean anything is still very strong, though mainly held by foreigners I think.

(48–9)

John McChesney

'Marvell's *The Garden*', *Explicator*, vol. 10   1951

Although it has been more than once noted that the 'melon' of Marvell's fifth stanza is derived from the Greek 'malum', meaning 'apple', it is doubtful that there has been any comment on the noun 'peach', which, elliptical for 'Persicum malum', Persian apple, is another reference to the apple of Eden, or to the adjective 'curious', which in the seventeenth century carried in addition to the readily recognized meaning, 'exquisite or fine', the sense of the 'occult' (*N.E.D.*), with its connotations of the magical and evil. The apple, named four times in the stanza, since the nectarine is 'a variety of the common peach', is the evil fruit of the Garden of Eden which drops upon the poet's head and causes him, ensnared in the flowers of pleasure, to fall. Although the sacramental wine is pressed upon his mouth yet there is irony in the first line: What a life of temptation and sin I lead!

The observation that Marvell may have been influenced in the choice of the fruits which he names by Tasso's description of Armida's garden (Fairfax made his translation of Tasso in 1600; Marvell wrote *The Garden* a half century later) does not invalidate the significance of Marvell's four-fold reference to the apple.

(Item 4)

Don A. Keister

'Marvell's *The Garden*', *Explicator*, vol. 10 1952

Mr McChesney's comment on a stanza of Marvell's *The Garden* moves me to immediate reply.

In the first place, there is no *Greek* 'malum'. There is a *Latin* 'malum'. The classical Greek is 'melon'.

In the second place, the apple is not 'named' four times in the stanza. The apple is named once, the peach once, the nectarine once, and the melon once. It *may* be that Marvell (who possessed neither Skeat nor Webster nor the *N.E.D.*) was aware of etymological reflections among the words and intended his readers to be aware of them. I think it pretty unlikely.

In the third place, while 'curious' may sometimes have carried the additional meaning suggested, is it not possible that Marvell was seeking to push the 'occult' but by this time not very menacing associations into the background by using such (or am I being naïve?) pleasant and favorable words as 'wondrous', 'ripe', 'luscious', and (*pace* Mr McChesney) 'nectarine' (immediate association: nectar of the gods)? Marvell seems to be reinforcing the usual meaning of the adjective when it was applied to food – exquisite or choice.

In the fourth place, the poet says that the apples, *ripe* ones (plump, sweet, highly edible) drop *about* his head, not (oh, lord, and shades of Newton!) *upon* it, knocking him out and causing him to fall on the grass!

And in the fifth place, making the wine 'sacramental' is an *acte gratuite* if I ever saw one. If the wine *is* sacramental, several questions present themselves. Where is the rest of the sacrament, the bread? Is the poem an evidence of Marvell's Protestantism, since he partakes of the wine; or have we here an indication of his essentially sacerdotal view of the function of the poet? Anyway, note the chronology: the sacramental wine is pressing itself upon the poet *before* the fall, *i.e.* before he can possibly have any need for it. The paradox requires elucidation.

I think everyone would agree that *The Garden* is a very skilfully written poem. Each stanza is a step in an argument, developing out of the preceding one and leading into the next. The point being made in the stanza in question is 'What a wonderfully sensuous life I am now leading!' The development illustrates the sensuousness to the swooning point. The images are at least partly sexual – the earth and its fruitfulness being feminine, the 'I' being masculine, both possessing and possessed in amorous embrace. The *body*, then, at the end of the stanza is completely occupied with its senses, and the *mind* is free to 'withdraw into its happiness' in the next stanza and by annihilating 'all that's made' it allows the *soul* to escape and have its mystical experience. Then comes the return to the work-a-day world in the last two stanzas.

Mr William Empson's etymologies are sometimes useful, but I think the famous 'apple-melon' one is a red herring in this poem. Of course, the Garden of Eden is alluded to, and Christian attitudes towards sex and sin necessarily furnish part of the general context of the poem. But its essential figure seems to me to be penetration-and-withdrawal, not rise-and-fall. The center of the poem is the line 'Waves in its plumes the various light'. Every preceding line leads (but with wit and some playful deviousness) towards it; every succeeding line leads away from it.

(Item 24)

Frank Kermode

'The Argument of Marvell's *Garden*', *Essays in Criticism*, vol. 2
1952

I

The Garden is an *étude d'exécution transcendante* which has been
interpreted by so many virtuosi in the past few years that a stiff-
fingered academic rendering is unlikely to be very entertaining. However, since it appears that the brilliant executants have been making
rather too many mistakes, there may be some value in going slowly
over the whole piece.

It may be useful to point out in advance that these mistakes are
of three kinds. The first is historical, as when Mr Milton Klonsky,
writing in the *Sewanee Review* (vol. 58, pp. 16–35), seizes on a passage
in Plotinus as the sole key to the poem. He is wrong, not because there
is no connexion at all between Plotinus and Marvell's lyric, but because he has misunderstood the relationship and consequently exaggerated its importance. He fails to observe that Marvell, like other
poets of the period, uses philosophical concepts, including those of
neo-Platonism, in a special way, with reference not to the body of
formal doctrine in which those concepts are originally announced, but
to genres of poetry which habitually and conventionally make use of
them. The process is familiar enough; for example, the nature of the
relationship between pastoral poetry and philosophic material such as
the debates on Action and Contemplation, Art and Nature, is toler-
ably well understood. It is not customary to find the only key to the
works of Guarini or Fletcher in some Greek philosopher; but these
poets have not, like Donne and Marvell, been distorted by the solemn
enthusiasm of modern exegetes. In a sense all philosophical propositions in Marvell are what Professor Richards used to call 'pseudo-
statements', and his is a 'physical' rather than a 'platonic' poetry.
However, rather than risk myself in these deep waters, I shall support
myself on a raft of Mr Wellek's construction: 'The work of art . . .
appears as an object *sui generis* . . . a system of norms of ideal concepts
which are inter-subjective. . . .' Above all, it is possible 'to proceed to
a classification of works of art according to the norms they employ'

and thus 'we may finally arrive at theories of genres.'[1] The point is that we must not treat these 'norms' as propositions, for if we do we shall fall into the toils of Mr Klonsky. Miss Ruth Wallerstein, who has worked so hard and so sanely to liberate seventeenth-century poetry from modern error, is none the less guilty of Mr Klonsky's fault, in her *Studies in Seventeenth Century Poetic*, 1950. Not only the indolent cry out against the suggestion that *The Garden* needs to be explicated in terms of Hugo of St Victor and Bonaventura. Doubtless there is, for the historian of ideas, a real connexion between the poem and the Victorine and neo-Platonic systems of symbolic thought; for there is a connexion between Plato and 'Trees'. However interesting this may be, it has nothing to do with what most of us call criticism. If we read *The Garden* as historians of poetry, and not as historians of ideas, we shall resist all such temptation to treat the 'norms' as ideas, even if it proceeds from Diotima herself, to whom Professor Richards succumbed in a recent lecture on the poem.

The second kind of mistake is one which, particularly when it assumes its more subtle shape, we are all liable to yield to, though it appears to be seductive even in its usual grossness. Sufficient, however, to say that *The Garden* must not be read as autobiography. 'What was Marvell's state of mind as he wandered in Fairfax's Yorkshire garden?' is a very bad question to ask, but it is obviously one which comes readily to the minds of learned and subtle interpreters; both Marvell and Donne have suffered greatly from this form of mis-applied scholarship, and it is comforting to reflect that the date of *The Garden* is quite unknown, so that it cannot be positively stated to be the direct record of some personal experience at Nun Appleton. It could conceivably have been written much later. The pseudo-biographical critic is wasteful and deceptive; he diverts attention from the genre just as certainly as Mr Klonsky does when he presents a picture of the poet torturing himself with Chinese boxes of Forms or Mr Empson when he invites us to reflect upon the Buddhist enlighten-ment (*Some Versions of Pastoral*, pp. 119–20).

The third kind of critical failure is clearly, in this case, the most important, for the others would not have occurred had there not been this cardinal error. It is the failure to appreciate the genre (the system

1 'The Mode of Existence of a Literary Work of Art', *Critiques and Essays in Criticism, 1920–1948*, ed. R. Stallman, 1949, pp. 210–23.

of 'norms' shared by other poems) to which *The Garden* belongs.
Despite the labours of Miss Bradbrook, Miss Lloyd Thomas,[1] and
Miss Wallerstein, poets like Théophile, Saint-Amant, Randolph,
Lovelace, Fane and Stanley have simply not been put to proper use in
the criticism of Marvell. This is the central difficulty, and the one
which this paper is intended to diminish. The first necessity is to
distinguish between the genre and the history of the ideas to which
the genre is related.

II

'We cannot err in following Nature': thus Montaigne, 'very rawly
and simply,' with this addition: 'I have not (as Socrates) by the power
and virtue of reason, corrected my natural complexions, nor by art
hindered mine inclination.'[2] This is a useful guide to that aspect of
'naturalism' in the thought of the late Renaissance which here concerns us. The like consideration governs all the speculations of the
older Montaigne; Nature is to be distinguished from Custom; the
natural inclinations are good, and sensual gratifications are not the
dangerous suggestions that other and more orthodox psychologies
hold them to be. Sense and instinct seek and find their own temperance without the interference of reason. It is good to satisfy a natural
appetite, and it is also, of course, innocent. Thus men behaved, says
Montaigne, in the Golden World, and thus they still behave in the
Indies.

The question how far Montaigne believed in his own 'primitivism'
seems to me a difficult one, but it scarcely concerns us at the moment.
It is legitimate to use him as spokesman for naturalism; and before
we leave him it will be prudent to glance at some of his references to
Plato, in order to have at hand some record of the naturalist reaction
to the Platonic theory of love. In short, as the foregoing quotation implies, Platonic love is rejected. No longer 'an appetite of generation
by the mediation of beauty', love is in fact 'nothing else but an in-
satiate thirst of enjoying a greedily desired subject' (vol. 3, p. 105).

1 M.C. Bradbrook, 'Marvell and the Poetry of Rural Solitude', *R.E.S.*, vol.
17, 1941, pp. 37–46; M.C. Bradbrook and M.G. Lloyd Thomas, *Andrew
Marvell*, Cambridge, 1940.
2 Montaigne, *Essays*, trans. John Florio, Everyman, vol. 3, p. 316.

'My page makes love, and understands it feelingly; read Leon Hebraeus or Ficinus unto him; you speak of him, of his thoughts and of his actions, yet understands he nothing you mean ...' (vol. 3, p. 102). Much more sympathetic are 'the ample and lively descriptions in Plato, of the loves practised in his days' (vol. 3, p. 82). If one is not overcareful – if, for instance, one fails to discriminate between the orations of Socrates and those who precede him, one may without much difficulty extract from the *Symposium* itself very different theories of love from those developed by Ficino or Milton. In Marvell's own youth antithetical versions of Platonism flourished contemporaneously at Cambridge and at Whitehall.

So far we have concerned ourselves, very briefly, with the informal naturalism of Montaigne, and hinted at a naturalistic version of Plato. What of the poetry which concerns itself with similar issues? One thinks at once of Tasso, and specifically of that chorus in his *Aminta*, *O bella etá de l'oro*, which was so often imitated and debated in the poetry of the age. In the happy Golden Age lovers concerned themselves with their own love and innocence, and not with honour, that tyrant bred of custom and opinion, that enemy of nature. In the garden of the unfallen just, whatever pleases is lawful. The paradise of these fortunate innocents is abundant in its appeal to the senses; law and appetite are the same, and no resolved soul interferes with the banquet of sense offered by created pleasure. Thus an ancient pastoral tradition accommodates new poetic motives, and poetry, though affirming nothing, strengthens its association with the freer thought of its time. The formal opposition to Tasso's statement is properly made in poetry which belongs to the same genre; and it may be found in the Chorus in Act IV of Guarini's *Il Pastor Fido*. Parallel debates could go on in the great world, and in the little world of poetry; the debate about naturalism was a serious one, since it involved theological censures. The poetical debate is of a different quality. The proper answer to Tasso is Guarini's. A genre of poetry developed which assumed the right to describe the sensuality of a natural Eden, and a specialized kind concentrated on sexual gratifications as innocent, and the subject of unreasonable interference from Honour. The proper reply is, again, in terms of the 'norms' of the genre, and there is evidence that the very poets who stated the extreme naturalist case were quite capable of refuting it. One might call the 'norms' of the refutation an anti-genre. *The Garden* is a poem of the anti-genre of the naturalist paradise.

Marvell therefore rejects the naturalist account of love, and with it that Platonism which was associated with the delights of the senses. The poets of the Renaissance were profitably aware of the possible antitheses in Platonic theories of love, just as they were aware of Plato's argument against their status as vessels of the truth.[1] Spenser makes comfortable bedfellows of two Platonisms in his *Hymns*; the two Aphrodites easily change into each other in poem and emblem. Nothing is more characteristic of Renaissance poetry than the synthesis of spiritual and erotic in poetic genre and image. It was encouraged by centuries of comment on the *Canticum Canticorum* and the eclecticism of mystics as well as by the doctrinaire efforts of Bruno to spiritualize the erotic Petrarchan conceits. Much more evidence could be brought, if it were necessary, to establish the existence of genre and anti-genre in Platonic love-poetry. They not only co-exist, but suggest each other. Marvell could pass with ease from the libertine garden to the garden of the Platonic *solitaire*, soliciting the primary *furor* of spiritual ascent. (The ease of such transitions was partly responsible for the development of another genre – that of the palinode.)

The Garden stands in relation to the poetry of the gardens of sense as the *Hymn of Heavenly Beauty* stands in relation to the *Hymn of Beauty*. It is poetry written in the language of, or using the 'norms' of, a genre in a formal refutation of the genre. In fact, this was a method Marvell habitually used, sometimes almost with an affectation of pedantry, as I have elsewhere shown of *The Mower Against Gardens*.[2]

III

The garden is a rich emblem, and this is not the place to explore it in any detail; indeed I shall say nothing of the symbolic gardens of the Middle Ages which were still alive in the consciousness of the seven-

1 See F. A. Yates, *The French Academies of the Sixteenth Century*, 1947, pp. 128 ff. From Plato (*Symposium* 202A, *Republic* 477 et seq.) through the Pléiade to Sidney there ran the argument that poets were not competent to make philosophical statements; they affirm nothing.
2 *N. & Q.*, vol. 197, 1952, pp. 136–8.

teenth century. The gardens to which Marvell most directly alludes in his poem are the Garden of Eden, the Earthly Paradise, and that garden to which the Stoic and Epicurean, as well as Platonist, retire for solace or meditation. The first two are in many respects one and the same; the third is the garden of Montaigne, of Lipsius, and of Cowley. I shall not refer to the *Hortus conclusus*, though at one point in my explication of Marvell's poem I allude to a Catholic emblem-writer. Doubtless the notion of Nature as God's book affects the poetic tradition; it certainly occurs in poems about solitude at this period. But I think it is misleading to dwell on the history of the idea.

Of the complexity of the Earthly Paradise, with all its associated images and ideas, it is not necessary to say much: it is of course a staple of pastoral poetry and drama, and the quality of Marvell's allusions to it will emerge in my explication. But a word is needed about the garden of the solitary thinker, which Marvell uses in his argument against the libertine garden of innocent sexuality.

It is to be remembered that we are not dealing with the innocence of Tasso's Golden Age, where there is a perfect concord between appetite and reason, or with the garden of innocent love that Spenser sketches in *Faerie Queene*, IV x, where 'thousand pairs of lovers walked, Praising their god, and yielding him great thanks,' and 'did sport Their spotless pleasures, and sweet love's content'. The libertines use the argument of the innocence of sense to exalt sensuality and to propose the abolition of the tyrant Honour, meaning merely female chastity. This is the situation of the *Jouissance* poetry which was fashionable in France, and of which Saint-Amant's well-known example, excellently translated by Stanley, is typical. It is equally the situation of Randolph's *Upon Love Fondly Refused* and his *Pastoral Courtship*, Carew's *Rapture* and Lovelace's *Love Made in the first Age*. In Randolph's Paradise there is no serpent – 'Nothing that wears a sting, but I'[1] – and in Lovelace's

No serpent kiss poisoned the taste
Each touch was naturally chaste,
And their mere sense a miracle.[2]

1 *Poems*, ed. G. Thorn-Drury, 1929, p. 110.
2 *Poems*, ed. C. H. Wilkinson, 1930, p. 147.

And so it is throughout the libertine versions of sensual innocence. The garden, the place of unfallen innocence, is identified with a naturalist glorification of sensuality. The garden which is formally opposed to this one by Marvell is the garden where sense is controlled by reason and the intellect can contemplate not beauty but heavenly beauty.

It was Montaigne, this time in his Stoic role, who gave wide currency to the pleasures of *solitary* seclusion. The relevant ideas and attitudes were developed into a poetic genre. Many poets certainly known to Marvell practised this genre, among them Fane and Fairfax and the French poets, notably Saint-Amant, whose *Solitude* demonstrates how easily he moved in this, the antithesis of the *Jouissance* mode. This famous poem was translated by Fairfax and by Katharine Phillips. This is the poetry of the meditative garden, whether the meditation be pseudo-Dionysian, or Ciceronian, or merely pleasantly Epicurean, like Cowley's. There is, of course, a play of the senses in which woman has no necessary part, though the equation of all appetite with the sexual appetite in the libertines tends to ignore it; this unamorous sensuality is firmly castigated by Lipsius in his treatment of gardens. If the garden is treated merely as a resort of pleasure, for the 'inward tickling and delight of the senses' it becomes 'a very sepulchre of slothfulness'. The true end of the garden is 'quietness, withdrawing from the world, meditation', the subjection of the distressed mind to right reason.[1] The true ecstasy is in being rapt by intellect, not by sex.

Retirement; the study of right reason; the denial of the sovereignty of sense; the proper use of created nature: these are the themes of Marvell's poem laboriously and misleadingly translated into prose. As poetry the work can only be studied in relation to its genre, though that genre may be related to ethical debates. To the naturalist *Jouissance* Marvell opposes the meditative *Solitude*. The fact that both these opposed conceptions are treated in the work of one poet, Saint-Amant, and a little less explicitly in Théophile and Randolph also, should warn against the mistaking of seriousness for directness of reference to ethical propositions. *The Garden* uses and revalues the 'norms' of the genre: it is not a contribution to philosophy, and not the direct account of a contemplative act.

1 *De Constantia, Of Constancy*, trans. Sir J. Stradling, ed. R. Kirk and C.M. Hall, 1939, pp. 132 ff.

IV

Henry Hawkins, the author of the emblem-book *Partheneia Sacra*, adopts a plan which enables him, in treating the emblematic qualities of a garden, to direct the attention of the pious reader away from the delights of the sense offered by the plants to a consideration of their higher significance. As in Marvell, sensual pleasure has to give way to meditation.[1] We now proceed to the explication of Marvell's poem, with a glance at Hawkins's wise disclaimer: 'I will not take upon me to tell all; for so of a garden of flowers, should I make a labyrinth of discourse, and should never be able to get forth' (p. 8).

The poem begins by establishing that of all the possible gardens it is dealing with that of retirement, with the garden of the contemplative man who shuns action. The retired life is preferred to the active life in a witty simplification: if the two ways of life are appraised in terms of the vegetable solace they provide it will be seen that the retired life is quantitatively superior. The joke is in the substitution of the emblem of victory for its substance. If you then appraise action in terms of plants you get single plants, whereas retirement offers you the solace of not one but *all* plants. This is a typical 'metaphysical' use of the figure called by Puttenham the Disabler. The first stanza, then, is a witty dispraise of the active life, though it has nothing to distinguish it sharply from other kinds of garden-poetry such as libertine or Epicurean – except possibly the hint of a secondary meaning 'celibate' in the word *single* and a parallel sexual pun on *close*,[2] which go very well with the leading idea that woman has no place in this garden.

The Innocence of the second stanza cannot itself divide the poem from other garden-poems; for Innocence of a sort is a feature of the libertine paradise, as well as of the Epicurean garden of Cowley and indeed most gardens.

Your sacred plants, if here below,
Only among the plants will grow –

lines which are certainly a much more complicated statement than that of *Hortus* – seem to have stimulated Mr Klonsky to astonishing

1 *Partheneia Sacra*, ed. Iain Fletcher, 1950 (reprint of 1633), p. 2.
2 Proposed by A. H. King, *English Studies*, vol. 20, 1938, pp. 118–21.

feats. But the idea is not as difficult as all that. Compare *Upon Apple-ton House* –

For he did, with his utmost skill,
Ambition weed, but conscience till,
Conscience, that Heaven-nursed plant,
Which most our earthly gardens want.
(353–6)

Your sacred plants, he says, addressing Quiet and Innocence, are un-like the palm, the oak and the bays in that if you find them anywhere on earth it will be among the plants of the garden. The others you can find 'in busy companies'. The joke here is to give Quiet and her sister plant emblems like those of the active life, and to clash the emblematic and the vegetable plants together. The inference is that Innocence may be found only in the green shade (*concolor Umbra* occurs at this point in the Latin version). Society (with its ordinary connotations of 'polish' and 'company') is in fact all but rude (un-polished) by comparison with Solitude, which at first appears to be lacking in the virtues Society possesses, but which possesses them, if the truth were known, in greater measure (the Ciceronian-Stoic 'never less alone than when alone' became so trite that Cowley, in his essay *Of Solitude*, apologized for referring to it).

We are now ready for a clearer rejection of libertine innocence. Female beauty is reduced to its emblematic colours, red and white (a commonplace, but incidentally one found in the libertine poets) and unfavourably compared with the green of the garden as a dispenser of sensual delight. This is to reject Saint-Amant's 'crime innocent, à quoi la Nature consent.'[1] A foolish failure to understand the superiority of green causes lovers to insult trees (themselves the worthier objects of love) by carving on them the names of women. (This happens in Saint-Amant's *Jouissance*.) Since it is the green garden, and not women that the poet chooses to regard as amorous, it would be farcically logical for him to carve on the trees their own names. The garden is not to have women or their names or their love in it. It is natural (green) and amorous (green – a 'norm' of the poem) in quite a dif-ferent way from the libertine garden.

Love enters this garden, but only when the pursuit of the white and

1 *Œuvres Complètes*, ed. Ch.-L. Livet, 1855, vol. 1, p. 119.

red is done, and we are without appetite. (Love is here indiscrimi-
nately the pursued and the pursuer. Weary with the race and exertion
(*heat*) it 'makes a retreat' in the garden; hard-pressed by pursuers it
carries out a military retreat.) The place of retreat has therefore Love,
but not women: they are metamorphosed into trees. The gods, who
might be expected to know, have been misunderstood; they pursued
women not as women but as potential trees, for the green and not for
the red and white. Marvell, in this witty version of the metamor-
phoses, continues to 'disable' the idea of sexual love. Here one needs
quite firmly to delimit the reference, because it is confusing to think of
laurel and *reed* as having symbolic significations. It is interesting that
this comic metamorphosis (which has affinities with the fashionable
mock-heroic) was practised for their own ends by the libertine poets;
for example, in Saint-Amant's *La Metamorphose de Lyrian et de Sylvie*,
in Stanley's Marinesque *Apollo and Daphne*, in Carew's *Rapture*, where
Lucrece and other types of chastity become sensualists in the libertine
paradise, and very notably in Lovelace. Thus, in *Against the Love of
Great Ones*:

Ixion willingly doth feel
The gyre of his eternal wheel,
Nor would he now exchange his pain
For clouds and goddesses again.

(Poems, p. 75)

The sensuous appeal of this garden is, then, not sexual, as it is in the
libertines. It has, none the less, all the enchantment of the Earthly
Paradise, and all its innocence: this is the topic of the fifth stanza.
The trees and plants press their fruit upon him, and their gifts are in
strong contrast to those of the libertine garden,

Love then unstinted, Love did sip,
And cherries plucked fresh from the lip,
  On cheeks and roses free he fed;
Lasses like autumn plums did drop,
And lads, indifferently did crop
  A flower, and a maidenhead.

(Poems, p. 146)

The fruits of green, not of red and white, are offered in primeval abundance, as they are in the Fortunate Islands or in any paradise. Everything is by nature lush and fertile; the difference between this and a paradise containing a woman is that here a Fall is of light consequence, and without tragic significance. ('Ensnared with *flowers*, *I* fall on grass.') In the same way, Marvell had in *Upon Appleton House* (stanza 77) bound himself with the entanglements not of wanton limbs, in the libertine manner of Carew, Randolph and Stanley, but of woodbine, briar and bramble. The same imagery is still in use for amorous purposes in the poetry of Leigh.

In this garden both man and nature are unfallen; it is therefore, for all its richness, not a trap for virtue but a paradise of perfect innocence. Even the fall is innocent; the sensuous allurements of the trees are harmless, and there is no need to 'fence the batteries of alluring sense'. It is evident that Empson and King were quite right to find here a direct allusion to the Fall.

Modern commentators all agree that the sixth stanza, central to the poem, is a witty Platonism, and of course this is so. The danger is that the Platonism can be made to appear doctrinal and even recherché when in fact it is reasonably modest, and directly related to genre treatments of love in gardens. There is, however, a famous ambiguity in the first two lines: how are we to take 'from pleasure less'? It can mean simply (1) reduced by pleasure, or (2) that the mind retires because it experiences less pleasure than the senses, or (3) that it retires from the lesser pleasure to the greater. The first of these might be related to the doctrine of the creation in *Paradise Lost* VII 168f. – 'I am who fill|Infinitude, nor vacuous the space.|Though I uncircumscribed myself retire,|And put not forth my goodness. . . .' This would be consistent with the analogy later drawn between the human and the divine minds. But the second is more likely to be the dominant meaning, with a proper distinction between mind and sense which is obviously relevant to the theme ('None can chain a mind|Whom this sweet chordage cannot bind'). The third meaning is easily associated with this interpretation. The mind withdraws from the sensual gratification offered in order to enjoy a happiness of the imagination. In terms of the genre, it rejects the *Jouissance* for the *Solitude* – indeed, Saint-Amant, in a poem which prefers the contemplative garden, writes of it thus:

Tantost, faisant agir mes sens
Sur des sujets *de moindre estofe*,
De marche en autre je descens
Dans les termes du philosophe;
Nature n'a point de secret
Que d'un soin libre, mais discret,
Ma curiosité ne sonde;
Et, dans ma recherche profonde,
Je loge en moy tout l'univers.
Là, songeant au flus et reflus,
Je m'abisme dans cette idée;
Son mouvement me rend perclus,
Et mon âme en est obsedée.

(1 32; my italics)

To put it another way, one prefers a different kind of ecstasy from that of the libertine, described by the same poet in his *Jouissance*, which Stanley translated. Saint-Amant represents his solitary as acquiring from nature knowledge of the forms, and the next two lines of Marvell's stanza seem to do likewise. The metaphor is not unfamiliar — 'Some have affirmed that what on earth we find The sea can parallel for shape and kind' — and the idea is that the forms exist in the mind of man as they do in the mind of God. By virtue of the imagination the mind can create world and seas too which have nothing to do with the world which is reported by the senses. This is the passage which seems to have caused such trouble to commentators, who look to learned originals like Plotinus and Ficino for the explanation: but in fact the Platonism here is dilute and current.

It is commonplace of Renaissance poetic that God is a poet, and that the poet has the honour of this comparison only because of the creative force of fancy or imagination. Nor is the power exclusive to poets. The mind, which 'all effects into their causes brings',[1] can through the imagination alone devise new and rare things: as Puttenham says, 'the fantastical part of man (if it be not disordered) is a representer of the best, most comely and beautiful images or appearances of things to the soul and according to their very truth' (p. 19). Puttenham shuns 'disordered fantasies . . . monstruous

1 Sir John Davies, *Nosce Teipsum* (*The Intellectual Powers of the Soul*, stanza 5).

imaginations or conceits' as being alien to the truth of imagination, but it is conceivable that Marvell, in his suggestion of the mind's ability to create, refers to a more modern psychology and poetic, with its roots in the Renaissance, but with a new emphasis. Thus Cowley in his Pindaric *The Muse* says that the coach of poetry can go anywhere:

And all's an open road to thee.
Whatever God did say,
Is all thy plain and smooth, uninterrupted way.
Nay, ev'n beyond his works thy voyages are known,
    Thou hast a thousand worlds too of thine own.
Thou speak'st, great queen, in the same style as he,
And a new world leaps forth, when thou say'st, Let it be.

And in a note he obligingly explains this:

The meaning is, that poetry treats not only of all things that are, or can be, but makes creatures of her own, as centaurs, satyrs, fairies, etc., makes persons and actions of her own . . . makes beasts, trees, waters, and other irrational and insensible things to act above the possibility of their natures as to understand and speak nay makes what gods it pleases too without idolatry and varies all these into innumerable systems, or worlds of invention.

These other worlds are thoughts in the mind of man as the world is a thought in the mind of God. Empson is probably right in his guess that *straight* means 'packed together' as well as 'at once'. The whole idea is illuminated by a passage of extraordinary interest in Leigh (who was imbued with that passion for optics which later became common among poets) in which the reduced images of the eye are contrasted with the illimitable visions of the mind. The mind contains everything undiminished by the deficiencies of sense.[1] The mental activity which Marvell is describing is clear; it is the working of the imagination, which, psychologically, follows sense and precedes intellection, and is therefore the means of rejecting the voluptuous suggestions of sense; and which 'performs its function when the sensible object is rejected or even removed.'[2] The mind's newly created

1 *Poems*, ed. Hugh Macdonald, 1947, pp. 36 ff.
2 Gianfrancesco Pico della Mirandola, *De Imaginatione*, ed. and trans. H. Caplan, 1930, p. 29.

worlds are, in the strict sense, phantasms, and without substance: and since they have the same mental status as the created world, it is fair to say that 'all that's made' is being annihilated, reduced to a thought.

But a green thought? This is a great bogey, but surely the thought is green because the solitude is green, which means that it is also the antithesis of voluptuousness? Here the normative signification of green in the poem is in accord with what is after all a common enough notion – green for innocence. Thus, in *Aramantha* Lovelace asks:

Can trees be green, and to the air
Thus prostitute their flowing hair?
(*Poems*, p. 112)

But I cannot think the green has any more extensive symbolic intention. Green is still opposed to red and white; all this is possibly only when women are absent and the senses innocently engaged.

The stanza thus alludes to the favourable conditions which enable the mind to apply itself to contemplation. The process is wittily described, and the psychology requires no explanation in terms of any doctrinaire Platonism, whether pseudo-Dionysian, Plotinian, or Florentine.

The seventh stanza is also subject to much ingenious comment. The poet allows his mind to contemplate the ideas, and his soul begins a Platonic ascent. Here there are obvious parallels in the English mystics, in Plotinus, in medieval and Florentine Platonism; but we must see this stanza as we see the rest of the poem, in relation to the genre. Failing to do this we shall be involved in an endless strife between rival symbolisms, as we are if we try to find an external significance for *green*. As it is, there is no need to be over-curious about the fountain; its obvious symbolic quality may have an interesting history, but it is primarily an easily accessible emblem of purity. As for the use of the bird as an emblem of the soul, that is an image popularized by Castiglione,[1] and used by Spenser of the early stages of the ascent:

Beginning then below, with th'easy view
Of this base world, subject to fleshly eye,
From thence to mount aloft by order due,
To contemplation of th'immortal sky,

1 *The Book of the Courtier*, trans. Thomas Hoby, Everyman, p. 338.

Of that soar falcon so I learn to fly,
That flags awhile her fluttering wings beneath,
Till she herself for stronger flight can breathe.

(*Hymn of Heavenly Beauty*, 22–8)

Spenser has just passed from the consideration of woman's love and beauty to the heavenly love and beauty. The bird which prepares its wings for flight is evidently a symbol with as settled a meaning as the dew, which Marvell also shared with many other poets.

The hungry soul, deceived with false beauties, may have 'after vain deceitful shadows sought' – but at last it looks 'up to that sovereign light, From whose pure beams all perfect beauty springs' (*H.H.B.*, 291, 295). Marvell's bird 'Waves in its plumes the various light'. Once more we might spring to Ebreo or Plotinus or even Haydocke, but we shall do better to note how this same image is used in literature more closely related to Marvell.

Les oyseaux, d'un joyeux ramage,
En chantant semblent adorer
La lumière qui vient dorer
Leur cabinet et leur plumage –

thus Théophile, in his ode, *Le Matin*.[1] In *Partheneia Sacra* Hawkins uses the dove as other poets use the dew or the rainbow –

Being of what colour soever, her neck being opposed to the sun will diversify into a thousand colours, more various then the Iris itself, or that Bird of Juno in all her pride; as scarlet, cerulean, flame-colour, and yielding a flash like the carbuncle, with vermilion, ash-colour, and many others besides. . . . (p. 202)

Marvell's use of the Platonic light-symbolism is therefore not technical as it might be in Chapman, but generalized, as in Quarles or Vaughan, and affected by imagery associated with the garden genres. We are thus reminded that the point about the ascent towards the pure source of light is not that it can be achieved, but that it can be a product of *Solitude* rather than of *Jouissance* and that it is an alternative to libertine behaviour in gardens. It is the ecstasy not of beauty but of heavenly beauty.

1 *Œuvres Complètes*, ed. M. Alleaume, 1856, vol. 1, pp. 174–5.

The eighth stanza at last makes this theme explicit. This is a special solitude, which can only exist in the absence of women, the agents of the most powerful voluptuous temptation. This has been implied throughout, but it is now wittily stated in the first clear reference to Eden. The notion that Adam would have been happy without a mate is not, of course, novel; St Ambrose believed it. Here it is another way of putting the case that woman offers the wrong beauty, the wrong love, the red and white instead of the green. Eve deprived Adam of solitude, and gave him instead an inferior joy. Indeed she was his punishment for being mortal (rather than pure Intelligence?). Her absence would be equivalent to the gift of a paradise (since her presence means the loss of the only one there is). This is easy enough, and a good example of how naturally we read references to the more familiar conceptions of theology and philosophy as part of the play of wit within the limited range of a genre.

In the last stanza the temperate quiet of the garden is once more asserted, by way of conclusion. (The Earthly Paradise is always in the temperate zone.) The time, for us as for the bee (a pun on 'thyme') is sweet and rewarding; hours of innocence are told by a dial of pure herbs and flowers. The sun is 'milder' because in this zodiac of flowers fragrance is substituted for heat; Miss Bradbrook and Miss Lloyd Thomas have some good observations here. The time computed is likewise spent in fragrant rather than hot pursuits. This is the *Solitude*, not the *Jouissance*; the garden of the *solitaire* whose soul rises towards divine beauty, not that of the voluptuary who voluntarily surrenders to the delights of the senses.

This ends the attempt to read *The Garden* as a poem of a definite historical kind and to explore its delicate allusions to a genre of which the 'norms' are within limits ascertainable. Although it is very improbable that such an attempt can avoid errors of both sophistication and simplification, one may reasonably claim for it that in substituting poetry for metaphysics it does no violence to the richness and subtlety of its subject.

(225-41)

Pierre Legouis

from 'Marvell and the New Critics', *Review of English Studies*, new
series vol. 8   1957

When our secretary asked me to read a paper before this conference
it was suggested that the title might run: 'Second thoughts on
Marvell.' But upon examination the dreadful reality revealed itself
starkly to me: I had *no* second thoughts on Marvell, at least not on his
poetry. Since my bulky book came out in 1928 I have had to revise
my views on his wife, or rather non-wife. And by discovering his
presence at Saumur in 1656 Mrs Duncan-Jones has opened to me new
vistas on the religious thought of his later years. As an historian I
should have liked to give you today a picture of that small French
town, then at the height of its intellectual fame. But this could hardly
have led to a discussion, and discussion is what the organizers of the
conference are after. Do not blame *me* then if this paper adopts a
provocative, nay an aggressive, tone and roundly attacks all those
who have presumed, in the last twenty-eight years, to discover new
meanings in Marvell's poems. For I shall use the term 'new criticism'
in a very inclusive sense, regardless of the division of opinion between
schools or coteries, English and American, even confounding Cantabs
with Oxonians. Whether they like it or not, to an impartial and
sufficiently remote observer they all derive from Professor Empson's
Seven Types of Ambiguity, 1930. Further than that in their pedigree I
will not go. The philosophical and psychological basis for their
method I shall ignore. Were I a blunt Englishman I should say I
neither know nor care whence it originates. By their fruit I will know
them. Have they brought forth any interpretation, both new and
valid, of any poem, stanza, or line?

Though in his afore-mentioned book Mr Empson discussed severa
poems of Marvell's and performed some remarkable feats with theml
his main contribution to the Marvellian new look is the article on *The
Garden* published in *Scrutiny*, vol. 1, 1932. Indeed *The Garden* has
since been the most frequently re-examined of Marvell's poems, and,
my time being limited, I shall concentrate on it almost exclusively.

Here is a sample of Mr Empson's method. Stanza 6, as you know,
opens:

Meanwhile the mind, from pleasure less,
Withdraws into its happiness;

From pleasure less. Either 'from the lessening of pleasure . . .' or 'made less by pleasure . . .'. Since three meanings, in Mr Empson's theory, are better than two, his omission of the real meaning conclusively shows that he never saw it: 'from a pleasure that is inferior' (see *O.E.D.* under *Less*, 2), viz. sensuous pleasure, the mind withdraws into a happiness that is specifically its own, viz. contemplation. Here Mr Empson does exactly what many a bright student has been doing for the last thirty-four years in translations set by me: not seeing the obvious meaning of a phrase and seeing entirely improbable ones instead, *gallice* 'faire un contre-sens'. So that, to parody a regal remark, we are amused, but we are not impressed.

However, Mr Empson does not stop *en si beau chemin*, but proceeds with the next couplet:

The mind, that ocean where each kind
Does straight its own resemblance find;

Here my friend Margoliouth's standard edition provides him with the true meaning, in the form of a quotation from *Pseudodoxia Epidemica*, to which I have added one from Butler and this from Cleveland:

Some have affirmed that what on earth we find
The sea can parallel for shape and kind.

But, in order to form one of his beloved dyads, Mr Empson remarks the sea also is a conscious mirror, and 'if calm reflects everything'. I answer, with gross literalness, that the sea will not reflect 'each kind' (of animals or plants) unless you previously hang them above it, a process involving even more difficulties than Noah was faced with when called upon to build the Ark. Such a vagary as Mr Empson's, forgivable only in a reader reduced to his twentieth-century knowledge, or ignorance, of natural history, is here positively harmful, since it distracts the mind (our mind) from the historical meaning, the only one that Marvell meant, the obvious one for mid-seventeenth-century men.

It was to be expected that a religious and a sexual ambiguity, or a religiously-sexually, or a sexually-religious, ambiguity should be extracted from some part of the poem. The stanza selected for this treatment is the fifth, and especially its final couplet:

Stumbling on melons, as I pass,
Ensnared with flowers, I fall on grass.

Mr Empson wonders whether admiring readers 'have recognized that the Alpha and Omega of the stanza are the Apple and the Fall', since 'Melon . . . is Greek for apple'. Indeed I had not. Nor had I noticed that the stanza 'is the triumph of Marvell's attempt to impose a sexual interest upon nature'. I had fondly imagined, so far, that the poet had left, for a time at least, the 'sexual interest' behind him, in London Cavalier society, and explicitly sacrificed women to trees in stanzas 3 and 4. But now I am quite prepared to reconsider these 'melons' in a new light. Only I must ask myself why Marvell also placed them (erroneously or not) on the soil of the Bermudas: is it to 'ensnare' the Greekless Puritan emigrants who foolishly thank God for them? He 'throws the melons at our feet'. Indeed I wonder why nobody has yet (to my knowledge) given a psychoanalytic explanation of these 'melons': in Greek they are apples. Mr Empson reminds us, and in French 'pommes' is sometimes applied, in a very informal style, to those globular charms that have made Marilyn Monroe and Gina Lollobrigida famous in our time. As a result no doubt of repression, the English Puritans, probably in a dream, find these instruments of the Fall of Man enticing them to 'fall on grass'.

If you say I exaggerate I shall refer you to the next full-scale commentary on The Garden, a much ampler one than Mr Empson's. Mr Milton Klonsky apparently has a full right to the title of 'new critic', since his article 'A Guide through The Garden' appeared in the Sewanee Review, vol. 58, 1950. He adopts a good many interpretations from Mr Empson, particularly that of the melons being the forbidden fruit, and Marvell's fall on the grass 'a corruptive action'. The 'ripe round feminine forms' are, moreover, recognized, not only in the Greek melons and the English apples, but also in the peaches (possibly with an anticipation of the American 'she is a peach'), the nectarines, and even the grape. As an inevitable consequence 'the sensuality which had been steadily rising up to now is climactically discharged', whatever this may mean.

But Mr Klonsky's article is not all fun. He has warned us in his pre-
amble that the poem could be thoroughly understood only through
the study of Plotinus's *Enneads*. I have no *a priori* objection to such an
approach, provided the obvious sense of the poem suffers no distortion,
but this is just what befalls it here. Mr Klonsky wants to prove that
Marvell – or Marvell's 'protagonist' as he curiously calls him – is
guilty of 'sensuality', and he punishes, or cures, him with death, the
result of which appears in stanza 6, already quoted. Now, says Mr
Klonsky, 'the soul and the body are dissevered'. They are, in a way,
since the mind cuts itself off from sensation, but why obtrude death
here? And, what is even worse, why introduce an idea of guilt where
the poem gives a happy gradation from the inferior (less) but quite
legitimate pleasure of a vegetable life, to the higher pleasure of
contemplation, itself only a step to the ecstasy in the next stanza? Mr
Klonsky's introduction of guilt is, to use his own phrase, 'a corruptive
action'.

I must now go back a dozen years or so and say a word of the useful
'Notes' on *The Garden* contributed by Mr A.H. King to *English
Studies* in 1938. But should he rank among the new critics except in
point of date? His careful examination of the English text in connexion with the Latin one satisfies the rules of caution laid down by
the old criticism at almost every point. If he refers to Mr Empson's
Apple-and-Fall interpretation he tones it down considerably. On the
other hand I agree with him that in *The Garden* Marvell's 'approach
should be kept distinct from the mortally earnest approach to Nature
of a Romantic poet like Shelley' (indeed I had said so in my book) –
but I disagree with the epithet 'mincing' applied by Mr King to
Marvell's 'approach': as if there were no other choice than that
between Romanticism and effeminacy. I should rather say that the
Romantic poets lack a certain form of *pudor*, which Marvell has, while
he can be serious enough under the surface. And against Mr King's
restrictive criticism of 'a green thought in a green shade' I must
protest, because he takes up a remark of mine (in a footnote) that
'green' can mean 'naïve' and regrets my 'building nothing on this'.
I shall retort that *he* builds more than the remark will bear, for, as I
had been careful to say, the usual senses of green, including this one,
prove inadequate here, and there is mystery in the phrase.

An even more detailed study than Mr Klonsky's followed closely.

It was no less 'new' since it appeared in *Essays in Criticism*, vol. 2, 1952. It bears the title 'The Argument of Marvell's *Garden*'. With its author, Mr Frank Kermode, I often agree, all the more readily since he rather confirms (tacitly) than contradicts what I had said of yore. If I have a complaint against him, it is that he goes too far in the right direction, e.g. when he dismisses autobiographical interpretation. Attention paid to the genre, however profitable, does not constitute the sum total of criticism, and Mr Kermode rather overworks the notion. The terms 'genre' and 'species' are relative, as we learnt at school; but while the seventeenth century acknowledged the pastoral as a genre it would not have recognized the genre of 'garden poetry' as defined by Mr Kermode. Even today the more modest term 'theme' might prove more suitable here.

Anyhow, in the so-called genre, poems by Théophile and Saint-Amant are included. Of course, as early as 1930, Mr Geoffrey Woledge had called attention to them in connexion with Lord Fairfax and his daughter's tutor, and had said they were in the same 'tradition'. Miss Bradbrook, in 1941, had considerably enlarged the claim on behalf of the French *libertins*, and Miss Ruth Wallerstein had followed suit in 1950. These three critics had chiefly stressed the literary resemblances between Marvell and his French predecessors. I must say I remained somewhat sceptical, because when preparing my book I had read these poets and been struck more by the differences, still literary, between them and Marvell, who, by the way, could not scan a French line though he could read French prose easily enough. But I would not refuse the honour paid to my country and kept silent. Now Mr Kermode, curtly dismissing his English or American predecessors, stresses the sufficiently obvious moral differences between Marvell and Saint-Amant, or Théophile, and sets out to prove that Marvell wrote to contradict, or to refute, them in the same style. Mr Kermode even erects *The Garden* into an 'anti-genre'. Here I must come in and, paradoxically for a Frenchman, accuse an Englishman of too systematic a treatment of the problem. There is little polemical spirit in *The Garden*. The only satiric touch, the word 'fond' applied to male lovers, denotes smiling intellectual superiority rather than moral reprobation. Neither are the ladies at all severely handled: their 'white or red' (natural it seems) is indeed placed lower than the 'lovely green' of the plants, but, as the Latin version testifies,

Marvell grants them a very moving beauty: 'Virgineae quem non suspendit gratia formae ?'[1] They surpass the snow in whiteness and the purple in redness – only the green stands in a class by itself. But here again Mr Kermode reacts against his predecessors – except Mr King – this time by denying that there is anything special in this word 'green'. He calls the 'green thought' the 'great bogey'. This seems to me to be carrying to excess the reaction against such philosophizing and scholasticizing of the epithet as Miss Wallerstein's. Certainly the thought is green because the solitude is green, but does it really end there ?

To prove that he is a 'new critic' *stricto sensu* in spite of his fondness for genre, Mr Kermode pronounces it evident that Empson and King were right to find in stanza 5 'a direct allusion to the Fall' and dilates on the 'famous ambiguity' in the beginning of stanza 6: 'from pleasure less'. He indeed admits the only sensible interpretation (omitted by Mr Empson) but he does so in a half-hearted and shamefaced manner. Yet his conclusion on the passage tallies with mine: 'the Platonism is here dilute and current'. I had spoken, apropos of *A Drop of Dew*, but with general application to Marvell's poetry, of 'platonisme diffus'. However, when he comes to stanza 7, Mr Kermode, still in virtue of his system, unduly lessens Marvell's originality. To the lines

Casting the body's vest aside
My soul into the boughs does glide:
There like a bird it sits and sings,

he discovers many parallels. But they entirely fail – in particular those culled by him in Saint-Amant and Théophile fail – to give the impression of the poet's identification with Nature that Marvell's metaphor gives, and here resides the unique value of that moment. For, while no one could deny the allusion to heaven in the last line but one, 'till prepared for longer flight', it sounds rather perfunctory. Marvell certainly wants to go to a still better place some day, but no less certainly he does not want to go yet. He is fully satisfied with a condition very similar to that described in a famous passage of *Upon Appleton House*, where he talks with the birds 'in their most learned original'. His past belongs to Woman, his future to God, but his

1 Whom does the grace of beauty not unsettle? [Ed.]

present belongs to Nature alone. And at the risk of shocking religious
souls, I consider that the premature intrusion of God into Mr Kermode's commentary spoils the instant. Truth to say, Marvell himself
does not remain thus poised, and the next stanza, the eighth, cannot
but come as an anticlimax with its reference – a playful one – to the
earthly Paradise. Yet, says Mr Kermode, it clinches the 'Argument';
here Marvell 'at last makes [his] theme explicit' and confounds the
libertins by stating that the right sort of solitude 'can only exist in
the absence of women, the agents of the most powerful voluptuous
temptation.' But surely Eve is not Adam's mistress in either sense of
the word: she is his wedded wife (Marvell says 'mate') and the poet
does not here renounce love but marriage. We now know for certain,
thanks to Professor F.S. Tupper, that the man Marvell stuck to the
last by the wisdom then revealed to him. He remained so far a hedo-
nist that he never married. As his eighteenth-century editor, Captain
Thompson, R.N., put it for all time: 'He had no wife and his gal-
lantries are not known.'

(382-7)

The Nymph Complaining for the
Death of her Fawn

E. S. Le Comte

'Marvell's *The Nymph Complaining for the Death of her Fawn*', *Modern Philology*, vol. 50   1952

To all appearances, *The Nymph Complaining for the Death of her Fawn* is a pastoral delineating with 'a pretty skipping grace' and many *concetti* a girl's tender relation with and mourning for her pet that 'wanton troopers riding by|Have shot'. The poem, a favorite with anthologists even before Palgrave added a portion of it to *The Golden Treasury* in 1883, undoubtedly has had a good number of appreciators, and, of these, none (including T. S. Eliot, who certainly cannot be accused of lack of sensitivity in these matters) had taken it other than literally until the appearance of *Andrew Marvell* by M.C. Bradbrook and M.G. Lloyd Thomas, Cambridge, 1940. These ladies advanced (pp. 47ff.) the startling thesis that the poem is an allegory on the Crucifixion. In the critics' own words, ' *The Nymph Complaining for the Death of her Fawn* opens with straightforward and charming naturalism; it ends by drawing largely on *The Song of Solomon* and its identification of the fawn with Christ.' No formal protest having been registered against this view, there is some danger that the silence of more than a decade may be interpreted as signifying universal consent. In fact, Marvell's standard editor, Professor H.M. Margoliouth, was favorably disposed, in his review: 'I am not convinced that they are wrong. If they are right, the poem takes on altogether new color and significance' (*R.E.S.*, vol. 17, p. 221; compare Ruth Wallerstein, who takes a middle position, *Studies in Seventeenth-Century Poetic*, Madison, 1950, pp. 335–6). It may not be belaboring the obvious then, to argue that the poem is *not* about the Crucifixion and to show incidentally what, in so far as the poem has a traceable background, that background is. On the positive side, this paper will offer more than one reason for believing that the poem is what Émile Legouis (in Legouis and Cazamian's *History of English Literature*) calls it, 'semi-mythological'.

The Bradbrook–Thomas interpretation comes in the form of an *aperçu*, we being mostly left to work out the details as best we can. And, contrary to the implication of the sentence quoted above, it appears to be the first paragraph of the poem, not the last, which holds out the best prospect for such an interpretation: [quotes lines 1–24].

Here are blood, prayers, sin, Heaven's King, and sacrifice. In a Christian poet the combination is certainly provocative, and, if the poem continued in this strain, we should have a right to suspect allegory. It is true that there are already grave theological problems, in such a case. Allowing that the 'wanton troopers' are the slayers of the Savior, can it be said, 'nor could|Thy death yet do them any good'? But the main point is that twenty-four lines in a poem of one hundred and twenty-two lines do not make it an allegory, and even the last couplet quoted above (the most provocative of all) fits into place as part of the poem's pattern of hyperbole and conceit, half-Italianate, half-metaphysical, whereby, the fawn is magnified, at mankind's – and particularly womankind's – expense. Marvell, whose Eden in *The Garden* is conspicuous for barring Eve, is being beguilingly antifeminine in his insistence on how much whiter the fawn is than the nymph:

>   And oft
> I blushed to see its foot more soft,
> And white, (shall I say than my hand?)
> NAY any Lady's of the land.
>   (59–62)

He is reacting against the Petrarchan tradition by removing woman from the pedestal, substituting a fawn, and making the woman the wooer. Whereas poets going back to Horace (*Car.*, i 23) and Ovid (*Met.*, xi 771f.) and including Wyatt (the poem commencing, 'They flee from me') had maidens flee men like fawns, Marvell's fawn – and what a sweet revenge it is! – literally as well as figuratively leaves Marvell's nymph far behind (lines 63–70). The poem, like any good poem, has overtones, but these are not religious: rather they have to do, as in other of Marvell's poems, with the Eden (or nature) versus civilization issue.

The second verse paragraph deals, one would think, the deathblow to the Bradbrook–Thomas thesis:

> Unconstant Sylvio, when yet
> I had not found him counterfeit,
> One morning (I remember well)
> Tied in this silver chain and bell,

Gave it to me: nay and I know
What he said then; I'm sure I do.
Said he, look how your huntsman here
Hath taught a fawn to hunt his dear.
But Sylvio soon had me beguiled.
This waxed tame, while he grew wild,
And quite regardless of my smart,
Left me his fawn, but took his heart.

(25-36)

In all common sense – however unfashionable that has become in criticism – does this tone, do these undoctrinal puns, permit us still to believe that the fawn is Christ? And who is Sylvio? The name suggests nothing, except a figure in a pastoral poem. Is Sylvio a pagan lover from whom the nymph turned to Christ? In the first place, the two influences were side by side for a time. In the second place, how can Sylvio be said to have been the giver of the fawn ('Tied in this silver chain and bell'!), if the fawn is Christ? It does not work out. It will not bear a moment's thought.

And in the fourth verse paragraph, this is said:

Had it lived long, I do not know
Whether it too might have done so
As Sylvio did: his gifts might be
Perhaps as false or more than he

(47-50)

How can this be said of the Savior? How can this be said, even if – the only possibility – it is meant to indicate lapse of faith on the part of the church, the nun, the Virgin Mary, or whoever the nymph is supposed to be according to the Misses Bradbrook and Thomas? Quoting lines 93-8, these critics grant, 'It would be difficult to do this now without being blasphemous.' But the above inversion is still more dangerous.

Let us grant what must be granted. There is a deer here and a deer in the Song of Solomon: 'My beloved is like a roe or a young hart' (ii, 9). In both works the deer skips (ii, 8), as young deer are wont to do. Also there are lilies common to both: the biblical 'beloved ... feedeth among' them (ii, 16); Marvell's does something similar: [quotes lines 77-92]. Where is the crown of thorns here?

It is most confusing to say that 'the whiteness of the fawn . . . is of course symbolic of the Agnus Dei'. It is true, a lamb is mentioned:

Now my sweet fawn is vanished to
Whither the swans and turtles go:
In fair Elysium to endure,
With milk-white lambs, and ermines pure.

(105–8)

But who are the ermines? One imagines that, if Marvell had wished to be so understood, he would have used a lamb instead of a fawn, or if, like Dryden in *The Hind and the Panther*, he had intended something allegorical by his deer, he would have found ways of consistently intimating as much. Instead, he ends, as he began, with a series of conceits:

First my unhappy statue shall
Be cut in marble; and withal,
Let it be weeping too: but there
Th' engraver sure his art may spare;
For I so truly thee bemoan,
That I shall weep though I be stone:
Until my tears, still dropping, wear
My breast, themselves engraving there.
There at my feet shalt thou be laid,
Of purest alabaster made:
For I would have thine image be
White as I can, though not as thee.

(111–22)

What parting shot of doctrine is here? One can discern, at most, an amalgamation of Cyparissus, the youth who so notably grieved for his accidentally slain pet deer (Ovid *Met*., x 106ff.; Spenser, *The Faerie Queene*, I vi 17), and Niobe. As for white deer, they can be found outside the Song of Solomon. Petrarch himself has one (meaning by it Laura), *Rime*, 90, the sonnet beginning, 'Una candida cerva sopra l'erba.' The white roebuck is a commonplace in folklore (a fact which Robert Graves has lately publicized in *The White Goddess*). Life itself still furnishes albinistic fallow deer. Marvell could have got both fact and legend from the section on deer in Pliny's

278 E. S. Le Comte

Natural History: 'Sunt aliquando et candido colore, qualem fuisse traditur Q. Sertorii cervam, quam esse fatidicam Hispaniae gentibus persuaserat' (viii 117). (Lines 66–8, quoted below, reproduce accurately viii 113: 'semper in fuga adquiescunt stantesque respiciunt, cum prope ventum est, rursus fugae praesidia repetentes'.) Plutarch in his life of that general tells more about the famous white hind of Sertorius, how he feigned it was given him by the goddess Diana and communicated to him divine messages. It is possible that among the 'three hundred head of deer' (Augustine Birrell, *Andrew Marvell*, New York, 1905, p. 31) in the park at Nunappleton was a white fawn. But this is to oppose the extreme of mysticism with the extreme of literalism. Let us say Marvell's fawn is white in sign of beauty, superiority, and innocence. The color and everything else about the fawn are amply accounted for without resort to biblical allegory; on the other hand, there is much, too much, in the poem that mocks any attempt at a theological reading.

Note that it is 'troopers' who shot the fawn – which connotes, then as now, soldiers. The *Oxford English Dictionary*, recording no appearance of the word before 1640, states: 'The term was used in connexion with the Covenanting Army which invaded England in 1640.' If allegory is our game, why may we not say that the fawn stands for Merry England, mortally wounded in the Civil War?

> For it was full of sport; and light
> Of foot, and heart; and did invite,
> Me to its game. . . .
>
> (41–3)
>
> It is a wondrous thing, how fleet
> 'Twas on those little silver feet.
> With what a pretty skipping grace,
> It oft would challenge me the race:
> And when 't had left me far away,
> 'Twould stand, and run again, and stay.
> For it was nimbler much than hinds;
> And trod, as on the four winds.
>
> (63–70)

Things will never be again what they were in Marvell's youth, not to push further back to the Elizabethans (who got their culture through

Italy – Sylvio is an Italian name). This is Marvell's 'Farewell, rewards and fairies'.

Two – or, rather, three – can easily play at this game of letting our thoughts wander. It is not even to be denied, considering the fact of the Civil War and the fact of Marvell's (or any seventeenth-century Puritan's) intimacy with the Bible, that the poet's thoughts *could* have wandered in both these directions, at times, as he wrote. But this is mere psychobiographical conjecture – or autobiographical wool-gathering – rather than defensible interpretation of a poem whose lines are straight and clear, however much fun the frivolity of trying to twist them. Not every fancy or free association that may dart into a reader's head is fair. One reader who was questioned as to the meaning of the poem replied without hesitation that it represented a girl's lament for her lost virginity. The reader went on to substantiate this view in painful detail, beginning with the word 'wanton'!

Let us freely admit, without straining grotesquely for Christian 'color and significance,' that *The Nymph Complaining for the Death of her Fawn* is less pious than, say, *The White Doe of Rylstone*. It does not follow, as night the day, that Wordsworth's is the better poem. Heaviness is not all. Poe, in singling out Marvell's poem on the occasion of its appearance in S. C. Hall's *The Book of Gems* in 1836, flatly took issue with the editor by denominating it 'poetry of the *very loftiest order*'. And for Poe the poem was lighter than for other readers, since he strangely and characteristically, ignoring Sylvio and the tone of the opening lines, insisted on calling the nymph a 'child', 'the little maiden'.

To come back to those opening lines, the part to which it is proposed to sacrifice the whole, they admit of a pagan interpretation – and that is more what the rest of the poem seems to require. In line 104 'Diana's shrine' is mentioned. The nymph has turned away from men, become a practitioner of chastity and lover of deer, like Diana. Marvell is not likely to be using the word 'nymph' just casually to mean girl. Diana was *the* nymph, *nympha nympharum*, and her followers were nymphs. In connexion with the opening suggestion of recompense for a slain fawn, one is probably supposed to remember, if anything, not Christ, but the sacred stag which Agamemnon and his party slew (*they* were troopers, on the way to the Trojan War) while hunting in the grove of Artemis at Aulis, and on account of which the goddess exacted the sacrifice of Iphigenia. That such an exchange would be worth while in the present case is denied by Marvell's nymph:

There is not such another in
The world, to offer for their sin.

The attitude in the first verse paragraph is, as Grosart noted, similar to Blake's in *Auguries of Innocence*: 'A robin red breast in a cage|Puts all Heaven in a rage' and 'A horse misused upon the road|Calls to Heaven for human blood,' etc. Pity for the stricken deer is shown by Shakespeare (*As You Like It*, II 1, 33ff.), Drayton (*Poly-Olbion*, XIII 147ff.), and Montaigne (*Essais*, II 11), and the antivenery literature includes More's *Utopia* (II 6), Erasmus' *Encomium Moriae* (19), Plutarch's *De solertia animalium* (i–ii), and goes back to Pythagoras and the Pythagoreans (see Ovid *Met.* xv 75ff.).

What set the Misses Bradbrook and Thomas off in an allegorical direction? Was it, perhaps, *another* poem? It was, judging by the footnote on page 49: 'The whole poem may be related to the death and metamorphosis of Fida's hind in William Browne's *Britannia's Pastorals* (Book I, Songs 4 and 5). Browne's nymph represents religious Faith and the hind, Truth.' This suggestion is not original with these critics – it goes back to the edition of Margoliouth, who, in turn, is repeating Robert Poscher (*Andrew Marvells poetische Werke*, Vienna, 1908, p. 30). The only proposal that has so far been offered for a source for Marvell's poem, it is not very cogent. The nearest that Browne's hind comes to being shot by hunters is that a shepherd's dog barks at it; thereupon, without fear, it walks up to Fida in a friendly way (Song 3), only to be later (Song 4) devoured by the man-monster Riot; on which occasion we are given, not Fida's implorations, but the hind's. The happy ending has it that from the mangled remains springs up the maiden Aletheia (observe that Browne, like Dryden, makes unmistakable *his* allegories).

If we must have a source for the simple situation in Marvell's poem, we can do better by turning to a more famous poet than Browne – Virgil. In the seventh book of the *Aeneid*, lines 475ff., we are told how the Fury Alecto stirred up war between the Rutulians and the Trojans in Italy by causing Ascanius, while out hunting with his men, to wound mortally, with his arrow, the pet stag of – the

name is not without interest – Silvia. We are provided with details
(Browne offers none) of what this pet, stolen from its mother's udder,
meant to the girl, how she had tamed it and adorned its antlers with
garlands, and was wont to comb and bathe it. It became accustomed
to its mistress's table, 'mensaeque adsuetus erili', inspiration enough
for Marvell's couplet,

With sweetest milk, and sugar, first
I it at mine own fingers nursed.

(55–6)

Moaning and with the blood flowing, the stag finds its way back to
its mistress, who reacts as one would expect.

Silvia prima soror palmis percussa lacertos
Auxilium vocat et duros conclamat agrestis,[1]

says Virgil. 'O help! O help!' cries Marvell's nymph, whose name,
if she is to be assigned one, is Silvia rather than Pietà.

(97–101)

Karina Williamson

'Marvell's *The Nymph Complaining*: A Reply', *Modern Philology*, vol.
51 1954

In his article in 1952, Professor Le Comte was right to expose the
flaws in Miss Bradbrook and Miss Lloyd Thomas' theory of the
religious significance of Marvell's poem; but neither his objections
nor his alternative explanations seem to me to justify his assertion that
'the poem, like any good poem, has overtones, but these are not
religious', or his suggestion that the recognition of any religious
associations is a frivolous distortion of the 'straight and clear' lines of
the poem. His remark, 'Not every fancy or free association that may
dart into a reader's head is fair,' raises the crucial point; if the biblical
associations which Miss Bradbrook and Miss Lloyd Thomas claimed
to detect were as 'free' and unwarranted as Professor Le Comte
suggests, their interpretation would indeed be indefensible; but in
my view there is enough evidence to show that the poem certainly

1 First Sylvia, the sister, beating her arms with her hands, calls for help and
shouts to the hardy country folk! [Ed.]

has 'religious overtones', even if they are not sufficient to justify a cohesive religious interpretation.

In any case, Professor Le Comte misrepresents Miss Bradbrook and Miss Lloyd Thomas when he attributes to them the thesis that 'the poem is an allegory on the Crucifixion'; their interpretation is not so circumscribed. Their suggestion is that the poem presents 'a very complete hierarchy of love,' in which 'the love of the girl for her fawn is taken to be a reflection of the love of the Church for Christ'; they even enter a caveat, warning that 'to relate is not to obliterate differences. Marvell's very nicety of control of the transitions has impressed on the reader the need for making distinctions' (pp. 49–50). The only justification for Professor Le Comte's reading of their theory is the footnote on page 49 referring to lines 93–8, with which they compare the earlier lines about the troopers, 'who now seem to have slain that which would have redeemed them.'

The cardinal reason for supposing that the poem is intended to have religious associations is that the central passage seems so clearly to draw on the Song of Solomon. Professor Le Comte makes light of this point, but it cannot be dismissed so readily; the parallels are very striking, even more than is shown in the quotations given by Miss Bradbrook and Miss Lloyd Thomas (probably they thought it already obvious), so I give an expanded version. Compare with lines 71–92:

I have a garden of my own,
But so with roses overgrown,
And lilies, that you would it guess
To be a little wilderness.
And all the spring time of the year
It only loved to be there.
Among the beds of lilies, I
Have sought it oft, where it should lie;
Yet could not, till itself would rise,
Find it, although before mine eyes.
For in the flaxen lilies shade,
It like a bank of lilies laid.
Upon the roses it would feed,
Until its lips ev'n seemed to bleed:

And then to me 'twould boldly trip,
And print those roses on my lip.
But all its chief delight was still
On roses thus itself to fill:
And its pure virgin limbs to fold
In whitest sheets of lilies cold.
Had it lived long, it would have been
Lilies without, roses within.

the Song of Solomon:

The voice of my beloved! behold, he cometh leaping upon the
    mountains, skipping upon the hills (cf. Marvell, line 65).
My beloved is like a roe or a young hart ... (Song of Sol., ii, 8–9).
My beloved is mine and I am his: he feedeth among the lilies.
Until the day break and the shadows flee away, turn, my beloved,
    and be thou like a roe or a young hart upon the mountains of
    Bether (ii, 16–17).
I am come into my garden, my sister, my spouse: ... I have eaten
    my honeycomb with my honey; I have drunk my wine with my
    milk (v, 1; cf. Marvell, line 55).
My beloved is white and ruddy. ... His cheeks are as beds of spices,
    as sweet flowers: his lips like sweet lilies, dropping sweet myrrh.
    ... His mouth is most sweet (v, 10, 13, 16; cf. Marvell, lines58–9).
My beloved is gone down into his garden, to the beds of spices, to
    feed in the gardens, and to gather lilies.
I am my beloved's, and my beloved is mine: he feedeth among the
    lilies (vi, 2–3).
By night on my bed I sought him whom my soul loveth: I sought
    him but I found him not (iii, 1).

Possibly, also, the fawn's 'chain and bell', which Professor Le Comte
finds so ludicrous in a religious context, may have been suggested by
the 'chains of gold' around the neck of the lover (i, 10). I am not
trying to suggest that the parallels are logically exact – the lover's lips
are like lilies, while the fawn's are rose-stained[1] – but that the verbal

1 But see P. Carey's 'Crucifixus pro nobis,' Seventeenth Century Lyrics, ed.
Ault, 2nd edn, London, 1950, p. 262, referring to Christ in the cradle,
His lips are blue
(Where roses grew).

similarities are too frequent and striking to be accidental. It is difficult to believe that an educated reader of Marvell's time could have missed these associations when we remember how familiar the Song of Solomon would have been to him. Besides the many commentaries and expositions on it published in the sixteenth and seventeenth centuries, numerous metrical versions testify to its popularity in literary circles. I have found mention of seventeen printed versions between 1549 and 1659, including ones by Quarles, George Sandys, Drayton, and a lost version by Spenser (if his printer is to be relied upon). In addition to these, there are in the Bodleian alone five MS translations or paraphrases in verse, of the seventeenth century, including one by Marvell's friend, Lord Fairfax; while the use made of the Song in seventeenth-century emblem books and poetry in general is incalculable. It was conventional to address Christ, or speak of him, in terms of the Song of Solomon, as in Herrick's carol for Christmas, *The Star-Song*:

Tell us, thou clear and heavenly tongue
Where is the Babe but lately sprung?
Lies He the lily-banks among?

(1–3)[1]

and in Vaughan's *Dressing*:

O thou that lovest a pure and whitened soul!
That feed'st among the lilies till the day
Break, and the shadows flee . . .

(1–3)[2]

which is just a paraphrase of the Song, ii, 16–17. Professor Le Comte's comment after lines 91–2 – 'Where is the crown of thorns here?' – is irrelevant. It is the relationship between the church and Christ (or the Virgin and Christ in Roman Catholic interpretations), not the suffering of Christ, that is supposed to be prefigured in the Song of Solomon.

Of course, use of the Song language is no guaranty that a religious allusion is intended (the passage in Chaucer's tale of January and May[3]

1 *Poetical Works*, ed. Moorman, Oxford, 1915, p. 367.
2 *Works*, ed. Martin, Oxford, 1914, p. 455.
3 *Complete Works*, ed. Robinson, Oxford, 1933, p. 149, lines 2138 ff.

is a famous example of the exploitation of it for secular purposes), but that would be the normal deduction; and here there has already been a certain direction of associations into religious channels through the use of terms with a specifically religious denotation: 'prayers', 'heaven' and 'Heaven's King', 'saint', 'holy frankincense', 'deodand' ('the priestcraft word', according to Hickering [1705], quoted by O.E.D.)

Moreover, an awareness of the poem's religious resources makes other phrases two-edged. The fawn treading 'as on the four winds' becomes reminiscent of the Psalmist's vision of God, 'who walketh upon the wings of the wind' (civ, 3; cf. also xviii, 10), an image which found its way into the Sarum Missal; the comparison of the fawn's tears to 'the wounded balsam' may be connected with the idea of the wounded Christ as the 'Balsam of souls' (Vaughan, *The Search*, line 44),[1] 'Whose breast weeps balm for wounded man' (Crashaw, *The Hymn of Saint Thomas*, line 46).[2] With the whole passage in Marvell, compare Herbert's *The Sacrifice*:

Therefore my soul melts, and my heart's dear treasure
Drops blood. . . .
These drops being tempered with a sinner's tears
A balsam are for both the hemispheres.

$$(21-2, 25-6)^3$$

Professor Le Comte finds in the nymph's renunciation of human love (lines 37-40, 53-4, 109ff.) a likeness to Diana: 'The nymph has turned away from men, become a practitioner of chastity and lover of deer, like Diana. Marvell is not likely to be using the word "nymph" just casually to mean girl. Diana was *the* nymph, *nympha nympharum*, and her followers were nymphs.' A nymph, whether divine or human, was essentially virginal; 'A virgin, a fair young maid' is the definition in Bullokar's dictionary (1616), and 'nymphs of the woods' are defined as 'virgin-goddesses' by Coles (1676). The conception of virginity is as appropriate to the 'undefiled' bride of

1 *Works*, p. 406.
2 *Poems*, ed. Martin, Oxford, 1927, p. 293. Curiously enough, in *The Weeper* Mary Magdalene's tears, like the fawn's, are likened both to the balsam (stanza 12) and to 'the amber-weeping tree' (stanza 8).
3 *Works*, ed. Hutchinson, Oxford, 1941, p. 27.

the Song of Solomon (see iv, 12; v, 2; vi, 9) and to subsequent
'brides of Christ' as to Diana and her followers. I do not see that the
two sets of associations are incompatible.

Professor Le Comte asks 'who are the ermines?' Unlike the swans,
turtles (often merely a synonym for doves) and lambs they have no
precise connexions with religion (the swan is the type of Christ and
of Mary in Roman Catholic literature),[1] but their appropriateness is
surely obvious: they were noted for their whiteness, like the fawn
itself, and a legend for purity. The legend found its way into Dyche's
dictionary in the eighteenth century: 'The animal is milk white, and
so far from spots, that 'tis reported that he will rather die or be taken
than sully its whiteness' (1735); but it was already well known in
the seventeenth (see John Hall's The Ermine).

Others of the issues which Professor Le Comte raises are more
serious. If we admit the connexion between the fawn of the poem and
the roe (= Christ) of the Song of Solomon and recognize the possibility of other religious associations being present, as in lines 23–4,
which could have obvious Christian implications, we ultimately have
to face the question of how far the analogies are meant to stretch. And
here some of Professor Le Comte's objections to a complete indenti-
fication of the fable with the story of the Crucifixion seem to me
unanswerable. The most important are the dubious theology of lines
5–6 (though it is arguable that this applies only to the murderers);
the impossibility of fitting the passage relating to Sylvio (lines 25–36)
into any reasonable interpretation on Christian lines; and, indeed,
the total lack of specific allusions (other than the actual slaying of the
fawn) to the events of the Passion. The suggestion of a possible source
in the story of Sylvia's stag in the Aeneid, on the other hand, though
very likely correct, does not explain away the religious allusions.
What, then, is their function? My view is that the poem certainly has
'religious overtones' but that they are intended as overtones, not as
a ground bass. In other words, they are not meant to supply another
level of significance parallel to, or expressed through, the literal
surface meaning but to intensify that 'meaning'. One is reminded of
Empson's remark in connexion with the Heliades image: 'one expects

1 Cf. Crashaw, Upon Our Lord's Last Comfortable Discourse with His Disciples,
Poems, p. 95; and Henry Hawkins, Partheneia Sacra, 1633, p. 27, where the swan
is an emblem of the Virgin.

a simile with reserves of meaning';[1] part of the power of this poem lies in its reserves; they help to give to an apparently slight story that effect of seriousness which T.S. Eliot notices.[2] They are part of the 'wit' of the poem, a 'wit' involving 'probably, a recognition, implicit in the expression of every experience, of other kinds of experience which are possible.'[3] Lines such as

There is not such another in
The world, to offer for their sin.

(23-4)

are effective, not for their 'hyperbole and conceit' in Professor Le Comte's phrase, but because, within the poem, they seem so true. The experience manifested in the poem is felt to belong to the total order of human experience.

(268-71)

1 *Seven Types of Ambiguity*, 2nd edn, London, 1949, p. 168.
2 'Andrew Marvell,' *Selected Essays*, 2nd edn, London, 1949, p. 300.
3 ibid., p. 303.

Upon Appleton House

Maren-Sofie Røstvig

from *The Happy Man*, revised edition 1962

The entire design of Marvell's poem seems grounded on a single theological or religious concept, to wit the contrast between innocence and corruption. The quest for moral and spiritual regeneration is pursued through regional history (the history of the religious establishment at Nunappleton), the history of England (in the allusions to the civil war), and universal history (the allusions to the major events of the Old and the New Testament).[1*]

Biblical allusions are particularly important. On viewing the landscape both Benlowes and Marvell are reminded of the crossing of the Red Sea and the river Jordan, of the miraculous provision of manna and quails in the desert, of Christ's love sacrifice on the cross, and of the religious devotee's union with Christ in a holy death which murders sense. To this Marvell adds references to the building of the tower of Babel and to Noah and the Ark. The ancient Church fathers had given these Biblical events quite specific typological meanings, and unless we are familiar with their interpretations, we shall fail to realize the implications clearly intended by Benlowes and Marvell. We must therefore study the symbolical value of these events, remembering that medieval and Renaissance theologians submitted both books of revelation (the Book of God's Word and the book of God's Work) to a searching, multi-levelled technique of interpretation. A deeper, spiritual sense was sought behind the historical events and behind the surface of things. It can scarcely be doubted that this habitual quest for various levels of meaning exerted the strongest influence on the type of poetry considered here.

In his study of *Symbolism in Medieval Thought* H. Flanders Dunbar explains how the rock might have three levels of meaning beyond its literal use as descriptive symbol:

It may stand for Christ, . . . or it may exemplify that which each soul should be to its fellows . . . or finally the rock may mean the foundation of the heavenly kingdom. In other words, every natural

* The notes appear on p. 293.

object may be taken allegorically as telling of the life of the Logos; tropologically, as conveying teaching as to the inner life of man; and anagogically as containing revelation of the life in glory. Every symbol should be understood at one and the same time in all of these significations . . . Each natural object, whether animate or inanimate, had its particular meaning on each of these levels.[2]

Marvell's poem displays a similar semantic complexity. Behind the literal, surface meaning lie both political allegory and a deeper, more spiritual sense. The political allegory has been ably explained by Don Cameron Allen.[3] I shall therefore focus on the purely religious or philosophical aspects. In the course of his exposition D. C. Allen takes notice of certain parts which may be interpreted typologically or anagogically,[4] but this type of insight symbol is not pursued systematically.

An excellent survey of the traditional interpretation of the main events of the Old Testament is given by Jean Daniélou, S. J., in his book *From Shadows to Reality. Studies in the Typology of the Fathers.*[5] I have also found Rosemond Tuve's book on George Herbert very useful.[6] The following exposition of some main points in the typology of the Church Fathers is based on the former.

The basic principle of typology is found in the belief that human existence constitutes an imperfect order which prepares for and prefigures an order of perfection. This perfection is achieved when natural man turns into spiritual man. The achievement of this process is the purpose of all the events in the Old Testament and the New. God's scheme for the redemption of the fallen Adam stands reflected in the four fundamental types of the Old Testament: the ark of Noah, the crossing of the Red Sea, the Mosaic Law, and the entry into the promised land. In the words of Jean Daniélou: 'All the outstanding persons and leading events of Scripture are both stages and rough outlines to prepare and prefigure the mystery which is one day to be fulfilled in Christ.'[7] Thus paradise lies in the future as well as in the past; the New Paradise was realized with the coming of Christ, and each Christian becomes a New Adam in his turn through Holy Baptism, 'which is thus revealed as a new creation and a return to Paradise.'[8] Paradise may therefore be realized in the Christian life, as Marvell suggests in his homage to Fairfax, whose garden is a literal Paradise. The ark of Noah is particularly rich in typological significance. The deliverance of Noah and the deliverance of Moses are the two main works of God in the Old Testament, and they are often associated together. Noah and Moses are types of Christ, their actions foreshadowing his. With the Flood is associated the sea beast Leviathan, a type of wickedness, just as in the crossing of the Red Sea Pharaoh and his horsemen represent the devil, or sin. Both are overcome by Christ. The Flood is

the figure of Christ's triumph over the sea dragon through his descent into Hell: he is the true Noah who has experienced the swelling of the waters of death, and has been delivered by God to be the beginning of a new world; it represents also Baptism wherein the Christian is buried with Christ in the water of death through the symbol of the baptismal waters, figuratively undergoing the punishment due to sin and being free with Christ and henceforth belonging to the new creation . . .[9]

Baptism therefore is a spiritual version of Noah's deliverance from the Flood, and also of the deliverance wrought by God through Moses when he commanded the Red Sea to divide.

A further turn of the interpretative screw is achieved on considering the interpretation submitted by Philo, whose influence on Origen and St Ambrose was profound. Philo interpreted *Genesis* as a Platonic myth. Thus the creation of Adam represented the creation of mind, while the creation of Eve represented the creation of sensation, or the life of the senses. As St Ambrose commented: 'Very rightly is mind represented by the symbol of man, and feeling by that of woman.'[10] Marvell's rejection of women therefore signifies a rejection of mere sense; at this point the teachings of Hermes and the Church Fathers coincide. Similarly Philo interprets the rescue of the Israelites from the Egyptians as a transition from a state dominated by the body (the Egyptians representing the bodily passions) to a state dominated by mind. As we shall soon see, Marvell, too, associates Pharaoh's horsemen with the physical passions, from which he seeks, and finds, deliverance in his 'yet green, yet growing ark'. In this manner the journey through the desert becomes a type of the soul's passage through life. The passions must be overcome, and this is achieved through the progressive enlightenment afforded by the Logos. Both

Benlowes and Marvell are intent on depicting such a spiritual journey. Both refer to the act of retirement as a retreat into a fortress, from which the soul wages a pious war against the world, the flesh, and the devil. And, in so doing, both refer to the five senses as the *Cinque-Ports* over which the strictest guard must be kept.[11]

We can now turn to the poem itself. As already stated, its main motif is the quest for redemption and innocence regained, a quest closely associated with the fortunes of the Fairfax family. Thus the rescue of the 'Virgin Thwaites' from her gloomy nunnery was a rescue from a state dominated by Evil ('I know what fruit their gardens yield,|When they it think by night conceal'd') to the holy state of matrimony. In the same manner the retirement of the Lord General was prompted by the wish to avoid the depravity inherent in the world; it represents the triumph of conscience over ambition, of mind over the world of sense. Fairfax's environment reflects the same contrast between innocence and corruption. Over against his modest house appears 'proud Cawood Castle' as a visual manifestation of the ambition of its 'prelate great' (stanza 46). The beauty and sweetness of his garden makes the poet bewail that 'luckless apple' which made man mortal and laid waste 'The garden of the world' (stanza 41). The corruption which thus gained entrance into man, Nature, and the body politic is allegorized in the stanzas describing how the 'traitor-worm' destroys the oak so that it may be felled by the lightest stroke. The cruel massacres of the mowers (types of soldiers engaged in civil war) provide a graphic illustration of that state of war which marks the postlapsarian state.[12] The chaotic state of the world is again strongly stressed in the concluding stanzas which denounce it as 'a rude heap together hurl'd;|All negligently overthrown,|Gulfs, deserts, precipices, stones'. The lesser world of the garden contains the same elements, but in 'more decent order tame'.

The forces of innocence form a strong contrast to the forces of evil. In attacking the Nunnery and exposing the 'wooden saints' and 'relics false' the first Fairfax becomes a type of the Protestant hero, 'whose offspring fierce|Shall fight through all the universe'. On a smaller scale he imitates the redemptive action of Christ by rescuing a human soul from corruption to sanctity. A second strong contrast is that between the cruel massacres of the mowers and the spiritual warfare conducted by the Lord General against the world and his own five senses. The concluding section focuses on Maria Fairfax as the symbol of innocence. She is seen as the archetype of that beauty and innocence which marks the garden of Nunappleton. By virtue of the sanctity of its residents, Fairfax's estate becomes 'Heaven's centre, Nature's lap,|And Paradise's only map'. The internal and external worlds are interdependent in the familiar manner of the Renaissance. When redeemed from vice, pride, and ambition, man bestows the same redemption upon Nature, just as conversely the corruption of Adam and Eve once had brought death and decay into the world.

Once it is seen that Marvell's poem is organized in this manner, its unity becomes apparent. The historical episode concerning the abduction from the Nunnery becomes relevant, and so does the political allegory, and the various compliments to Fairfax and his daughter. The individual, the church, the body politic, and Nature must undergo the same process of purgation. As in *The Garden* the method employed involves a contemplative retirement into rural scenes and a focusing of all the powers of the mind on God. To the contemplating mind the chief events in the universal history of man yield up their inner, spiritual significance, at the same time that deeper insights are gained from a close study of the Book of God's Work.

References
1. For an exposition of this literary tradition, see E. Katherine Dunn, 'The Medieval Cycle as History Play: an Approach to the Wakefield Plays,' *Studies in the Renaissance*, vol. 7, 1960, pp. 76–89. The main point of universal history is to unfold God's plan for His chosen people. St Augustine's *City of God* is the *locus classicus* for the Christian theology of history according to which the history of the world is divided into a cosmic 'week' consisting of seven periods: the creation, the covenant with Noah, the covenant with Abraham, the exodus, the reign of David, the Babylonian captivity, and the incarnation of Christ. In such a history questions of chronology are irrelevant, since one is concerned with the inner meaning of events, these being interpreted as types of the events connected with Christ and God's scheme of redemption.
2. H. Flanders Dunbar, *Symbolism in Medieval Thought*, Yale University Press, 1929, pp. 19 f.
3. Don Cameron Allen, *Image and Meaning: Metaphoric Traditions in Renaissance Poetry*, Baltimore: Johns Hopkins Press, 1960, pp. 115–53.
4. Thus he comments on the fact that Noah's stay in the Ark for forty days is a type of Christ's retreat into the wilderness for forty days in order to contemplate his mission. If Marvell intended his allusion to the former

event to provoke associations with the latter (if, in other words, he views
Noah as a type of Christ), his re-enactment of Christ's passion in stanzas
77 and 78 has been carefully prepared for. See also Allen's interpretation of
Maria Fairfax as a personification of divine wisdom.

5. Published by Burns and Oates, London, in 1960.
6. Rosemond Tuve, *A Reading of George Herbert*, London, 1952. This study
   provides interesting information about the various avenues through which
   certain typological significances had become sufficiently familiar for poets
   to be able to draw upon them for the sake of their generally accepted
   symbolic value.
7. Jean Daniélou, S.J., *From Shadows to Reality*, London, 1960, p. 11.
8. ibid., p. 19.
9. ibid., p. 83.
10. ibid., p. 64.
11. Compare lines 285-8 and 349-50 with the following excerpt from the
    prefatory poem (*Pneumato-Sarco-Machia: or Theophila's Spiritual Warfare*):

> Then be sure
> That all thy outworks stand secure . . .
> Design
> With constant care a watch o'er every part;
> Ev'n at thy Cinque-ports, and thy heart
> Set sentinels. Let Faith be captain o'er
> The life-guard, standing at the door
> Of thy well-warded breast . . .

> Quoted from G. Saintsbury, ed., *The Caroline Poets*, vol. 1, Oxford,
> 1905, p. 322.

12. It is possible that Du Bartas, as translated by Sylvester, may have prompted
    Marvell to associate the massacring mowers with Moses and the punish-
    ment which he inflicted on the erring Israelites for their adoration of the
    golden calf. Du Bartas had compared the furious onslaught of the 'zealous
    prophet' to that of a group of reapers:

> . . . each where [he] strows his way
> With blood and slaughter, horror and dismay:
> As half a score of reapers nimbly-neat,
> With cheerful eye choosing a plot of wheat,
> Reap it at pleasure, and of Ceres' locks
> Make handfulls sheaves, and of their sheaves make shocks;
> And through the field from end to end do run,
> Working a-vie, till all be down and done.

> *Du Bartas His Divine Weeks And Works*, London, 1621, p. 372. The passage
> occurs in the Second Week, the Third Day and the Third Part (*The Law*).

(I 172-7)

Robin Grove

from 'Marvell', *Melbourne Critical Review*, vol. 6 1963

The kind of comedy I think most characteristic of Marvell's poetry at its finest is neither a whimsical fancifulness nor a knowing play on words and traditional images, though both manners may sometimes be part of the wit. The range of Marvell's wit has an order and congruity far more impressive than the humorous elegance he can effect, and I would indicate it in the *Horatian Ode*, where it is altogether present in every line, rather than in the more evidently witty *Appleton House*, where the insights teasingly proffered are only occasionally relevant to the graceful diversions of imagery and the lighthearted tricks of language. It seems almost perverse that an article as intelligent and serious in purpose as S. L. Goldberg's (*Melbourne Critical Review*, 1960) should take for its starting-point a poem that scarcely demonstrates Marvell's real strength. *Appleton House* is for the most part insignificant as poetry, though it is impregnated with Marvell's brilliant and lively sense of comedy. The sharpness of perception and the rapidly proposed images make an odd effect in the often inert poetry, for Marvell seems capricious or evasive in his dealings with imaginative experience, exploiting effects that remain unsubstantiated by the quality of the verse. The shifting tone, the elusive imagery, the varying manners the poem assumes indicate something more than a delicate and easy talent for pastoral, but they fail to validate that inquiry into philosophical speculations which *Appleton House* seems to undertake.

While wholly in agreement, then, with Mr Goldberg's comments on the great variety of tone and the ingenious play of Marvell's imagination, I would suggest that these qualities represent an activity on the part of the poet different from the 'exploration of human values in their diverse relationships with reality' that Mr Goldberg's article is concerned to elucidate. If this were Marvell's aim in *Appleton House* we should be forced to count the poem a failure. The slack verse and the disparity between the development of the themes and the quality of the writing make such a claim impossible. Despite some brilliant passages I do not think *Appleton House* a good poem, but it is acceptable *because* the poetry (characteristically) will not allow us to accept its philosophizing as anything but a game. Mr Goldberg has indicated this playful manner, but he attributes a far greater importance to the witty effects of such a manner (the significance suggested by that Meadow-Sea) than the jocular, relaxed poetry can support.

The poem is, of course, an extended jest, and its humour may pursue the most fugitive impressions as more sober statement could not. We may confidently call the mode of the first seven stanzas one of caricature, which we find diverting by the neatness with which observation is made to answer to the rules of the game of wit:

Who of his great design in pain
Did for a model vault his brain,
Whose columns should so high be raised
To arch the brows that on them gazed.

(5-8)

The confusing and often contradictory heaping of conceit upon pun and paradox is typical of the game the poetry plays, but the mind's bewilderment makes difficult any reflection upon the *meaning* of this game. The image of Nunappleton House as a 'sober frame' to hold the 'wanton mote of dust', which the opening stanzas evoke, is curiously irrelevant to what we feel as the life and interest of the poetry: that is, the swiftly changing metaphors and the surprising wit dissolving each conceit into its successor. Verse such as this does not prompt us to an understanding of the various tendencies (humility and naturalness, for instance) that Nunappleton is said to represent. What instead engages the imagination, though lightly, is the play of the mind over distracting and eccentric metaphors. The paucity of rhythmic invention, the easy movement and the simple rhymes hardly suggest a poetry concerned to order, and to question by its ordering, experience of richly imaginative power. What we find is something far closer to the comic lines of stanza 12:

Near to this gloomy cloister's gates
There dwelt the blooming virgin Thwaites,
Fair beyond measure, and an heir
Which might deformity make fair.
And oft she spent the summer suns
Discoursing with the subtle nuns . . .

Brilliantly effective though such comedy can be, it will scarcely satisfy us for long. Our pleasure is due to the lightness of phrase, the exact turn of language and fall of the rhyme; but we expect a poetry that is not merely amusing itself. The development lacks coherence and proportion – though these are the very virtues that are praised in Nunappleton House – and we feel the marked profusion of images to be not so much compelling as tiring. Marvell appears intent on the intimation of a subtle and ambiguous speculative position, but instead we prize the witty swiftness of intelligence and the startling images that are cleverly given an air of mock-seriousness. As for the rest, the interest of the poetry is not in any examination of the human significance of Nunappleton House, but in a piling up of conceits, the unexpected comic rhyme and the contortions of the nuns' argument. Yet the rhythm is often flaccid and monotonous, and not only the inhabitants of the Nunnery are absurd, but Fairfax also is obliged to submit to the game being played-out by the verse.

But, waving these aside like flies,
Young Fairfax through the wall does rise.
Then th' unfrequented vault appeared,
And superstitions vainly feared.
The relics false were set to view;
Only the jewels there were true.
But truly bright and holy Thwaites
That weeping at the altar waits.

(257–64)

Even where the poem evokes a sense of more serious and more sinister issues it does so with the same detached air of caricature:

For such indeed are all our arts;
Still handling Nature's finest parts.
Flow'rs dress the altars; for the clothes,
The sea-born amber we compose;
Balms for the grieved we draw; and pastes
We mould, as baits for curious tastes.
What need is here of man? unless
These as sweet sins we should confess.

(177–84)

As a criticism of the life of the Nunnery this must seem little more than frivolous. The smooth rhythms and facile rhymes encourage a rapid progression of the argument which, with its knowingly-placed implications ('Nature's finest parts') gives the illusion of an unmasking of the nuns' corruption – but the easy texture of the verse can only measure the guilty cynicism of the Nunnery against a superficial worldliness. The familiar poise of manner that we observe in the confident turn of the argument ('What need is here of man? unless|These as sweet sins we should confess') is no more than deceptive, for the distancing by this slight formality seems to indicate a discreet play of irony about the subject, the striving for a finer balance of feeling that will be adequate to the suggestions of the words. In fact, the poetry is oddly static and the mocking tone of the wit generates no new imaginative insight, but leaves us with an inert and single attitude toward the scene.

> For if the virgin proved not theirs,
> The cloister yet remained hers.
> Though many a nun there made her vow,
> 'Twas no religious house till now.
>
> (277–80)

Stanza 26 commences a new advance of the poem, notable for the tactful balance which is struck between seriousness and a relaxed tone whose slight formality supports the gracefully developed simile of the flower regiments. But the dignity and freshness of the best of these stanzas too often gives way to an insistent lack of rhythmic sensitivity and, despite the image of the garden-fortress with its implicit (and controlled) ambiguities, the poetry labours at its conceits until they seem mere emblems that have lost their own power of suggestiveness:

> The nursery of all things green
> Was then the only magazine.
> The winter quarters were the stoves,
> Where he the tender plants removes.
>
> (339–42)

As the passage continues it becomes plain that there is something self-breeding about these analogies and conceits. The effect of self-stimulating images, each distracting attention to itself, each adroitly placed but organized in an external, almost mechanical progression, is incompatible with the delicately precise balance of apprehension that the ironies of the garden-fortress would require of the reader. We are aware not of the probing mind and its urgent need to be delivered of a complex vision, but of a deft fancy that links the images in an external logic. It is a victory of the mode of the poetry, and the subjugation of the vision that should use it.

There is, however, an exquisite politeness qualifying the self-importance of these analogies. Too many poets write extravagant verses in praise of their patrons, but Marvell's hyperbole does not admit unthinking acceptance or equally unthinking rejection; one cannot praise a Fairfax in poetry that is simply conventional and conventionally insincere. By adopting so self-consciously the expected devices and poses Marvell reveals the falseness of such praise. At the same time in an occasionally rich and diverse poetry he gives substance to the very real compliment to Fairfax that is hidden beneath the ornate surface of the poem. The elaborate artifice of the writing is matched by a comedy of grotesque conceits and extended analogies, so that while the verse can be an engrossing game, it is recognized as ust that and no more. *Appleton House*, highly mannered and literary though the stratagem is, does not pretend to praise Fairfax: he is (we might assume) too great for such a common measure.

Yet this does not constitute the poetic strength of *Appleton House* any more than that strength is to be located in the quasi-philosophical judgements arising out of Marvell's reflections on the house and the surrounding countryside. The general slightness of the verse and the almost Jesuitical cunning with which Marvell has devised these sophisticated implications for the urbane Understander contrast strongly with the supple, alive poetry of the finest stanzas:

And now to the abyss I pass
Of that unfathomable grass,
Where men like grasshoppers appear,
But grasshoppers are giants there:
They, in their squeaking laugh, contemn
Us as we walk more low than them:
And, from the precipices tall
Of the green spires to us do call.

To see men through this meadow dive,
We wonder how they rise alive.
As, under water, none does know
Whether he fall through it or go.
But, as the mariners that sound,
And show upon their lead the ground,
They bring up flowers so to be seen,
And prove they've at the bottom been.

(369–84)

The gravely moving rhythm, with its natural inflections and quietly-controlled cadences, is exactly attuned to a discreet intimacy between author and audience. Those fantastic evolutions of imagery are checked by a faint air of comic pedantry that shows itself in the delicate forwarding of the argument ('as . . . but . . . so') and the half-concealed preparation for a simile of the mariners. There is even a certain gallantry in the lightly-given justification for the poem's telescoping of perspectives: after all, the vision of the 'unfathomable grass' *is* really evoked in the pausing and rounding of the rhythm, and in the superb organization of the whole stanza, where the travelling of the glance from the abyss to the spires each time discovers a new aspect of the scene. We are not invited to accept a merely fanciful elaboration of a conceit, but a vision that has its own validity and is subject to its proper laws. Amused though the poetry may be, it is also perfectly serious – the 'squeaking laugh' of the towering grass-hoppers is both sinister and comic.

But *Appleton House* does not achieve that significant complexity it seems to have within its grasp. The excellence of the poetry is sporadic and the quality quite unrelated to the (apparently dialectical) shifts of perspective that take us deeper and deeper into the natural scene. So, following these splendid stanzas, there is much that is dull or disturbingly whimsical. Indeed, the verse is sometimes a complete evasion of feeling and appears an elaborating of spurious vitality. The final impression is of an ornamental and fanciful half-life.

Bind me ye woodbines in your twines,
Curl me about ye gadding vines,
And O so close your circles lace,
That I may never leave this place:

But, lest your fetters prove too weak,
Ere I your silken bondage break,
Do you, O brambles, chain me too,
And courteous briars nail me through.

(609–16)

Here the Crucifixion is no more than a decorative pantomime, with
its 'silken brambles', 'gadding vines' and 'circles lace' (the line
works both ways), so instead of passion, agony or transcendence there
is only artifice. The use of associations surrounding the words is
irresponsible, for no real effort is made to come to terms with the
imaginative life they bring into the poem. Whatever value we discern
in this as a stage in the poem's development will depend upon the
imaginative coherence of that development. Finding, however, that
the exploration is attempted in such uneven poetry, it is difficult to
claim that this scene in the wood is placed against a genuinely
inclusive vision made actual elsewhere.

As Mr Goldberg has pointed out, the final section should portray
the humanity that is 'both a model for nature and its fulfillment, the
ideal *stasis* of its energies', but such challenging complexity does not
exist in the verse that transforms the scene into something unreal and
precious. The ability of the poetry to maintain a balanced complication of feeling (such as we found in the 'unfathomable grass') has
begun to flag, and the air of amused indulgence in surprising or
specious conceits, lively humour and nicely-measured artificialities is
overwhelming. What remains is not the balance but the complication.

The poem is ingenious, capricious and delightfully self-aware of its
ability to entertain the most diverse, swift-moving succession of
images, and to participate wholly in the jest, yet to create from this
libertine wit a poetry that sometimes transcends the limitations of the
fanciful. I am convinced that Marvell's mockery of his own captivat-
ingly absurd effects must be accepted as a civilized politeness by which
he defers the claims of his art to be – covertly or overtly – speculation.

(31–6)

Harold E. Toliver

from 'Pastoral and History', *Marvell's Ironic Vision* 1965

> But I have for my music found
> A sadder, yet more pleasing sound:
> The stock-doves, whose fair necks are graced
> With nuptial rings, their ensigns chaste;
> Yet always, for some cause unknown,
> Sad pair unto the elms they moan.
> O why should such a couple mourn,
> That in so equal flames do burn!
>
> (*Upon Appleton House*, 521–8)

The elm tree and the doves are undoubtedly suggested by the actual Fairfax estate that Marvell ostensibly describes, but the gardens of literature are fused with the actual scene. The basis for the dove's emblematic qualities, as in those of the bee, lay in the early naturalists and in the amplifications of various bestiaries which connected it to 'our Saviour'.[1] Commenting upon the Canticles ('vox turturis audita est in terra nostra'), Hugh of St Victor finds that by the voice of the dove is meant the sorrow of the weary mind devoted to God.[2] The dove-soul comes to the garden and builds its nest of 'deliverance and safety' in the branches of the scriptural tree. When it sings its mournful song, the perceptive ear recognizes Christ's laments upon the cross and the soul's own sorrow when remembering the mystery of the crucifixion. Hugh's forest, like Marvell's, thus becomes a scriptural milieu with the tree-cross as its center and a mystic lesson to be read in its leafage.

1 *Physiologus latinus versio y*, ed. Francis J. Carmody, *University of California Publications in Classical Philology*, vol. 12, 1933–4, p. 131.
2 See J.-P. Migne, *Patrologia Latina*, 1854, 177:25; cf. comments by Pliny, X:52; Philo I: 24–29; St Gregory, *Moralium*, 19:1 (Migne, 76:97); Quarles IV xii; Crashaw, *To the Name of Jesus: A Hymn*, *On a Prayer Book sent to Mrs M. R.*, *On the Assumption* and *On a Treatise of Charity*; Vaughan, *H. Scriptures*; Bede's commentary on Matt. 31 in Migne, 92:173–74; and other versions of the scriptural forest in Vaughan's *Jesus Weeping*, *Retirement* and *The Revived*; J. Mason Neale and B. Webb, *Du Symbolisme dans les Églises du Moyen Age*, Bourasse, 1847, p. 12.

The doves also suggest to Herman Hugo the marriage of the chaste soul to Christ. In *Pia Desideria* (II 14), which presents the scriptural forest in emblem form, a penitent sinner kneels before an apple tree in which Christ is crucified, apples and leaves hanging about so as nearly to absorb him into the tree. The prayer he utters is a mixture of Christian and classical pastoral tropes:

O! who will shade me from this scorching heat?
See on my head how the fierce sunbeams beat!

.　　.　　.　　.　　.

Then you I praise, dear groves, and shady bowers,
Blest with cool springs, and sweet refreshing flowers,
Then with th' èxpanded poplar would o'erspread,
Or leafy apple shade my weary head.

And Christ answers:

Implore refreshment from the apple's shade ...
Beneath my shadow ease your weary grief.
Behold my arms stretched on the fatal tree!
With these extended boughs I'll cover thee:
Behold my bleeding feet, my gaping side!
In these free coverts thou thyself mayst hide.
This shade will grant thee thy desired repose,
This tree alone for that kind purpose grows.

There, pensive, the speaker continues, 'I'll bewail my wretched state,| Like a sad turtle widowed of her mate'; his tears will flow like Christ's blood as he embraces the fatal tree and writes this 'sad inscription': 'Two lovers see, who their own deaths conspire!|She drowns in tears, while He consumes in fire.'

The mixture of secular and divine Eros and of world-weariness and religious hope is more explicit here than in Marvell. And in an emblem, unlike a regular poem, the fusion of Christ and forest can be made graphic. That Marvell intends something similar, however, seems very likely to be the purpose of the biblical-erotic language in the description of the grove and the explicit guidance offered by stanza 73. The paradoxical song – the 'Sadder, yet more pleasing sound' – of the doves replaces the song of the nightingale, the poet's

304 Harold E. Toliver

bird (in Herbert's *Jordan, 1* and Vaughan's *Idle Verse*, the bird of nonreligious poets). The doves have more endurance and more contact with the world of thorns than the nightingale, for whom 'The thorn, lest it should hurt her, draws|Within the skin its shrunken claws' (stanza 65). Like Hugo's repentant sinner, they are consumed by the fire of celestial love but at the same time 'drowned in the tears' of that love's imperfection in its historical form: 'O why should such a couple mourn,|That in so equal flames do burn!' Like Damon in *Clorinda and Damon* Marvell is a kind of voyeur-participant in a divine Eros that transcends both the autoeroticism of the reclusive life and and the violent heterosexuality of the amazons and Julianas that inevitably destroy the pastoral haven.

. . . Hence the erotic religious terms in which Marvell addresses the woodbines should come as no surprise:

Bind me ye woodbines in your twines,
Curl me about ye gadding vines,
And O so close your circles lace,
That I may never leave this place:
But, lest your fetters prove too weak,
Ere I your silken bondage break,
Do you, O brambles, chain me too,
And courteous briars nail me through.

(609–16)

When we have seen the grove as a *paysage moralisé* whose spiritual authority is clinched by brambles and briars, this will perhaps seem less an eccentric and unmotivated outbreak of masochism and dendro-eroticism than a logical outgrowth of the harsher, 'sadder' truth, symbolized by the doves, that alone is able to cope with a world so disordered. Unlike the 'sweet chordage' of *A Dialogue* or the 'winding snare' of *The Coronet*, nature's bondage must not be broken; it must bind tighter, until the thorns are felt. (A commonplace observation of Jonathan Edwards suggests why Marvell thinks of the nails in the context of the brambles: roses grow on briars to signify that 'pure happiness, the crown of glory, is to be come at no other way than by bearing Christ's cross, by a life of mortification.'[1])

1 *Images or Shadows of Divine Things*, p. 43.

This passionate apostrophe, like the rest of the woodland experience, is projected in a semi-humorous mood, as though reading in this increasingly outmoded book of nature required taking refuge behind a shield of irony. The commitment to the 'mystic book' seems vital enough, however. The 'sensuous self-identification', the 'sense of unity', and the 'masochistic passivity' that critics have found in the passage depend upon the validity of the symbols. Marvell knows the 'play' to be an imaginative and childlike gesture, as he indicates in stanza 74, but he is nevertheless taken by the 'actors' that present the divine pageant. Although his awareness of the stage as stage is greater than Vaughan's or Traherne's in comparable forest scenes, he is no less serious.

(117–20, 122–3)

Kitty Scoular

from *Natural Magic* 1965

When Marvell came to organize his patron's landscape somewhat more ambitiously in his other estate-poem, *Upon Appleton House, to my Lord Fairfax*, it was again by reconciling opposing qualities, and by demonstrating multiplicity in unity. The controlling sense behind the poem is that Fairfax's 'little world commands the great'.[1] The estate is presented paradoxically as 'a retreat from the world, as it is man's; into the world, as it is God's'.[2] The greater world is annihilated, not by denying its values and characteristics, but by showing how they are included with completeness in the estate, which is presented as the realization of the poets' myths of imaginary places, Arcadia, the Bower of Bliss, Jerusalem, Elisium, and as the fulfilment of several fashionable paradoxes,

As if it had by Nature's cunning hand
Been choicely picked out from all the rest,
And laid forth for ensample of the best.[3]

1 Edward Benlowes, *Theophila*, XIII 20.
2 Cowley, *Essays*, 1668, 'Of Agriculture'.
3 *Faerie Queene*, II vi 12. Francis Bacon described gardens as 'in small compass a model of universal nature made private'.

Comprehensiveness was a contemporary ideal in landscape-painting.[1] Nor was Marvell the only poet of the time to regard place or person in this way. Mildmay Fane's witty poem, *To Sir John Wentworth, upon his Curiosities and Courteous entertainment at Summerly in Lovingland*,[2] is built upon the same idea. Summerly contains all nature's wonders 'in epitome' (a phrase popularized by Donne with reference to the beloved lady).

The fablers of old, I guess, might find
Some objects t'help invention, but the mind
Was sure prophetic, for whatever is
Described for rare by them, 'twas meant by this.

The strangeness of the place is related to the variety of excellences included within such small scope, provided by the European 'Civility' of its owner.

Now as contracted virtue doth excel
In power and force, This seems a miracle;
Wherein all travellers may truly say,
They never saw so much in little way:
And thence conclude their folly, that did steer
To seek for that abroad, at home was near
In more perfection.

It was by using for his own ends the conventions associated with different sorts of poem that Marvell suggested that he found encompassed in the Appleton estate 'All that's made', whether in nature or in art, 'a monopoly of all the pleasures and delights that are on earth, amassed together, to make a dearth thereof elsewhere'.[3] The themes related to country life which he recalled and combined into a new whole included the meditation on the superiority of the humble

1 See H. V. S. Ogden, *J.H.I.*, vol. 10, 1949, pp. 159–82, and with Margaret S. Ogden, *English Taste in Landscape in the Seventeenth Century*, 1955. For contemporary statement, see Rémy Belleau, *Le Pinceau*; Maurice Scève, *Le Microcosme*, 1562, 111; Sylvester, 5th edn, 1621, p. 139; William Browne, *Britannia's Pastorals*, 1 ii 819–58; Henry Peacham, *Graphice*, 1612, 'Of the Graces of Landscape.'
2 *Otia Sacra*, p. 153.
3 Henry Hawkins, *Partheneia Sacra*, p. 6, *The Garden*.

life to the life of ambition,[1] the history and patriotic praise of a place,[2] the enumeration of a day's activities in the country, with its *aubade*, its morning-walk, and its account of nightfall,[3] the journey,[4] the allegorical description of the interior garden, and the poem of contemplation passing from one object to another with the purpose 'to know the Heavenly use of earthly things'.[5] All these patterns of artifice are to be found within *Upon Appleton House*, unified by a style whose core is the discovery of resemblance between things apparently unlike, and between different kinds of life, heroic and rustic, biblical and contemporary, exotic and local, small and great, erotic and ascetic, pious and profane. Reason is combined with the irrational, magic with the mundane, and the categories of painting drama, and science are shown to have some relevance to the Fairfax demesnes. There is not another place-poem of the same length from the seventeenth century which has as its intention the display of such varieties.

... The poem's journey ends when the salmon-fishers bring their boats up from the river,

And, like Antipodes in shoes,
Have shod their heads in their canoes.

(771-2)

The wit of this final stanza, which has earned Mr Eliot's disapproval, is an extension of more than one contemporary literary joke. A poem that was full of creatures suspended between two elements would conclude fitly with the mention of 'rational amphibii', oddly resembling that other amphibian, the tortoise, with which the poem

1 See M.-S. Røstvig, *The Happy Man*, for an account of the important seventeenth-century poems on this theme.
2 See William Warner, *Albion's England*; Drayton, *Poly-Olbion*.
3 See S. R. Watson, 'Milton's Ideal Day: Its Development as a Pastoral Theme', *P.M.L.A.*, vol. 67, 1942, pp. 404-20.
4 See R. A. Aubin, *Topographical Poetry in XVIII-Century England*, New York, 1936, chaps. 1, 7, and bibliography.
5 From a poem by Fairfax himself in Bodleian MS. Fairfax 40, p. 485. Cf. John Hagthorpe, *Divine Meditations*, 1622; Ann Bradstreet, *The Tenth Muse*, 1650, 'Contemplations'; Benlowes, *Theophila*, xii, xiii; Saint-Amant, *Œuvres Poetiques*, 1629, 'Le Contemplateur'; Sarbiewski, *Lyricorum libri IV*, Cologne, 1625, third epode, p. 212.

had begun. Du Bartas, remembering Pliny, had described the large
Arabian tortoise from which a boat might be made.

But of one tortoise, when he list to float,
Th' Arabian fisherman can make a boat;
And one such shell, him in the stead doth stand
Of hulk at sea, and of a house on land.[1]

Marvell took the notion a stage farther and transformed fishers into
tortoises. The world consists of one shell within another: over all is
'the dark hemisphere', and within are men and animals similarly
housed and enclosed.

The 'Antipodes, such as walk with their feet against ours'[2] became
useful metaphorically to describe such wonders as a hall of mirrors,
turning the world awry:

Nay, to reverse the miracle, with ease
We are become our own Antipodes.[3]

So the coming of night distorts the order of the universe, making
men and things seem what they are not; and yet this very semblance
is the assertion of another kind of order, in which great is contained
in little. The inhabitants of the Appleton estate need not go *alio ...
sub sole* (the Virgilian phrase rendered 'their Antipodes' by Cowley)[4]
to find delight and profusion. There is a time of day when even the
oddest miracles of the ends of the earth are comprehended within their
own boundaries.

When Maria Fairfax walked by the water she was not subject to it,
but performed miracles by her very presence. There was hardly a

1 Sylvester, 5th edn, p. 93. Philemon Holland's *Pliny*, IX 10, 1634 edn, i 241,
runs; 'There be found tortoises in the Indian sea so great, that one only shell
of them is sufficient for the roof of a dwelling house. And among the islands
principally in the Red Sea, they use tortoise shells ordinarily for boats and
wherries upon the water'. Z. Heyns, *Emblemata Moralia*, Rotterdam, 1625,
III, fols. 6ᵛ–7ʳ, 'Vivitur parva bene', illustrates this lore.
2 Quoted from Lactantius, *Institutes*, III 24, by Bishop Wilkins, *A Discourse
concerning A New World and Another Planet*, 1640, pp. 7–8. Cf. Augustine, *Of
the City of God*, XVI 9.
3 *Parnassus Biceps*, 1656, p. 32. Cf. Poole, *English Parnassus*, 1657, p. 285,
Evening: 'The morning of the Antipodes'.
4 *The Works of Mr Abraham Cowley*, 1668, p. 106, *A Translation out of Virgil*
from *Georgics* ii 511–12, on the country life versus travel.

garden in Tudor poetry without some lady central to it, either
Elizabeth or some more private person, or Venus, or Lady Nature
herself. Sometimes her features were compared to the universe,
sometimes she was given magic powers over it. In one poem 'there is
a garden in her face', in another her robes are a cosmic image, in
another she draws the admiration of the creatures, enchanting them,
making them perform the impossible. Sometimes she is offered gifts
from the world's abundance by her lover. Seldom is the lord of nature
treated so variedly as the lady (though the behaviour of the wood-
creatures towards Marvell, and his rustic cope, are traditional patterns).
In Maria true womanhood is presented, in opposition to the evil
power over nature and people typified in the nuns.

> 'Tis she that to these gardens gave
> That wondrous beauty which they have;
>
> .   .   .   .   .
>
> She yet more pure, sweet, straight, and fair,
> Than gardens, woods, meads, rivers are
>
> (689–90, 695–6)

She is superior to the sonneteers' ladies, to Elizabeth, to the nuns, even
to the Catholic Queen of Heaven, for 'all virgins she precedes'.[1]
Maria is the Lady of the Evening, and is given associations which
Collins reserved for Eve herself a century later: she is chaste, retiring,
modest. As night falls on the river, Marvell imagines the 'eben shuts'
of the shadows to be closing upon it, 'eben' suggesting both the colour
of the shadows themselves, and the trees by the water's edge which
cast them, darkened to look like exotic ebony by the disappearance of
the sun. In his poem La Solitude, the contemporary French poet
Théophile de Viau had created a river-nymph to open the crystal
door of the water.[2] The 'shuts' or shutters of this poem suggest the
same kind of odd transformation of the river into a house, closing up
in the evening.

1 The poem may be, among other things, a literary riposte to contemporary
praise of the Virgin Mary, such as there is in Partheneia Sacra.
2 Œuvres Complètes, ed. Alleaume, Paris, 1856, i 176:

> De ceste source une Naiade,
> Tous les soirs ouvre le portail,
> De sa demeure de crystal,
> Et nous chante une sérénade.

So when the shadows laid asleep
From underneath these banks do creep,
And on the river as it flows
With eben shuts begin to close;
The modest halcyon comes in sight,
Flying betwixt the day and night;
And such an horror calm and dumb,
Admiring Nature does benumb.

(665–72)

In this stanza the connective 'so' might be merely a loose introductory word; but it is the initiation of a simile. Maria resembles some of the most mysterious creatures in her own landscape. Her affinities are with the halcyon and the comet, belonging to the middle-regions, participating both in earth and in heaven.

Other miraculous birds had caused wonder before Marvell's; other poets used similar words:

Let me stand numbed with wonder, never came
   So strong amazement on astonished eye
   As this, this measureless pure rarity.[1]

'Benumb' was used precisely by Marvell with a double reference. The landscape, regarded anthropomorphically, was experiencing the ecstasy of a trance at the appearance of the blessed lady. To the eye, it had become still, fixed in a solid state. The two meanings are held together, the human and the scientific, since the external appearance of things is an emblem of inner significances. These two kinds of meaning are interfused in the following stanza also.

The viscous air, wheres'e'er she fly,
Follows and sucks her azure dye;
The jellying stream compacts below,
If it might fix her shadow so;
The stupid fishes hang, as plain
As flies in crystal overta'en;
And men the silent scene assist,
Charmed with the sapphire-winged mist.

(673–80)

1 In Robert Chester, *Love's Martyr*, Marston's accompanying poem on the phoenix and the turtle.

Here the contemporary vocabulary of magnetism is interwoven with a traditional literary imagery, derived from the classical epigrammatists. It is necessary not only to say that the bird gives its colour to the evening sky, but to explain this as a scientific process. A passage in Sir Thomas Browne's *Vulgar Errors* throws light on the matter:

Another way of their attraction is also delivered that is, by a tenuous emanation or continued effluvium, which after some distance retracteth into itself; as is observable in drops of syrups, oil and seminal viscosities, which spun at length, retire into their former dimensions. Now these effluviums advancing from the body of the electric, in their return do carry back to bodies whereon they have laid hold within the sphere or circle of their continuities; and these they do not only attract, but with their viscous arms hold fast for a good while after.[1]

Besides the adjective 'viscous', the verb 'to suck' was used technically in descriptions of magnetism: the spirit of iron was thought to be sucked by the loadstone.[2] So the air attracted the colour of the halcyon to itself.

Other poets before Marvell had described birds' shadows on the surface of the water.

But as the raven late, he next sends out
The damask coloured dove, his nimble scout,
Which thrills the thin air, and his pinions plies,
That like to lightning, gliding through the skies,
His sundry coloured feathers by the sun,
As his swift shadow on the lake doth run,
Causeth a twinkling both at hand and far,
Like that we call the shooting of a star.[3]

Drayton's image is predominantly a visual one; but by introducing a semblance of cause and effect, Marvell produced a conceit which at

1 *Enquiries into Vulgar and Common Errors*, II 4.
2 See Oswald Crollius, *Philosophy Reformed and Improved*, 1657, translated by H. Pinnell, p. 45. In William Cartwright, *The Gnat, Plays and Poems*, ed. G. Blakemore Evans, Madison-Wisconsin, 1951, p. 478, 'suck' is used of the action of jet upon straws.
3 Drayton, *Noah's Flood*, in *Complete Works*, ed. J. W. Hebel, iii 349.

once presents a facet of the landscape, the coming of stillness and darkness over the water as the bird flies across, and a value-judgement, the extreme worth of the bird, so that even the catching of its shadow is important. The halcyon has brought night with it, and not merely accompanied it.

One of the most notable features of this poem is its presentation of transitional states and changes in the face of things. Marvell himself was attempting to fix shadows, to make something permanent of impermanence; and this twilight passage is the climax of that part of the poem's meaning. Like Marvell, Herrick was fascinated by 'doubtful twilight', by the concealment of one thing within another. There are certain resemblances between this passage and *The Lily in a Crystal*.[1] Behind them lie some lines from the Latin poets, and a kind of descriptiveness to be found in the romances. The power of the lady operates not in the full blaze of day, but in the half-light which stands for mystery; the beauty of things consists not only in their order, but in the enfolding of one kind of excellence within another. The lily is 'More fair in this transparent case,|Than when it grew alone;|And had but single grace.' The halcyon hovering over 'The stupid fishes' brings about the fulfilment of their beauty as they are fixed in the crystal water. The sun had first 'In blushing clouds' concealed 'his head'; the windows of the river were closed, and now the fish are entombed; and these successive veilings of the landscape suggest first Maria's modesty, and then the power of her goodness. In Herrick's poem the 'Scene' was the veil or curtain (a relatively new meaning of the word),[2] 'cast over,|To juggle with the sense'. Though an awareness of the deceptiveness of twilight is not absent from Marvell's lines, his emphasis lies rather on the wonder aroused both in the creatures and in the men who are spectators (who 'assist' in the Latin root-sense of the word). 'Charmed' bears the treble sense of delight, hypnotization by a spell, and the ecstasy which is the culmination of an act of contemplation.

(163–5, 171–6)

1 *Hesperides*, no. 193 in *Poetical Works*, ed. L. C. Martin, Oxford, 1956, p. 75.
2 *N.E.D.* records the first use in 1638, with associations with the meaning 'scenery', applied to the stages.

The Gallery

Winifred Nowottny

from *The Language Poets Use* 1962

The strategy in this poem [*The Gallery*] is to raise a question about his relation to Clora, real or posed, firstly by accentuating all that is *voulu* in Clora and in his own attitude to her. A tone of non-commitment is established at the very beginning by the evident wilfulness of the conceit of making the soul into a gallery of portraits of Clora. One does not view the soul, nor contrive it at will, nor invite people to inspect it and say whether they are pleased. All that follows this opening must be felt as subtly non-obligatory, a polite fiction. If the poet chooses to contrive his soul in this way, that is his business. Various pictures of Clora follow; we are never allowed to forget that they are merely pictures, and all different. Marvell is at pains to make it clear that Clora is not really what any one picture shows her to be: 'Here thou art painted in the dress|Of an inhuman murderess' (stanza 2); 'But, on the other side, th'art drawn|Like to Aurora in the dawn' (stanza 3); 'Like an enchantress here thou show'st' (stanza 4); 'But, against that, thou sit'st afloat|Like Venus in her pearly boat'(stanza 5). The sixth stanza brings into explicitness the reiterated suggestion that these pictures are only pictures and that they are mutually-contradictory inventions:

These pictures and a thousand more,
Of thee, my gallery do store;
In all the forms thou canst invent
Either to please me, or torment:

(41–4)

and these lines are followed by a conceit so outrageous that it is a contradiction in terms:

For thou alone to people me,
Art grown a num'rous colony;

(45–6)

then follows a description of the lady as a gallery far more interesting to a connoisseur than either Whitehall or Mantua; the citing of real places deliberately underlines the unreality of the gallery he has made – or allowed Clora to make for his benefit. There is not one stanza of the poem in which Marvell does not labour to suggest that the picture gallery is a figment and every picture in it is only a picture: he wills the gallery and Clora wills the contents. Indeed it is uncertain who is responsible for the attitudes struck in the pictures – Clora, or the poet who appreciates them. It is all a highly-civilized game, which will last only as long as both of them want to play.

Having built up all this, both by the diction and by the displayed unreality of the conceit, Marvell now beautifully places the *volte-face* of the poem. It is still a gallery, still a game; one could pull it down, one could refuse to play; and yet – as the last stanza suddenly reminds us – there are degrees of unreality:

But, of these pictures and the rest,
That at the entrance likes me best:

(49–50)

the picture he chooses as the best is the one at the entrance, at the beginning of love. Here, what is familiar in the diction and what is simple in the picture suggest that there is something artless about this picture. Its effect on the poet is that he is no longer the wholly detached connoisseur of unreal attitudes: he has made a choice, he is affected. What affects him is what is completely unaffected, a purely visual object. But yet, a visual object *in a gallery*. Is it quite unaffected? Was she not, even at the beginning, affecting to be the picture of simple beauty, adorning herself with innocent flowers? No doubt it doesn't finally matter whether or not that was affectation too; he liked her when she pretended to be simple and was just there to be looked at. And despite all the subsequent pictures, the first one is still there, and somehow more real than the others – despite the fact that the first lured him into an experience which turned out to be very different from what it promised. The tone of all this – the detachment at once ironic, tender, and willingly deceived – depends for its achievement firstly on the displayed artificiality of the conceit and of the pictures described within it. But it depends too on a structural element which stands, in a sense, outside the display of contrivance and the stressed artificiality in the diction. This structural element is a relational element. The tour round the gallery returns to the picture at the entrance; the last picture in the poem is the first in the gallery – which is to say that the last stanza of the poem alters all that has gone before by introducing a *da capo*, the relation *to go back to the beginning*. To remove the last stanza would take away the pediment on which the whole poem proves to have been standing. The effect of this pediment on the whole poem is difficult to pin down, for the good reason that the relation *to go back to the beginning* is, like all relations, clear in one way and infinitely ambiguous in another. The relation itself can be stated. *Da capo* states it. But what it means (means to anybody) depends on the members it relates. Here it relates members who have no definition except *vis-à-vis* one another. The first five pictures are more artificial than the sixth; yet the sixth is also inside a gallery, and an invented gallery at that. So the meaning of the relation *da capo* – when it relates members as ambiguous as these – is one that may well 'tease us out of thought', as Keats said of the Grecian urn.

(94–6)

Mourning

Winifred Nowottny

from *The Language Poets Use* 1962

I would suggest, then, that we should regard the humdrum potential ambiguities of language at large as raw material which the poet can process, if he so wishes, in such a way as to make it clear to the reader that there are more ways than one of thinking about the situation with which his poem deals, and, further, that when the raw material is so processed we should describe the poem not as 'an ambiguous poem' (because this tends to suggest muzziness of meaning, or defective meaning) but as 'an extraloquial poem' (because this will help to remind us that we are dealing with a poem that brings together in a simultaneous display a larger number of possible readings of a situation than we usually find provided for us in ordinary statements). A further advantage to be derived from adopting some new term that will free us from the embarrassment of talking about 'ambiguous poems' is that we shall not be constantly pushed into thinking that the only important thing about such poems is that they take up a Yes/No attitude to whatever they present. The expression of a Yes/No attitude, i.e. of ambivalence, is not the only use for extraloquialism. Moreover, though the language of poetry is often used to express or come to terms with ambivalence, and though in articulating ambivalence it may exploit the potential ambiguity of the common tongue, it is also true that ambivalence can be articulated without any such exploitation. To illustrate: Marvell in his poem *Mourning*, which questions the sincerity of Chlora's tears for her dead lover Strephon, devises as the climax of the poem two quatrains in each of which the words of the fourth line can be taken in either of two opposed ways: having told us that some people say that Chlora is weeping for joy, he goes on:

How wide they dream! The Indian slaves
That sink for pearl through seas profound,
Would find her tears yet deeper waves
And not of one the bottom sound.

I yet my silent judgement keep,
Disputing not what they believe:
But sure as oft as women weep,
It is to be supposed they grieve.

If 'sound' is taken as a verb, the quatrain says that the waters of
Chlora's tears are so deep that even the Indian pearl-divers could not
sound their depths; if however it is taken as an adjective, then the
quatrain says that if one were to procure divers experienced enough to
get to the bottom of these waves it would be found that none had
any solid ground beneath. Similarly with 'It is to be supposed they
grieve'; this may be taken to mean either that when women weep,
the obvious explanation is that they are really grieving – or that when
women weep, everybody is expected to make a polite pretence of
believing that they have properly demonstrated a proper amount of
concern. Here the poet's ironical insistence on keeping silent about his
own judgement of the case is maintained by using ambiguous syntax
and idiom. But when Catullus writes (*Carmen* 85),

Odi et amo. quare id faciam, fortasse requiris
  nescio, sed fieri sentio et excrucior

[I hate and love. Perhaps you ask why I do this
  I do not know, but I feel that it is so and I am in agony.]

the ambivalence of his feelings is expressed not through ambiguity
but through the contradictory assertions that he hates and he loves.

It will be helpful, then, to be able to avail oneself of a term that
stands clear of the contemporary practice of using 'ambivalent' and
'ambiguous' in ways that suggest that they are interchangeable terms.
Indeed it would seem that the contemporary tendency to couple
these terms has had the result that too little attention has been given
to poems in which linguistic ambiguity is used for purposes other
than the expression of ambivalence of feeling; recent criticism, making
play with the concept of ambiguity as a means of traversing the
antithetical categories registered in common vocabulary, has perhaps
persuaded us to think too much in terms of the reconciling of oppositions (as between hate and love, sorrow and joy, gain and loss, good
and evil). Perhaps, naturally enough, the prefix 'ambi-' has led us to
think in terms of 'Not Either-Or, But Both'. The prefix 'extra-' is
not likely to have this tendency.   (157–8)

The Satires

George de F. Lord

from the Introduction to his edition of *Poems on Affairs of State: Augustan Satirical Verse, 1660–1714* 1963

Political satire is related to historical events in two ways. It is a record of events, a 'history', however distorted by partial views and private motives. It also exerts influence, however slight, upon the events themselves. The political verse of the Restoration played a considerable part in the determination of large issues in England: the question of a Protestant or a Catholic succession, for one, and the relative power of royal prerogative and Parliament for another. Viewed either as 'history' or as an instrument of party warfare, Restoration political satire is marked by a circumstantial and highly personal approach to events. As history and as propaganda, it purports to tell the real story, to set the record straight, and its prime method is to present the reader with a plausible body of purported fact. For us who are studying these events three hundred years after they happened, two questions arise: how accurately do the *State Poems* reflect events ? To what extent did they influence events ?

From 1665 on, every aspect of public affairs in England was subjected to the satirist's increasingly minute and bitter scrutiny. Charles' personal faults, which might have been tolerated in a monarch whose political and religious inclinations were more congenial to his subjects, were magnified until he was depicted as another Sardanapalus. The mistresses, whose greed supposedly drained off vast sums appropriated for the national welfare and whose alien creeds threatened the liberties of Charles' subjects, were exposed to appalling, but sometimes justified, invective. Not a drunken frolic, nor a brawl at court, nor a bribe in Parliament, not an instance of cowardice or chicanery in the navy, nor one of hypocrisy or bigotry in the Church escaped satirical notice. The Restoration is a period unusually rich in detailed records: the diaries of Pepys, Evelyn, Dering, and Milward; the letters of Rochester and Savile, of Etherege, Marvell, and Henry Verney; the memoirs of Grammont, Barillon, North, Burnet, and Clarendon; the state papers and newsletters – all make it a richly-documented period. Nearly every item of even the slightest public interest in such sources is mentioned in the thousands of poems on public affairs which have survived. The most important of these, set in chronological order with their occasions and persons identified, comprise a priceless record. Their particularity and involvement and gossipy interest in everything that happened give them something of the appeal that we find in Pepys. The pictures they paint are always, to some extent, distorted. The mirror they hold up to flawed human nature is often flawed itself, but thanks to rebuttals and apologias and to the abundance of other dependable records in this period, the modern student of Restoration history and manners may still get at kinds of truth through this medium.

What, then, can be said of these poems as history? The writer of commendatory verse selects his details, softens his focus, and heightens his colors to produce an image heroic or benign of king, queen, or chancellor. *Second Advice* reveals, for example, the many unheroic realities that Waller omitted or glossed over in *Instructions to a Painter*. The satirist, on the other hand, despite the pretense of delivering unvarnished truth, distorts and colors realities for his own political and aesthetic purposes. Waller's panegyrical treatment of the war of 1665 reminds us that Marvell underrated the courage of James and the magnanimity of Clarendon.

In the preface to *Annus Mirabilis* Dryden implied, I believe, just such a discrepancy between the heroic or the satirical image and reality. In defending his adaptation of Virgilian tropes and phrases, he writes:

Such descriptions or images, well wrought, which I promise not for mine, are, as I have said, the adequate delight of heroic poesy; for they beget admiration, which is its proper object; as the images of the burlesque, which is contrary to this, by the same reason beget laughter; for the one shows nature beautified, as in the picture of a fair woman, which we admire; the other shows her deformed, as in that of a lazar or of a fool with distorted face and antic gestures, at which we cannot forbear to laugh, because it is a deviation from nature.

We go a step beyond Dryden's explicit statement to say that the 'fair woman' and the 'lazar' are essentially images of the same person, but a comparison of Dryden's massive apologia for the regime of Charles

II with, say, *Third Advice*, suggests that this is true. In *Annus Mirabilis* Dryden bent his energies on painting anew, with a palette of heroic colors, such figures as the King, the Duke of York, the Duke of Albemarle, whom the satirists depicted in livid colors and grotesque postures.

The juxtaposition of a heroic poem like Waller's *Instructions to a Painter* or *Annus Mirabilis* with satiric poems dealing with the same figures and events sheds new light not only upon the events themselves but on the techniques of the heroic and satiric modes in topical poetry. The poems of Waller and Dryden, of Marvell and Rochester, are mutually illuminating. In the first place the underlying aesthetic assumptions of both modes are thrown into relief by the comparison. The heroic mode, as Dryden's important comment suggests, is designed to 'beget admiration' or wonder; the satiric (or 'burlesque') to 'beget laughter'. The heroic mode aims at an imaginative identification of contemporary persons and events with the heroic tradition in epic or biblical accounts. The technique necessarily entails a careful selection from the available mass of fact, an idealizing or heightening of the details selected, and a cunning association of these details with mythic precedents. The satiric artist also selects from the available mass of fact, but pays particular regard to details which may appear as grotesque and incongruous. His technique depends upon a vivid and naturalistic treatment of detail, and, if he employs heroic associations, he does so in order to denigrate the present reality by contrast with an ideal past. Thus Dryden, in *Annus Mirabilis*, projects upon Charles II Aeneas' pious care for his people and his country's destiny, while Marvell draws grotesque analogues between Ovid's fabulous artificer and the cunning political architect he sees in Clarendon. An example of the difference between the two modes is found in the accounts of the wounding of the British Admiral Monck in the Three Days' Battle. Monck's breeches were shot away, and he suffered a minor wound in the buttock. Dryden permits himself a moment of grave levity before reasserting the epic mood:

Our dreaded Admiral from far they threat,
  Whose batter'd rigging their whole war receives.
All bare, like some old oak, which tempests beat,
  He stands, and sees below his scatter'd leaves.

Heroes of old, when wounded, shelter sought,
  But he, who meets all danger with disdain,
Ev'n in their face his ship to anchor brought,
  And steeple high stood propp'd upon the main.

At this excess of courage all amaz'd,
  The foremost of his foes a while withdraw:
With such respect in enter'd Rome they gaz'd,
  Who on high chairs the god-like fathers saw.

As Hooker judiciously remarks, 'Dryden's raillery is admirable by the
best standards of his age: it is a gentle thrust, serving to reveal or
heighten certain admirable qualities in the object of raillery – in this
instance, the Duke's unshaken courage.' In treating the same incident
Marvell employs mock-modesty and a Ciceronian disclaimer in
advising his painter:

But most with story of his hand or thumb,
Conceal (as Honour would) his Grace's bum,
When that rude bullet a large collop tore
Out of that buttock never turn'd before.
Fortune, it seem'd, would give him by that lash
Gentle correction for his fight so rash,
But should the Rump perceive't, they'd say that Mars
Had now reveng'd them upon Aumarle's arse.
                    (*Third Advice to a Painter*, 123–30)

Here something like heroic dignity is momentarily assumed to
emphasize by contrast the prevailing effect of broad humor. Heroic
personifications of Honor and Fortune wage a vain struggle with low
words like bum and arse. In the lines which follow this passage
Marvell, like Dryden, brings in further analogues from the heroic
tradition, but with an effect that is directly opposite to Dryden's:

The long disaster better o'er to veil,
Paint only Jonah three days in the whale,
Then draw the youthful Perseus all in haste
From a sea-beast to free the virgin chaste,
(But neither riding Pegasus for speed,
Nor with the Gorgon shielded at his need);

For no less time did conqu'ring Ruyter chaw
Our flying Gen'ral in his spongy jaw.
So Rupert the sea dragon did invade,
But to save George himself and not the maid,
And so arriving late, he quickly miss'd
E'en sails to fly, unable to resist.

(131–42)

In this account of Prince Rupert's attempt to rescue the beleaguered
Monck the mythical allusions to Jonah, Perseus and Andromeda,
and St George have a discordant effect. They underscore by contrast the irrelevance of heroic attitudes to the present 'long disaster'.
The effect of the passage runs counter to that which Dryden gains by
his sonorous lines on Rome's 'god-like fathers'. It awakens the
reader's skepticism whereas Dryden's weighty lines excite his awe.

These two passages represent a fundamental distinction between
heroic and mock-heroic verse. The heroic poet attempts to draw
over contemporary public affairs the sanctions of myth, of heroic
values, of a conservative tradition. The satirist invokes the same
sanctions to expose what he regards as instances of folly in contemporary affairs. One might add that the conflicting techniques and
strategies of the two genres tend to illustrate the basic ideological
oppositions of the century: on the one hand the appeal to faith in
traditional values, rituals, and myths, on the other the appeal to
empirical, skeptical and critical attitudes toward experience.

As I have already suggested, circumstances conspired in this period
to arouse such skeptical and critical attitudes toward authority. The
actual character and conduct of great Restoration figures often seem
like those found in satires in other ages. The truth could be stranger
than fiction, and the Restoration satirist of court life was rarely called
upon to strain his powers of invention. As Rochester wrote of his
enemy, Sir Carr Scroope,

                in thy person we more clearly see
That satire's of divine authority,
For God made one on man when he made thee,
To show there were some men as there are apes,
Fram'd for mere sport, who differ but in shapes.

In his famous portrait of Zimri Dryden took few liberties with the
historical Duke of Buckingham. The wits and bravoes of this period,
like Charles himself, were a self-conscious lot, and one suspects them
at times of trying to imitate hyperboles that imagination drew of
them. Sir Robert Howard sometimes seems to have modeled his
haughty demeanor on the heroes of his own dramas. One is driven
to wonder if Restoration life imitated art more than in other periods.
To what extent, for example, did Etherege invent Rochester in
creating Dorimant?

In matters of politics the same rule often applies. Marvell's satirical
account of England's defeat by the Dutch in 1667 and the Parliamentary and diplomatic maneuvers which accompanied it is a primary source for historians. In her scholarly edition of the Parliamentary diary of John Milward, Professor Caroline Robbins draws upon
Last Instructions continually for illustration and confirmation of her
author. When Charles II, with the aid of Clifford, 'the mad Cethegus
of the age', and Arlington, evolved in secret the Grand Design of
making England a dependency of Louis XIV and the Catholic Church,
the worst suspicions of the satirist fell short of the truth.

(1 xlii–xlvii)

Acknowledgements

For permission to use copyright material acknowledgement is made to the following:

For the article from T. S. Eliot, *Selected Essays*, to Faber & Faber Ltd and Harcourt, Brace & World Inc.; for the extract from the review by T. S. Eliot to the *New Statesman*; for the article from Christopher Hill, *Puritanism and Revolution*, to Secker & Warburg Ltd; for the extract from F. W. Bateson, *English Poetry: A Critical Introduction*, to Longmans Green & Co. Ltd and Barnes & Noble Inc.; for the extract from Patrick Cruttwell, *The Shakespearean Moment*, to Columbia University Press; for the lecture by J. B. Leishman to the British Academy; for the extract from the review by Susan Shrapnel to the editors of the *Cambridge Quarterly*; for the extract from William Empson, *Seven Types of Ambiguity*, to Chatto & Windus Ltd and New Directions Publishing Corporation; for the article by J. H. Summers to the Johns Hopkins Press; for the extract from Robert Ellrodt, *L'inspiration personelle et l'esprit du temps chez les poètes métaphysiques anglais*, to Librairie José Corti, Paris; for the extract from J. B. Broadbent, *Poetic Love*, to Chatto & Windus Ltd; for the article by S. L. Goldberg to the editors of the *Melbourne Critical Review*; for the extract from Yvor Winters, *Forms of Discovery*, to The Swallow Press Inc.; for the extract from the article by Cleanth Brooks to the University of Columbia Press; for the article by Douglas Bush to *The Sewanee Review*, The University of the South and the author; for the extract from John Crowe Ransom, *The New Criticism*, to New Directions Publishing Corporation; for the extract from J. V. Cunningham, *Tradition and Poetic Structure*, to The Swallow Press Inc.; for the extract from Barbara H. Smith, *Poetic Closure*, to the University of Chicago Press; for the extract from René Wellek and Austin Warren, *Theory of Literature*, to Jonathan Cape Ltd, Harcourt, Brace & World Inc. and the authors; for the extracts from Harold E. Toliver, *Marvell's Ironic Vision*, to Yale University Press; for the extract from R. S. Crane, *The Idea of the Humanities*, to the University of Chicago Press; for the extract from William Empson, *Some Versions of Pastoral*, to Chatto & Windus Ltd and New Directions Publishing Corporation; for the article by William Empson, to the *British Journal of Aesthetics*; for the article by John McChesney to the University of South Carolina; for the article by Don A. Keister to the University of South Carolina; for the article by Frank Kermode to the editors of *Essays in Criticism*; for the extract from the article by Pierre Legouis to The Clarendon Press, Oxford; for the article by E. S. Le Comte to the University of Chicago Press; for the article by Karina Williamson to the University of Chicago Press; for the extract from Maren-Sofie Røstvig, *The Happy Man*, to the Norwegian

Universities Press; for the article by Robin Grove to the *Melbourne Critical Review*; for the extract from Kitty Scoular, *Natural Magic*, to The Clarendon Press, Oxford; for the extracts from Winifred Nowottny, *The Language Poets Use*, to The Athlone Press of the University of London; for the extract from George de F. Lord's edition of *Poems on Affairs of State: Augustan Satirical Verse* to Yale University Press.

Select Bibliography

(Books and articles for which reference has been supplied in the Introductions, pp. 17–33, and 61–71, are not repeated here.)

Editions

H.M. Margoliouth, *The Poems and Letters of Andrew Marvell*, second edition, Oxford University Press, 1952.

W.A. McQueen and K.A. Rockwell, *The Latin Poetry of Andrew Marvell*, University of North Carolina Press, 1964.

George de F. Lord, *Andrew Marvell: Complete Poetry*, Random House, 1968.

Hugh McDonald, *The Poems of Andrew Marvell*, Routledge, 1952 (omits post-Restoration satires).

Books on Marvell

M.C. Bradbrook and M.G. Lloyd Thomas, *Andrew Marvell*, Cambridge University Press, 1940 (reprinted with corrections 1961).

Pierre Legouis, *Andrew Marvell, Poet, Puritan, Patriot,* Oxford University Press, 1965 (an abridged English version of Professor Legouis's *André Marvell: poete, puritan, patriote, 1928*).

J.B. Leishman, *The Art of Marvell's Poetry*, Hutchinson, 1966.

H.E. Toliver, *Marvell's Ironic Vision*, Yale University Press, 1965.

J.M. Wallace, *Destiny His Choice: The Loyalism of Andrew Marvell*, Cambridge University Press, 1968.

Books containing discussions of Marvell

A. Alvarez, *The School of Donne*, Chatto and Windus, 1961.

Joan Bennett, *Five Metaphysical Poets*, Cambridge University Press, 1964.

Douglas Bush, *English Literature in the Earlier Seventeenth Century*, second edition, Oxford University Press, 1962.

J. Hollander, *The Untuning of the Sky*, Princeton University Press, 1961.

J.A. Mazzeo, *Reason and the Imagination*, Routledge, 1962.

H.R. Swardson, *Poetry and the Fountain of Light*, Allen and Unwin, 1962.

C.V. Wedgwood, *Poetry and Politics Under the Stuarts*, Cambridge University Press, 1960.

Articles (general)

Paola Colaiacomo, 'Alcuni Aspetti della Poesia di Andrew Marvell', *English Miscellany*, vol. 11, 1960, pp. 75–111.

J.D. Rosenberg, 'Marvell and the Christian Idiom', *Boston Universit Studies in English*, vol. 4, 1960, pp. 152–61.

F.J. Warnke, 'Play and Metamorphosis in Marvell's Poetry', *S.E.L* vol. 5, 1965, pp. 23–30.

Articles on particular poems

Upon Appleton House

S.L. Goldberg, 'Andrew Marvell', *Melbourne Critical Review*, vol. 3 1960, pp. 41–56.

To his Coy Mistress

Joan Hartwig, 'The Principle of Measure in *To his Coy Mistress*' *College English*, vol. 25, 1964, pp. 572–5.

The Garden

G. Williamson, 'The Context of Marvell's *Hortus* and *Garden*' *M.L.N.*, vol. 76, 1961, pp. 590–8.

An Horatian Ode

L.D. Lerner, 'An Horatian Ode' in John Wain, *Interpretations*, Routledge, 1955, pp. 59–74.

Mourning

E.E. Duncan-Jones, 'Notes on Marvell', *N. & Q.*, vol. 98, 1953, p. 102.

The Nymph Complaining for the Death of her Fawn

E.H. Emerson, 'Andrew Marvell's *The Nymph Complaining for the Death of her Fawn*', *E.A.*, vol. 8, 1955, pp. 107–10.

G.H. Hartman, '*The Nymph Complaining for the Death of her Fawn*: A Brief Allegory', *Essays in Criticism*, vol. 18, 1968, pp. 113–35.

Pierre Legouis, 'Réponse à Jack E. Reese', *E.A.*, vol. 18, 1965, pp. 402–3.

Jack E. Reese, 'Marvell's *Nymph* in a New Light', *E.A.*, vol. 18, 1965, pp. 398–401.

Leo Spitzer, 'Marvell's *Nymph Complaining for the Death of her Fawn*: Sources versus Meaning', *M.L.Q.*, vol. 19, 1958, pp. 231–43.

The Unfortunate Lover

J. Max Patrick, 'Marvell's *The Unfortunate Lover*', *Explicator*, vol. 20, 1962, item 65.

Index

Extracts included in this anthology are indicated by bold page references.

Massinger, Philip (1583–1640) Playwright, best known for his
New Way to Pay Old Debts (1633) 70

Massingham, Harold John (1888–1952) Journalist, and author of
many books on birds and countryside; edited a *Treasury of
Seventeenth Century Verse* (1919) 32

Match, The 119

May, Thomas (1595–1650) Poet, dramatist; translated Lucan, and
so gained favour of Charles I; became Parliamentarian propagandist
in 1646. See A. G. Chester, *Thomas May* (1932) 71, 180–82

Mazzeo, J. A. 69

Mencius (371–289 B.C.) Chinese philosopher, teaching the original
goodness of human nature. *Works* translated by James Legge (1895) 235

Meynell, Alice (1847–1922) Poet, essayist, Catholic convert; poems
admired by Tennyson; weekly articles in the *Pall Mall Gazette*
reprinted in *The Colour of Life* (1896), praised by Meredith; admirer
of 17th-century poetry before it was fashionable. See V. Meynell,
Alice Meynell (1929) **43–6**

Milton, John (1608–74) Letters in Columbia edition of the *Works*,
ed. F. A. Patterson and others, 20 vols. (1931–40) 14, 25, 30–31, **35**,
40, 43–4, 47–8, 55, 57, 74, 100, 117–18, 133, 156, 174, 179, 246, 253
    Comus 48, 161, 173
    Defensio Secunda 113–14
    Il Penseroso 50
    L'Allegro 50, 152
    Lycidas 29, 143, 175
    Observations on the Articles of Peace 208
    Paradise Lost 260
    Samson Agonistes 56
    Sonnet on the Lord Protector 112–13, 116

Milward, John (1599–1670) Cavalier. See his *Diary*, ed. Caroline
Robbins (1938) 321, 326

Mitchell, Charles 69

Mitford, Mary Russell (1787–1855) Poet, essayist, dramatist; most
successful play, *Rienzi* (1828); known for sketches of village life,
Our Village (1824–32); friend of Coleridge and Lamb. See
V. Watson, *Mary Russell Mitford* (1949) 28

Montaigne, Michel de (1533–92) 252–3, 255–6
    Essais 280

More, Henry (1614–87) Cambridge Platonist; strove to reconcile
reason and Christianity; opposed Descartes' denial of extension to
spirit in *The Immortality of the Soul* (1659) and *Enchiridion
Metaphysicum* (1671) 69